NO. 10

NO. 10

The Geography of Power
at Downing Street

JACK BROWN

First published in 2019 by
HAUS PUBLISHING LTD
4 Cinnamon Row
London SW11 3TW
www.hauspublishing.com

A CIP catalogue record for this book is available from the British Library

ISBN: 978-1-912208-01-2
eISBN: 978-1-912208-77-7

Typeset in Garamond by MacGuru Ltd

Printed and bound in Great Britain by Clays Ltd

Contents

Acknowledgements

This book is the result of the Researcher in Residence initiative at No. 10 Downing Street, itself the product of a unique collaboration between No. 10; the Strand Group, the Policy Institute, and the Widening Participation Department at Kings College London; university access charity The Brilliant Club; and Hewlett Packard Enterprise. Without the involvement of these organisations, and the stewardship of Jon Davis of the Strand Group, there would be no Researcher in Residence role and there would be no book.

The book owes a great deal to the mentoring and encouragement of Jon and the whole Strand Group team. It was Peter Hennessy (Lord Hennessy of Nympsfield) who first generously observed that this project sounded like 'more of a book than an article'. That escalated quickly.

Assistance from within No. 10, the Cabinet Office, the National Archives, Churchill Archives Centre, Cambridge, and the Royal Institute of British Architects (RIBA) archives has been widespread and immensely helpful, but particular mentions are warranted for Helen Alderton, Simon Case, Mark Dunton, David Heaton, Jeremy Heywood (Lord Heywood of Whitehall), Peter Hill, Helen Lederer, Hannah Meyer, Andrew Riley, Roger Smethurst and Ed Whiting. I am also immensely grateful to those interviewees who spared me their time and shared their experiences and insights, not to mention making the whole process of researching this book a thousand times more enjoyable.

Chapter 5 of this book reproduces a series of posts written for the History of Government blog (https://history.blog.gov.uk/category/researcher-in-residence). It is reproduced with the kind permission of the publisher.

This book also benefits hugely from material provided by Research Assistant Jan Gökçen, whose work was invaluable. Any errors in interpreting this research, however, are entirely the fault of the author and not the researcher.

I am of course most grateful to my extended and loving family, and particularly to Jo. Thank you for your love, and your patience.

The trouble with history is that there's no future in it.
                    – Ken Clark to the author, circa 2014. He's still right.

Introduction

You shouldn't underestimate the influence of geography. The fact that these ancient houses are used for the head of government reflects in many ways how the government runs.[1]

– Andrew Turnbull

Proximity is power.[2]

– Robert Armstrong

Speaking in 1943 on the rebuilding of the Houses of Parliament, Winston Churchill observed that 'We shape our buildings and afterwards our buildings shape us.'[3] The Prime Minister was reflecting on how the small, oblong layout of the Commons, whilst proving very cramped if all Members were in attendance, kept the style of speaking conversational and the party system adversarial. The gravity of deciding to 'cross the floor' to join another party (a decision that Churchill was highly unusual in having taken twice) was reinforced by the design of the building, which sat the government and the opposition on opposite sides of the room, facing one another, poised for battle, with the most senior figures on each side leading the charge from the front benches. This oppositional layout remains influential today. Members are permitted to address one another only from their seats, and are forbidden from speaking from the floor of the House, in the area between the two red lines said to have been drawn two sword-lengths apart.[4]

Churchill also noted that a small chamber meant that 'quick, informal interruptions and interchanges' were possible even when the chamber was half full, brought about by catching the eye of the Speaker of the House when rising or half-rising to speak. In addition, on significant occasions, the cramped nature of the small chamber brought about 'a sense of crowd and urgency', giving 'a sense that great matters are being decided, there and then, by the House'.[5]

The chamber in the House of Commons is deliberately oppositional in its architecture, and its size and layout directly affect how business is conducted. Similarly, the size and layout of No. 10 directly limits the small number of staff that work in the Prime Minister's Office. Its confines dictate which few advisers have easy, direct and frequent access to the Prime Minister, and therefore who has influence over him or her. It provides the curious blend of the formal and informal, of work and leisure (as both home and office), that is central to being Prime Minister. Its relatively humble stature sends a message to the nation that the Prime Minister is neither regal nor presidential, but merely *primus inter pares* (first among equals) in the British system. Successive Prime Ministers have altered it, but it has also altered them.

This book

This book is not just the history of a building. It tells the story of how No. 10 and its occupants interacted in the postwar years, during the premierships of ten different Prime Ministers from 1945 to 1997. It centres on the reconstruction of No. 10 between 1960 and 1963, led by the architect Raymond Erith and taking place during Harold Macmillan's premiership. The study of this process reveals a great deal about the building and the job it houses. It reflects the fusion of informality, adaptability and strict small-'c' conservatism at the heart of Britain's unwritten constitution. It tells us a great deal about how we as a nation have shaped the office of Prime Minister, and how No. 10 itself has influenced the evolution of the role.

The phrase 'geography of power' is used to describe how the buildings that house the most powerful jobs in the country shape the conduct of these roles, and how their occupants in turn shape them. The phrase itself was borrowed from Peter Hennessy's *The Prime Minister*, where it was used to refer to George Downing, the eponymous builder of the street that would go on to become one of the most famous in the world. The phrase may well have been used elsewhere, but that is where it was drawn from in this case. It speaks to the role that physical places play in constraining or allowing the exercise of influence and access. It has also been suggested that the 'architecture of power' may have been more appropriate, and this could have been an equally valid title.[6] However, this is primarily a work of contemporary history, focusing on No. 10 during the premierships of ten postwar Prime Ministers, from Clement Attlee to John Major. To borrow a phrase from an influential contemporary historian for its title seems appropriate.

The book begins with a history of the building itself. Chapter 2 provides an overview of the functions that it has housed in the period 1945–97. Chapter 3 then looks at the layout of key rooms in No. 10, and their relation to the internal geography of power. Chapter 4 explores the geography of power outside the building, as well as considering some of the ways in which geography can be and has been subverted at No. 10. Chapter 5 tells the story of the reconstruction of the Downing Street houses and the adjoining Old Treasury from 1960–3, and explores its influence on No. 10's development. Chapter 6 investigates the building's role as a home, and Chapter 7 its role as a place for hosting visitors and projecting power. The final chapter provides a history of No. 10 under attack, demonstrating the building's resilience and adaptability throughout its long history, before some concluding thoughts.

The extent to which buildings shape the actions of individual political actors does of course have limits. Observing the manner in which journalists have covered the deteriorating physical state of the Palace of Westminster in recent years, the comedian David Mitchell noted the 'tedious satisfaction' that many commentators appeared to derive from overusing the 'leaden analogy' of the crumbling, outdated building for the functions (and the politicians) that it houses.[7] Studying the influence of No. 10 on successive Prime Ministers has involved a careful tightrope walk between providing real human insight into the conduct of arguably the most powerful job in the country, and tedious, overreaching metaphors and conclusions.

I hope that this book does not too often lose its balance. It is intended to blend some degree of insight into the inner workings of No. 10 with a wider interest in one of the most famous and influential buildings in

British history. It is the result of a year and a half as Researcher in Residence at No. 10, an initiative designed with the intention of making No. 10's history more widely accessible. I sincerely hope that it will not be the last such book produced by a Researcher in Residence.

A note on sources

This book makes extensive use of Prime Ministerial and other political memoirs, as well as the few excellent works that have studied No. 10 as a home and office to date, particularly those by Anthony Seldon, R. J. Minney and Christopher Jones. It also draws on archival material, primarily from the National Archives and Erith's personal archives, held by RIBA. Original interviews with some key figures are drawn upon, alongside previous interview material gathered by the Mile End Group at Queen Mary University of London and the Strand Group at King's College London.

However, writing the history of No. 10 itself is not without its challenges. The history of the building is intertwined with the role that it quickly went on to occupy, and the magnitude of this role often means that memoirs and biographies of those who have lived there often quite rightly focus on events and characters rather than place. Details as simple as which room a Prime Minister preferred to work from are recorded only occasionally. Much of No. 10's history has therefore been passed down by word of mouth, and is inherently fallible. One particular anecdote, from the former Cabinet Secretary and Principal Private Secretary at No. 10 Robert Armstrong (Lord Armstrong of Ilminster), illustrates this point particularly well:

> While I was Private Secretary, Mr. Heath had a dinner party for Sir Alec Douglas-Home on his seventieth birthday in 1973 and Mr. Macmillan was invited. He came to the party. When the party was over, he asked if he could see the Cabinet Room. I took him in. There was a dim light, but it was not brightly lit. But it was all there: the table and the chairs, the Prime Minister's telephone by it. Mr. Macmillan – aged about eighty by now – stood at the door and looked around the room, hand on his cane, and after a long pause:

"To think, that was the chair on which I was sitting, the telephone I was using, when I talked to Jack Kennedy during the Cuban missile crisis". I didn't have the heart to say, "Actually, Mr. Macmillan, you were in Admiralty House!"[8]

If even those who occupied the house are prone to historical confusion, then it is fair to assume that the historian may occasionally struggle too.

This does not make the work impossible – only challenging. Some governments, particularly those of Harold Wilson and Margaret Thatcher, featured multiple influential figures who, upon their departure from office, went on to eagerly produce reams of insightful studies on the machinery of No. 10 and the workings of the premiership. Others have produced much less. Internal documents from the Ministry of Works that detail the building's history do exist, and can be useful, but the source of key facts is often unclear, and the degree of historical rigour involved in putting them together is also questionable.

One final point needs to be made. Due to Downing Street's constant evolution and adaptation, the precise location of historic rooms may have altered slightly over time. More significantly, present-day No. 10 is an amalgamation of three separate historic buildings, the main two of which were joined together in 1735. The historic 'house at the back' is therefore an entire floor lower than the terraced house on Downing Street. As a consequence, the ground floor on the Downing Street side, when one enters the famous front door, is the first floor by the time one reaches the back of the house. This can make it difficult to locate a room by referring to floor numbers, as the ground floor at the back of the house, which opens onto the garden, is the basement when viewed from Downing Street. There are also several half-floors, where historic adaptations have led to short flights of stairs or raised ceilings that further confuse matters. For consistency, this book takes the 'ground floor' to be the floor on which one enters from the front door on the Downing Street side. The first floor is immediately above, and the basement immediately below, regardless of whether the rooms referred to are at the front or the back of the house.

1

The Building

It is the smallest, yet the greatest street in the world, because it lies
at the hub of the gigantic wheel which encircles the globe under the
name of the British Empire.

– Joseph Hodges Choate[1]

On first inspection, No. 10 Downing Street appears an unassuming
home for the British Prime Minister. Yet despite its outward appearance, this modest terraced property located just off Whitehall in London's SW1 postcode is a house like no other. Behind one of the world's
most iconic front doors lies a sprawling, labyrinthine building with
an incredible history. No. 10 has been the property of the First Lord
of the Treasury, a role that in modern times has become synonymous
with that of Prime Minister, for nearly 300 years.

Constructed in the 1680s, this historic building has remained a
constant at the heart of British governance ever since. At the time of
John Major's departure from No. 10 in 1997, it had seen fifty different Prime Ministers come and go. Since Arthur Balfour established
the precedent at the turn of the twentieth century, every subsequent
Prime Minister has at some point made Downing Street their home.
Alongside its residential role, No. 10 also serves as a twenty-four-hour
office for the Prime Minister and their staff, as well as a venue for
entertaining prestigious national and international guests.

This historic terraced London house has endured stoically through
the rise and fall of the British Empire, two world wars and countless diplomatic, political and economic crises. It has transitioned
from the Industrial Revolution to today's high-speed, open-all-hours

information age, and has accommodated technological change from the installation of electric lighting to the dawn of email.

Downing Street has also seen the world transformed around it. Its namesake was a former resident of the puritan colony of Massachusetts; it was at Downing Street, just short of a century later, that Prime Minister Frederick North, better known as Lord North, would receive the news that the American colonies were lost.[2]

It was from an upstairs window of No. 10 that Neville Chamberlain would proclaim 'peace for our time' to the assembled crowd in Downing Street in 1938, and it was within this same building that Winston Churchill's War Cabinet would decide to fight on against Adolf Hitler in May 1940. Five years later, Churchill would broadcast the end of the war in Europe from No. 10's Cabinet Room, and his successor, Clement Attlee, would subsequently announce the surrender of Japan from the same spot. Both Benjamin Disraeli's acquisition of the Suez Canal in 1875, and Anthony Eden's reluctant acceptance of its loss following the humiliation of the 1956 crisis, were directed from No. 10.[3]

Protesters have marched on Downing Street throughout its long history. The street was generally accessible to the public until security gates were erected at the Whitehall end in 1989, and protesters have thrown rocks at No. 10's windows on numerous occasions. Suffragettes chained themselves to its railings. Large wooden barricades were erected at the end of the street in the early 1920s as a security measure in response to the Anglo-Irish War. Less could be done when Zeppelins dropped bombs 'alarmingly near' to No. 10 during the First World War; German bombs would cause substantial damage to the building itself during the Second World War.[4] An Irish Republican Army (IRA) mortar also left its mark in 1991, landing in No. 10's garden during a meeting of the War Cabinet to discuss the Gulf War, exploding just after the Prime Minister had said the word 'bomb'.[5]

Throughout all this turmoil and transformation, No. 10 has remained remarkably consistent. Familiar and iconic, the building has provided an abiding presence in a rapidly changing world, remaining fundamentally the same over the years despite the constant evolution of Britain's politics and place in the world. No. 10's appearance and operation have been essentially unchanged, despite the transformation

Neville and Anne Chamberlain look out an upstairs window at
crowds assembled on Downing Street to celebrate the ill-fated
Munich Agreement, September 1938. Sadly, the 'peace for our
time' declared by Chamberlain would prove short-lived.

of its surroundings. It even survived the construction of George
Gilbert Scott's impressive Foreign Office (which became the Foreign
and Commonwealth Office in 1968) on the other side of Downing
Street in the 1860s, which dwarfed No. 10 in both scale and grandeur.
No. 10's notable architecture and world-famous front door remain a
significant selling point across the world. So popular was the iconic
door that a private company approached the government in the 1950s,
seeking to manufacture replica 'No. 10' front doors for sale to American tourists. The Ministry of Works perhaps unsurprisingly decided to
reject the request, however, believing that 'this would, to some extent,
detract from the dignity of the residence'.[6]

Despite its role at the heart of British government, No. 10 was not
designed for its current purpose. The Downing Street houses were
built cheaply, with the intention of turning a profit for their developer,

and were certainly not designed or intended to house the most powerful politicians in Britain. They have been repeatedly, incrementally adapted and refurbished, with only one serious and total reconsideration in their history. Their blend of resilience and adaptability with a reliance on precedent and tradition echoes that of British government and the Westminster system as a whole.

There are great lessons to be gleaned from the study of No. 10. The building's story is intimately intertwined with the stories of its occupants. The interaction between No.10's many historic residents and the building that they have temporarily occupied is revealing of their personalities and their approaches to occupying the office of Prime Minister. But, above all, the history of No. 10 is fascinating and unique.

Living at No. 10

What have the building's historic residents made of No. 10? The house has had more than its fair share of compliments from those who have occupied it over the years. William Pitt the Younger, during his first stay at No. 10 as Chancellor of the Exchequer in 1782, wrote to his mother describing his new residence as 'the best summer town house possible'.[7] Over 150 years later, postwar premier Clement Attlee would report settling into No. 10 easily, describing the house, with typical understatement, as 'very comfortable'.[8] Clarissa Eden, wife of Attlee's successor-but-one, Prime Minister Anthony Eden, thought No. 10 'the loveliest house in London'.[9] The Conservative Prime Minister Harold Macmillan praised No. 10 in his diary, noting that the building was 'rather large, but has great character and charm. It is very liveable'.[10]

The house is not just a home, but a centre of British national life. Olwen Carey Evans, daughter of the First World War Prime Minister David Lloyd George, recalled her time at No. 10 fondly: 'There was always something going on. Famous people came and went, and No. 10 seemed to be the hub of the universe.'[11] Macmillan echoed these sentiments, noting that the building had long been 'famous throughout the whole world as the hub or centre of British rule and influence'.[12] As one historian of the premiership describes, 'All the power lines lead to No. 10.'[13] Life at No. 10 is therefore rarely dull for those who live and work there.

British understatement?

No. 10's air of calming humility has been widely noted. As the building is a venue for national and international decision-making at the highest level, the weight of the world can often bear down heavily upon its shaky foundations. However, No. 10 is a stoic, even tranquil place. Churchill's Private Secretary John 'Jock' Colville described life at No. 10, even during the great strain of the Second World War, as a 'gentlemanly occupation'. Colville's No. 10 was 'a well-established private house of pre-war comfort', within which 'coal fires glowed in every grate, at the tinkle of a bell were ivory hairbrushes and clean towels in the cloakroom; and everything reminded the inhabitants that they were working at the very heart of a great empire, in which haste was undignified and any quiver of the upper lip unacceptable'.[14]

In addition to the air of relaxed professionalism, the relative modesty of the building, particularly when compared with other similarly purposed buildings internationally, is also charming. Joe Haines, Press Secretary to the Labour Prime Minister Harold Wilson, observed that the modest façade of No. 10 masked the incredible power that lay within:

> From the street outside it is a classic example of British understatement, hiding the treasures of art and history and experience that are within... Today it harbours only Britain's crises, but it was once the eye of the storms that shook the world.[15]

The contrast between the Downing Street terrace and the notably larger and significantly grander Foreign and Commonwealth Office building across the road is stark. Writing in 1908, the author Charles E. Pascoe observed the unusual contradiction between the two buildings' outward appearances and the significance of the functions that they housed:

The First Lord's residence is overshadowed by the statelier glories of the Foreign Office opposite. That imposing pile may rear its grand front over against the humbler dwelling; it may make parade of its fine archway and inner court; it may boast its sumptuous confer-ence room, its richly decorated apartments of State, its noble halls and stairways, its painted ceilings and the rest; but not one of the grand rooms has a tithe of the interest that belongs to the smallest chamber in that little house fronting it. A dingy little dwelling in sober truth [...] unknown to the millions of London, save by repute, whose history should be richer in anecdote and reminisce, could all be written down, than that of any building owned by the Crown.[16]

A place in history

The sheer historical importance of the decisions that have been made in No. 10 continue to make a great impression on its occupants. Mac-millan argued that the building had 'a meaning and a significance' which was essential to preserve.[17] Margaret Thatcher observed that 'All Prime Ministers are intensely aware that, as tenants and stewards of No. 10 Downing Street, they have in their charge one of the most precious jewels in the nation's heritage.'[18] For Thatcher, the portraits and busts of past Prime Ministers that decorated No. 10's otherwise unremarkable interior reminded the current occupant of the 250-year path of history onto which they now stepped.[19]

Thatcher's speech-writer Ronald Millar felt that this sense of history seeped not just from No. 10's ornaments and decorations but from the very walls of the building itself. Noting the building's plain-ness, Millar claimed that No. 10 'acquires a wonder and a magic' for those who know and consider the stories of the people who have 'run Britain from those premises and more than once saved it from its enemies':

And if you walk down its long corridor from the black front door to the white one at the end of that corridor which opens to the Cabinet Room, and stand in the doorway and look about you and remember those who have sat and taken the big decisions [...] why, then you're a dull stick if you are not stirred and humbled by the experience, for you are standing in the engine room of our country's history.[20]

Peter Hennessy has also noted that, alongside its calmness, the thing that strikes visitors to No. 10 is 'the near tangible feeling of a deep and richly accumulated past whose resonance is such that the walls almost speak'.[21]

The rabbit warren

Some have spoken of the historic building's cramped conditions in fond terms. Harold Macmillan found that 'one of the charms of the house lies in the number of small rooms which give a sense of intimacy'.[22] Harold Wilson described No. 10 as 'a small village'.[23] Bernard Donoughue, Head of the No. 10 Policy Unit under Wilson, describes how the 'cosiness' of No. 10 meant that 'there was little scope for hierarchy and standing on ceremony'.[24] Whilst the relatively small building, with its maze-like corridors and disorientating layout, can seem like an inconvenient place from which to run a government, its humbleness and intimacy can also make for a warm, welcoming and ultimately nimble operation.

There are, of course, alternative viewpoints. Henry Campbell-Bannerman, Liberal Prime Minister from 1905–8, described a 'rotten old barrack of a house'; his wife Charlotte 'a house of doom'.[25] Perhaps this is unsurprising, considering that Campbell-Bannerman was the only Prime Minister to die at No. 10. Margot Asquith, wife of Campbell-Bannerman's successor, Herbert Henry Asquith, recalled waiting outside in the car whilst her husband visited his ailing predecessor inside the building that would soon become their home: 'I looked at the dingy exterior of Number 10 and wondered how we could live there.'[26]

Margot Asquith did not subsequently warm to the labyrinthine property: 'It is an inconvenient house with three poor staircases [...] and after living there a few weeks I made up my mind that owing to the impossibility of circulation I could only entertain my Liberal friends at dinner or at garden parties.' To make matters worse, taxi drivers seemed not to know the address: '10 Downing Street ought to be as well known in London as Marble Arch or the Albert Memorial, but it is not.'[27]

As Margot Asquith observed, the unusual and complex layout of the Downing Street houses was far from convenient. In fact, her son Anthony and Chancellor Lloyd George's daughter Megan once both went missing within the house. Fearing abduction by Irish nationalists or disgruntled suffragettes, the police were called, before the children were found asleep in the lift, with the door open, on the house's top floor.[28] The daughter of Ramsay MacDonald, the first Labour Prime Minister to occupy the house, 'recalled being appalled by the rambling passages and by the sheer number of rooms'.[29]

Fit for purpose?

The building was not designed for its current purpose. In many respects, it is an ill-fitting home for the central business of government. Marcia Williams, Wilson's Personal and Political Secretary, offered a strongly worded summary of this position:

> The truth is that No. 10 is both a dreadful place to live and work in and also an exciting place to live and work in. It is not beautiful but it is impressive. Its designers have not succeeded in making it either an efficient office or a comfortable home. It seems to exude an air of condescending contempt for both roles.[30]

Williams was not alone in this outlook. Jonathan Powell, who arrived at No. 10 in 1997 as Chief of Staff to Tony Blair, described the place as 'extraordinarily ill-suited to be the headquarters of a modern government.'[31] Another member of the Blair team, reportedly more familiar with open-plan office working, described Downing Street as 'too genteel and peaceful', but also ultimately 'too compartmentalised' to prove an effective workspace.[32] Edward Heath's former Political Secretary Douglas Hurd said in 1979, 'It is hard to imagine anyone governing anything substantial from Number Ten.'[33]

A 'furnished house to let'

Alongside the impracticalities of working at No. 10, the curiously ephemeral nature of life in its occupancy can also play on the minds of its residents. Some Prime Ministers are able to make their mark on No. 10, either by virtue of being in office at the point when periodic renovations or redecorations are required, or by remaining in office for long enough to find the time to make alterations that reflect their personalities. Others are simply less interested in doing so. Margaret Thatcher made the improvement of the building's appearance an early priority, claiming that 'When we arrived No. 10 looked rather like a "furnished house to let", which in a way, I suppose it was.'[34]

Prime Ministers are continually aware that their stay at No. 10 could end at any moment. The Head of the British Government can be unseated with very little notice should they lose the confidence of their peers. Thatcher, herself the victim of a sudden ejection from No. 10 at the hands of her party rather than the electorate, was a prime example of this. Once public or party has decided that a Prime Minister has outstayed their welcome, the speed at which they can be removed is remarkable. Every occupant of No. 10 is aware of this, having themselves ousted their own predecessor, more often than not against their will.

Acutely aware of the temporary nature of Prime Ministers' occupation of the building and the role, the early twentieth-century author Pascoe mused on their fears and concerns:

> Who will sleep in this room twenty years hence? Nay, who will sleep here seven years from now? Do Prime Ministers dream strange dreams – a phantasmal and a hideous dream – I wonder, when they come in here of nights, worn out, from their ceaseless vigil in the Parliament House over yonder?[35]

Why would Prime Ministers, occupying what is widely regarded as the most powerful job in British politics, dream such 'hideous' dreams? Perhaps the answer lies in the precariousness of their position. Prime Ministers never cease to be vulnerable to power-hungry colleagues and the near-unlimited range of unforeseen surprises that Macmillan reportedly described as 'events, dear boy, events'.[36] All the while, both personal and private life are subject to constant and ever-increasing scrutiny. It's enough to cause anyone nervous nightmares.

In a building so rich with history, it is hard to forget that few Prime Ministers have left of their own volition. Nowhere is this more apparent than in No. 10's Grand Staircase, the architectural heart of the building. Here, portraits of every previous Prime Minister since Robert Walpole line the walls, a constant reminder of Enoch Powell's famous observation that 'All political lives, unless they are cut off in midstream at a happy juncture, end in failure.'[37] The historian W. L. Stephen noted of the staircase, 'It is not easy to take one's place in that distinguished company. The historic house is haunted by the ghosts of the disappointed and disillusioned.'[38] An anecdote from a former No. 10 insider reinforces this concept:

> Mr. Heath was a great admirer of Macmillan, and Macmillan came to see him in No. 10, I suppose quite early on in his period in office. Heath was in the Study upstairs. [...] I asked Mr. Macmillan whether we were going to go upstairs, and whether he would like to use the lift – he was eighty, after all. He said no, he'd like to go up the stairs, past all those [portraits of] eighteenth-century Prime Ministers. We went up the first flight and then along the landing. And then we went up the second flight, and Mr. Macmillan began going slower and slower, and I thought, he is going to flake out – have a heart attack or something – and I shall be blamed. Then he stopped completely. My heart was in my mouth. He peered at the pictures of Neville Chamberlain, Stanley Baldwin and Ramsay MacDonald, and then he turned to me and said, "A melancholy set of faces." He then steamed up the rest of the staircase.[39]

Whilst uncertainty of tenure is one factor for a Prime Minister in preventing No. 10 being a comfortable and relaxing home, many would argue that the looseness of their grip on the reins of the nation that they nominally control is another. Those who study the premiership, whether vocationally or academically, have noted a gradual increase in the resources at the centre of British governance. Some have perceived an increasing tendency towards centralisation, with No. 10 now more likely than ever to intervene in policy decisions across government.[40] However, many of the role's historical occupants have either struggled, or felt that they have struggled, to exercise the power that is commonly assumed to accompany the title of Prime Minister.[41] It has even been suggested that the physical size of No. 10 as a building has limited the power and resources of the role, producing 'a premiership modelled to the space available, rather than vice versa'.[42]

Whether the British Prime Minister has become over-mighty over time is a subject of constant and perennial debate. But it is certainly true that the premiership can be the most powerful, most frustrating or most vulnerable occupation in government. Even those who manage to cling to their position at the notional top, parking themselves firmly within No. 10, can find that staying too long has its own hazards. Norman Tebbit, who ran the 1987 Conservative Party campaign for Thatcher, observed of the later years of her premiership:

> The windows in this building are very big when the Prime Minister first comes in, and every year they get smaller and smaller and smaller and after ten years it is very difficult for a Prime Minister to see the world outside as opposed to the world of No. 10.[43]

A bunker mentality is a constant occupational hazard – an enduring temptation to be resisted when at Downing Street.

Whilst opinions clearly differ on No. 10's suitability, comfort and appeal as a place of work and a home for the Prime Minister, it is clear that it is both an unusual place and one that leaves a lasting impression on those that work there. It truly is a house like no other, its air so thick with accumulated history that for the unfortunate it can become suffocating. For the successful, it is invigorating, inspiring and electric. Ultimately, as Marcia Williams observed, 'Anybody who has ever worked at No. 10 never has to worry about a subject for conversation again.'[44]

Origins

How did this bizarre and unique place come to be? Certainly not by design. Upon entering No. 10's famous doorway today, the endless corridors, staircases and rooms that lead off from its Entrance Hall immediately illustrate the building's gradual and uncoordinated evolution. The complex and asymmetric layout of the rooms and floors of Downing Street branches out in all directions from the initial trunk: a row of cheap, square, terraced houses constructed in the 1680s. What began as a row of relatively unexceptional homes has evolved over the years into a much more impressive property, and No. 10 in particular has grown almost organically over the years to become an impressive and surprisingly effective home and office for the British Prime Minister. The story of Downing Street begins with the story of its builder, the man who gave the street its name.

George Downing

The initial short row of terraced houses on Downing Street was built between 1682 and 1684. George Downing himself was a fascinating character, and his reputation remains controversial. A former ship's chaplain and army preacher, Downing became one of the first graduates of Harvard University during a stint in the United States early in his life. On his return to England, he became close to Oliver Cromwell, and became Cromwell's Commonwealth Scoutmaster-General in 1649 – effectively, his chief spy. This role saw him take up an office next to Cromwell's, close to the site of what is now Downing Street.[45] In 1657, Downing was dispatched to The Hague as British Ambassador, and tasked with spying on the exiled British royals.

However, following Cromwell's death in 1658, and his subsequent replacement by his less able son Richard Cromwell, Downing was quick to sense weakness, and rapidly shifted his loyalties. Finding his way to Charles II in disguise, he begged forgiveness and pledged his allegiance to the Royalists. This cynical move saw him knighted in 1660, subsequently becoming a spy in Holland once more, this time at the service of royalty. Sending several of his former allies back to Britain for their trial and execution, including John Okey, the former captain of the army regiment Downing had once been attached to as a preacher, earned Downing his historical reputation for treachery. Samuel Pepys most famously described him as a 'perfidious rogue', and it is this phrase that has remained most famously attached to Downing in popular memory today, despite his connection to the home of the British Prime Minister.

Downing also acquired a reputation as a miserly man, with both Pepys and even his own mother describing him as such; despite being one of Harvard University's first graduates, Downing left a grand total of £5 of his accumulated wealth to his alma mater on his death.[46] His remarkable personal success was also matched by a reputational collapse within his own lifetime; a return to Holland later in his life, at the behest of the King, saw Downing flee back to Britain, where he would spend two months imprisoned in the Tower of London for cowardice. However, his many achievements as a diplomat and administrator, which include pioneering a system for the central collection of tax revenues and the issuing of war bonds, are now increasingly being recognised.[47] For good or for ill, Downing led an extraordinary life, later giving his name to an unremarkable set of buildings which would go on to serve a most remarkable purpose.

Downing Street

The area around Downing Street has played a significant part in national governance for centuries. Henry VIII first moved England's centre of power to Whitehall Palace (previously York Place) in 1530. This huge, sprawling palace was located between St. James's Park and the banks of the Thames, and ran half a mile up Whitehall from Westminster to Charing Cross. It was almost entirely destroyed by fire in 1698.[48]

Today's Downing Street roughly corresponds with the historical site of The Axe brewhouse, which operated near the palace in the sixteenth century. Around 1605, buildings on this site were home to the Keeper of the Palace of Whitehall, Thomas Knyvet, the man who arrested Guy Fawkes. When Whitehall Palace was active, Henry VIII's cockpit and tennis court were also located nearby, and the ruins of part of the historic cockpit are preserved in part to this day within the Cabinet Office's contemporary home at 70 Whitehall.[49] Throughout the 1600s, several members of the royal family inhabited buildings on or around the site of today's Downing Street.

Despite the remarkable history of the area, the Downing Street houses themselves were built on marshy ground, at minimal cost and to a low standard. The boggy ground was not Downing's fault. As difficult as it may be to imagine today, the site of the nearby Westminster Abbey was once effectively a small island, surrounded by tributaries of the River Tyburn at the point where it met the River Thames. The Thames was at that time untamed and significantly wider, and this rare dry spot amongst its marshy north bank was known as Thorney Island. The instability of the ground on which Downing Street was eventually constructed therefore predates Downing's involvement by some centuries. However, the developer's penny-pinching had a clear impact on the houses, with little effort made to mitigate the environment; No. 10 would soon begin to sink as well as fall apart. Downing's was also a very long legacy: 300 years after the construction of the houses at Downing Street, Churchill would describe them as 'shaky and lightly built by the profiteering contractor whose name they bear'.[50]

Downing had acquired the land that would eventually become the site of Downing Street from Cromwell in 1654. The Restoration saw the sale of the land cancelled, but Downing continued to pursue it. Just short of ten years later, after receiving his knighthood, Downing was able to convince the king to return the land to him.[51] This included the site of Hampden House, a large amalgamated property occupying much of the site of what is now Downing Street, which Downing sought to pull down. However, he was unable to build on the site until 1682, when the Hampden lease expired. A row of around fifteen houses was then constructed with impressive speed, with the house that is now recognised as No. 10 originally numbered as No. 5 Downing Street (or, rather, the plot itself was labelled 'Plot 5' on maps) until the late 1700s.

The first Prime Minister

Despite lending his name to the street, Downing himself did not live in any of his houses, and he died in 1684. In 1732, King George II decided to present part of what would become No. 10 to Robert Walpole, the Whig statesman and First Lord of the Treasury, widely regarded as the first Prime Minister. The term 'Prime Minister' itself was first used with some hostility, as an accusatory term for a minister seen as attempting to become overly dominant in what was – theoretically, at least – a collective system of government.[52] Far from being deliberately designed, the role of Prime Minister has evolved over centuries and experienced gradual, iterative change, as it has been stretched and reshaped to accommodate the demands of a changing world.

Walpole was the son of a wealthy Norfolk landowner. Prior to becoming a member of parliament (MP), he had managed his family's impressive estate. Already owning a substantial property portfolio, Walpole refused to accept the Downing Street address as a personal gift from the king. Instead, Walpole declared that he could only accept it in his capacity as First Lord of the Treasury. Holders of that office have inherited temporary ownership of the house for the duration of their tenure ever since, and it is the title of First Lord of the Treasury that is inscribed onto the letterbox of No. 10 to this day. Like the lion's-head door knocker and the light above the famous front door, this letterbox appears to date from the 1770s, with the design remaining essentially the same throughout countless replacements and renovations.[53]

Walpole persuaded the king that the property required expansion in order to make it fit for purpose. The building recognised today as No. 10 was therefore joined to the much grander 'house at the back' that was presented to Walpole in 1732.[54] This 'house at the back' had also previously been occupied by the Earl and Countess of Lichfield, amongst others, and was most recently home to the German nobleman Hans Caspar von Bothmer, who died the same year that the property was gifted to Walpole.[55] Its entrance faced northwards, onto Horse Guards, and it was a larger and more impressive property than the Downing Street terraces.[56] A small cottage on the Downing Street side of the property was also acquired and absorbed into the site of the new building upon the eventual relocation of its inhabitant, a Mr. Chicken, about whom little is known apart from his wonderful name. Chicken only moved out of Downing Street in 1734, one year before the first Prime Minister moved into No. 10.[57]

Although Walpole's decision not to accept the property as a personal gift seems public-minded, his motives may not have been entirely altruistic. Adapting No. 10 for its new purpose, and particularly joining the smaller terraced property on Downing Street to the 'house at the back', required substantial and expensive work. Further improvements were then required to make the house habitable, and Walpole commissioned the architect William Kent, who had worked on Houghton Hall, his grand home in Norfolk, to gut the interior and join the properties together around one central courtyard. Kent also moved the main entrance to the Downing Street side of the building, and constructed No. 10's Grand Staircase, which remains one of the house's most impressive features to this day.

In accepting the new and expanded No. 10 only in an official capacity, Walpole ensured that the extensive building works and renovations were performed at the taxpayers' expense rather than his own.[58] The exact cost of these works is difficult to pinpoint, as they were absorbed into the existing budget for some already-planned works on the adjacent Old Treasury building, rather than recorded separately. However, this overall figure shot up from an estimate of £8,000 to a final total of around £20,000, presumably due to the additional costs of the work on the new property of the First Lord of the Treasury. This further suggests that allowing the public purse to pay may have been a rather shrewd move on the part of the first Prime Minister.[59]

As the historian R. J. Minney describes, work on the new residence of the First Lord of the Treasury was superficially impressive, but hid deeper and more fundamental flaws in the building's construction:

> Money had been spent lavishly. The work was well done. A delightful home, spacious and decorated with taste, had been provided for the King's first minister. But neither Kent nor Downing had given much thought to the foundations [...] It was inevitable that the timber would rot and that the house should be in need of constant and costly attention.[60]

Despite this, the house still stands today. It has hosted the biggest decisions and some of the most significant events in British political history. But its constant need for refurbishment and rescue from its own inherent flaws has been a constant repeated motif throughout its lifespan.

Adaptation and early expansion

Whilst Nos. 10, 11 and 12 appear today as a row of modest terraced houses when viewed from Downing Street, No. 10 is much larger than it first appears, due to its being connected to the 'house at the back' by a series of corridors set around a central courtyard. As a consequence of its amalgamated nature, today's No. 10 looks from above like an offset square, extending northwards behind the façades of Downing Street's now world-famous south-facing terraced houses. After entering the famous front door, it is easy to lose track of your position within the building, amongst No. 10's endless corridors and ad hoc rooms.

As Sarah Hogg, Head of the Policy Unit under Major, observed, 'The physical oddities of Downing Street reflect its origins. It is an architectural marriage of Roundhead and Royalist, an allegory of British constitutional history.' [61] The architectural inconsistency of the property, from the historic 'house at the back' to the more modest terraced property built by Downing, is still detectable when walking through No. 10 today. The countless adaptations, renovations and alterations throughout No. 10's existence can also be detected, not only in the huge variety in the size and style of its rooms, but also in the asymmetry of its floorplan.

'Full of passages, stairways and rooms is No. 10', wrote Pascoe in 1908.[62] Downing Street's sprawling, labyrinthine layout is part of what makes it so unique, engendering great affection but also frustration. Pitt the Younger referred to No. 10 as a 'vast, awkward house'; Disraeli later preferred the word 'rambling'.[63] More recently, Hogg described a 'building like a Cluedo board'.[64]

The BBC's Christopher Jones preferred the metaphor of 'a political Tardis', its unassuming exterior masking a surprisingly complex and larger-than-expected interior, much like Doctor Who's famous time machine disguised as a police box. It could be argued that entering the historic building is like stepping back in time, but what Jones described as its disorientating 'endless corridors' and 'confusing number of staircases' also make it difficult for the first-time visitor to keep track of where they are in space.[65]

No. 10 is often compared to a rabbit warren; it is arguably more analogous to an ant nest in its complexity and asymmetry. This is the

A cleaner sweeps outside No. 10, 1947. Like Trigger's broom,
No. 10 has had so many parts replaced that it seems faintly
ridiculous to describe it as the same building.

result of an almost organic evolution over hundreds of years that has
matched that of the gradually shifting role at the centre of British government that it houses. Neither was designed or planned. Rather, both
have adapted, expanded and contracted throughout history to suit the
needs of the time. Even Downing Street itself has changed completely
– the road was a cul-de-sac until 1879, when No. 14 was knocked
down, opening access to the street at the St. James's Park end.[66] Today,
the street is inaccessible to the public from either end.

The adaptation of Downing Street has not come without cost. Ministry of Works files held at the National Archives note that, within thirty years of the first Prime Minister moving into Downing Street, the buildings were already being described as 'old' and 'much decayed'.[67] Work by prominent architects including William Kent and John Soane in the eighteenth and nineteenth centuries was accompanied by numerous major expenditures on repairs and rebuilding, including over £11,000 of works in the 'Great Repair' of the late 1700s (a sizeable sum for the time, and twice as much as the initial estimate), and modifications such as the installation of electric lighting in 1894 and central heating in 1937.[68] The majority of these works would prove more expensive than expected, and would repeatedly fail to address No. 10's structural issues.

Occupants

No. 10 was inconsistently occupied after Walpole departed the house upon his resignation in 1742. In the decades that followed, its on-and-off residents included several Chancellors of the Exchequer, such as Francis Dashwood, the hedonistic founder of the Hellfire Club and Prime Minister Henry Pelham's son-in-law, who, as the BBC's Jones notes, 'had absolutely no right whatsoever to be there, but who lived at No. 10 for eight years'.[69] Both Lord North and Pitt the Younger occupied the building alongside their families for relatively long periods during their premierships, but the nineteenth century saw No. 10 decline in usage and status. Over the course of half a century, the building became primarily an office, occupied only by clerks and secretaries, and at times lived in by no one. The mid-nineteenth century also saw the area around Downing Street fall into serious disrepute, and by 1846 there were an estimated 170 brothels and 145 gin parlours in the area.[70]

Despite major works throughout the 1800s, including Soane's iconic designs for No. 10's dining rooms, and consistent public expenditure on maintaining the building, it was surprisingly little used and little loved.[71] Neither Disraeli nor William Gladstone elected to live in No. 10 during their first terms.[72] As Jones notes, Victorian Prime Ministers were often 'wealthy aristocrats who much preferred to remain in their own splendid residences rather than squash in with the clerks in a Westminster back street'.[73] The poor state of the building, alongside the undesirable nature of the area around Downing Street, cannot have helped. Some premiers declined to even use No. 10 for work; in the nineteenth century, Cabinet meetings were often held in the much grander Foreign and Commonwealth Office building, particularly impressive after its revamp in the 1860s by the architect George Gilbert Scott.[74]

It wasn't until the twentieth century that Arthur Balfour, Conservative Prime Minister from 1902–5, established the convention that Prime Ministers would be assumed to live, as well as work, at No. 10. Balfour himself was unusual in having lived in No. 10 prior to his becoming Prime Minister, occupying the premises briefly from 1891–2 and during the premiership of his predecessor and uncle, Robert Gascoyne-Cecil (Prime Minister three times in 1885–8, 1886–92 and 1895–1902), whilst serving as Leader of the House of Commons and First Lord of the Treasury. This was the last time that the latter role was not synonymous with that of Prime Minister. Balfour continued to live at No. 10 throughout his premiership. In a manner typical of the evolutionary British political system, once the precedent was set, it was adopted by subsequent Prime Ministers and became an unwritten rule that has lasted ever since.

In an equally British fashion, however, this was a precedent that was followed by all who followed – except when it wasn't. Harold Wilson elected not to move in to No. 10 during his second term as Prime Minister from 1974–6. Two temporary forced relocations to nearby Admiralty House, located just a short distance up Whitehall, were also brought about – first by essential renovation works during Macmillan's premiership from 1960–3, and later by repairs after the IRA mortar attack in 1991. However, despite these notable caveats, it remains the case that Downing Street has at some point been the home of every Prime Minister since Balfour.

In this time, the building has endured a state of near-collapse due to neglect and structural decay, and has survived bomb attacks, some direct hits and some falling nearby, during both peacetime and two world wars. It has seen and accommodated the arrival of electric lighting, gas heating, the motorcar, television and the internet. The role of

Prime Minister has evolved, and in many senses expanded, over hundreds of years, and yet the basic fabric of the building that houses the job has remained essentially the same. Somehow, No. 10 has remained a reassuring constant at the heart of decision-making in a rapidly changing world.

Modern Downing Street

There is no key to No. 10's famous front door. Today, the door is operated by a security guard, who waits inside and monitors arrivals via closed-circuit television. The guard opens the door from inside in anticipation of wanted arrivals, giving the impression of high-profile visitors having mystical powers. Prior to 1997, a policeman would stand outside the door and knock when someone needed to be let in. The door itself has also changed; today, it is one of two identical pieces, with the other kept in storage and substituted whenever renovations are necessary. Both are made of reinforced steel, rather than oak.

Beyond the front door lies No. 10's Entrance Hall with its striking black-and-white chequered floor tiles, dating back to the 'Great Repair' of the 1760s and 1770s.[75] Portraits of Walpole and Pitt the Younger have dominated the walls immediately ahead for many years (although these portraits, like all works of art in No. 10, are not assured of permanent residence). In one corner sits an antique Chippendale hooded chair, with a drawer underneath for storing hot coals to warm the guards who once occupied them when protecting the building. The chair is said to be one of a pair of two such fine pieces of furniture, with the location of the other piece currently unknown.

A corridor to the left after entering No. 10 connects the three Downing Street houses together, leading through a series of (usually) open doors and past a staircase, to Nos. 11 and 12. To the immediate right after entering stands the bow-windowed room at the front of No. 10 that in the postwar years came to house the No. 10 Press Office. Straight ahead, a corridor leads from the Downing Street part of the building, past the courtyard at the centre of No. 10, to the grander Kent-built half of the building, which begins with the Cabinet

Anteroom. This is where ministers congregate before Cabinet meetings, sharing political gossip and preparing themselves, before entering the adjoining Cabinet Room to discuss the issues of the week.

The Cabinet Room, historically the office of the Prime Minister, is relatively spacious compared to many of the rooms in No. 10. However, it remains quite cramped due to the large coffin-shaped table that dominates it, and the two impressive double pillars that were installed when the room was enlarged and extended eastwards in 1783.[76] Behind the pillars, a baize door leads to a room historically occupied by the Prime Minister's most senior Private Secretaries (usually the Principal Private Secretary, the Prime Minister's most senior direct civil service adviser, and the Foreign Affairs Private Secretary). Beyond that, a more distant room is occupied by those Private Secretaries deemed to require less instant access to the Prime Minister.

Two similarly connected, albeit smaller, rooms spin off from the Cabinet Room at its opposite end; these rooms have been used for a variety of purposes throughout history, but in the postwar period were most commonly associated with political advisers. Traditionally, and throughout much of the period studied in this book, this network of rooms around the Cabinet Room represented the operational centre of No. 10 – the hub where the Prime Minister would work, and where access to him or her, either in person or through papers, was filtered through the Private Office or the Prime Minister's political advisers.

Adjacent to the Senior Private Secretaries' Office is the Grand Staircase, arguably the architectural centrepiece of No. 10. The three-sided, cantilevered staircase is impressive in its own right, but it is the collection of Prime Ministerial portraits, running up its walls in chronological order, that makes the Grand Staircase arguably the most striking part of the house. Each Prime Minister's departure from Downing Street is now followed by their image taking its place at the top of the staircase, with each existing picture being moved painstakingly down towards the basement of No. 10. The historian Anthony Seldon traces the origins of this tradition to Edward Hamilton, Permanent Secretary to the Treasury, who donated the initial set of portraits to No. 10 in 1906.[77] Downing Street's long history can be traced here, through not only the subjects but the portraits themselves. The earliest images

are engravings, up to and including that of Lloyd George, with subsequent premiers represented by photographs, although remaining in
black and white all the way through to today.[78]

At the bottom of the Grand Staircase lies the basement, home to the
Garden Rooms, the historic offices of No. 10's pool of typists, clerks
and administrative support staff. Their offices are located at the back
of the building, and one short flight of stairs down (but only a few
seconds' sprint) from the Private Secretaries' Room. Due to No. 10's ad
hoc construction, the knocking together of two buildings that created
it and its location on a significant slope, the Garden Rooms are located
at ground level, looking out directly onto the garden, despite being
one floor down from the Downing Street entrance and the famous
front door. This cannot help to improve the sense of disorientation
that first-time visitors are likely to feel.

Upstairs

Taking the stairs up, rather than down, a floor from the Private Secretaries' Room and the operational centre of No. 10 leads to the most
impressive part of the house. The State Rooms, consisting of three
former drawing rooms and two dining rooms – one large and one
small – are the finest rooms in Downing Street, and are today used primarily for functions and entertaining. Two of the three State Drawing
Rooms have been traditionally known by their colour, although the
tendency of different Prime Ministers to alter the colour schemes in
No. 10 can make this occasionally challenging.

At one end of the building lies the corner drawing room, widely
known as the White Room, despite its once being painted yellow
under the supervision of Neville Chamberlain's wife, Anne.[79] This
room was historically used as a bedroom by early Prime Ministers or
their wives, and has the dubious distinction of being the site of the
death of one Prime Minister and a Chancellor of the Exchequer.[80] As
well as temporarily changing its colour, Anne Chamberlain, perhaps
sensing the room's morbid legacy, masterminded a more lasting transformation of the room's purpose, changing it from a private space to a
room for entertaining.[81]

Despite initially using it as a bedroom, Anne Chamberlain decided to vacate the White Room due to her discomfort with the lack of privacy that the interconnected State Rooms provided. The Prime Minister's living quarters were moved another floor up, reflecting the expansion of the premiership, and the associated increase in the number of staff required at No. 10. In recent times, the White Room has most often been used for 'fireside chat'-style television interviews and photo opportunities for visiting dignitaries. Its ornate ceiling, which dates back to Thatcher's premiership but references a style hundreds of years older, features the daffodil, rose, shamrock and thistle that represent the United Kingdom of Great Britain and Northern Ireland's four constituent countries.

The next room along, joined to the White Room by double doors that can be fixed open during events, is currently known as the Terracotta Room, although its walls were once red, then blue, and it was painted green in the 1980s before its most recent incarnation.[82] The Terracotta Room in turn connects via another set of double doors to the largest of the State Rooms, known as the Pillared Room. The Pillared Room is often used for hosting and entertaining, with the Terracotta Room and White Room able to provide space for overspill if required. All three State Drawing Rooms are used to entertain guests and showcase No. 10's finest art and furniture.

Through another adjoining door from the Pillared Room lie two Soane-designed dining rooms. First is the Small Dining Room, historically used by some Prime Ministers as a personal or family dining room. Passing through double doors to the far end of the Small Dining Room, one arrives in the much larger State Dining Room, perhaps the most impressive room in No. 10. This room has a high vaulted ceiling and can accommodate 65 guests for meals. It has hosted a huge range of prominent guests, from royalty to politicians and other famous figures.

This floor is also home to the Prime Minister's Study, located next door to the White Room and just across an anteroom from the Grand Staircase. Formerly another bedroom, in the postwar era this room has been used by some Prime Ministers as an alternative working space to the Cabinet Room. Today, a painting of Margaret Thatcher looks out over the room from above the fireplace. Commissioned by Gordon Brown during his premiership, the portrait reflects Thatcher's habit of using the Study as a workspace, and has led to the room being informally referred to as the Thatcher Room by No. 10 staff today, although several other Prime Ministers also made great use of it.

Further upstairs

The Prime Minister's self-contained flat, adapted and renovated many times throughout history, is located another floor up in the building, remaining there today. However, since Tony Blair set a precedent, the Chancellor of the Exchequer has usually lived above No. 10. Due to the large size of the Blair family, it was agreed that the Prime Minister would instead live above No.11 Downing Street, which provides a larger living space.

Additional office space, increasingly at an absolute premium within No. 10, is provided primarily on the higher floors, including the offices of the Policy Unit and other staff that are not deemed to require immediate proximity to the Prime Minister. Accommodation for staff who are required to stay overnight has been provided on the top floor of No. 10, which was also once the home of the famous Downing Street switchboard, known affectionately as Switch and famed for their ability to track down anyone, anywhere, at any time.

If there has been a general pattern of change in No. 10 in the postwar years, it has been the expansion of office space within the building, alongside the gradual easing out of functions that do not require regular access – and therefore physical proximity – to the Prime Minister. Like the development of a city, the growth at No. 10's centre has led to an expansion into the building's 'suburbs', alongside the growing 'commuter town' that is the adjacent home of the Cabinet Office at 70 Whitehall. Only an elite few have been able to maintain their position at the very centre of the building, as we shall see in Chapter 3.

Over the years, No. 10 has changed alongside the role which it houses. Whilst its current situation emerged by historical accident, years of precedent and tradition have shaped its usage today. Change has been incremental and often reactive, and yet somehow it has been accommodated without serious reconsideration of the entire structure. In this respect, No. 10 is the perfect home for the British Prime Minister.

2

What Goes On Inside No. 10 Downing Street

It would not be possible to write a book about No. 10 Downing Street and the geography of power without at least a brief overview of the role that it houses. Others have written much more comprehensive and specialised studies of the premiership and the machinery that supports it at No. 10, and this chapter does not seek to reinvent that particular wheel. Rather, this chapter informs the following chapters by providing an overview of the role of Prime Minister and how it has changed over the years, as well as introducing the Prime Minister's Office that supports the premiership from within (and around) No. 10.

The Prime Minister

The role of Prime Minister in the British system, as mentioned in the previous chapter, was not one that was deliberated upon, carefully constructed and then enshrined in a written constitution. It is the product of hundreds of years of unwritten conventions and a gradual, informal evolution, as Prime Ministers have stretched and reshaped their remits. As with much in British politics, it is important to note that the Prime Minister's role is predicated on precedent rather than prescribed on parchment. As the politician David Steel described, 'There are no ground rules here. There are historical precedents but, basically, you make them up as you go along.'[1]

He has a point. Despite Robert Walpole being widely accepted to have become the first Prime Minister in 1721, the job's title only really began to be used in an official capacity from the late nineteenth century onwards, when it was written into the Treaty of Berlin by Benjamin

Disraeli and featured in Hansard's list of government ministers for the first time.[2] Its first mention in statute came as recently as 1917, when the Chequers Estate Act declared Chequers a Prime Ministerial residence.[3] By this point, No. 10 had been the property of the First Lord of the Treasury (a role that came to be synonymous with that of Prime Minister) for almost 200 years.

That it took so long for the role to be written down in a legal sense reflects the amorphous nature of the British constitution. As previously mentioned, the very term 'Prime Minister' first emerged as a title of derision for a minister who was seen as getting above themselves; twenty years after having become, in effect, the first Prime Minister, in 1741 Walpole elected to 'unequivocally deny that I am sole and prime minister' in front of the Commons.[4]

Whilst it has become the most powerful job in British politics, there is no definitive manual for an incoming premier to consult, and there is no formal document defining exactly what the Prime Minister can and cannot do. Their power can be phenomenal, but their vulnerability is intense. What they are able to achieve is often a product of personality as much as procedure. Ultimately, if the purpose, functions and powers of the Prime Minister seem difficult to pin down, that is because they are. As the US political scientist Richard Neustadt summarised, 'In Britain governing is *meant* to be a mystery. And so it is.'[5]

An evolving role

Over hundreds of years, the role of Prime Minister has acquired more and more functions, something that the historian Peter Hennessy has described as the 'stretching of the premiership'.[6] Some of these functions were slowly transferred from the monarch, as the role of the crown in the governance of Britain became gradually more ceremonial (although it remains far from exclusively so). Others are simply the product of a changing wider world, whether necessitated by new technologies or geopolitical shifts. Some powers have been wrestled away from rival ministers and members of the Cabinet by particularly confident and determined Prime Ministers. The premiership is unlikely to stay static into the future, and the direction of travel seems to be towards expansion.

The primary aspects of the role are well known: hiring and firing ministers; creating and abolishing government departments; chairing the Cabinet and having the final say if it is unable to reach a decision; attending summits and meeting world leaders; and generally being the public face of the government at home and abroad. But Prime Ministers are also responsible for everything from appointing Regius Professors at the universities of Oxford and Cambridge to launching nuclear strikes, and from awarding peerages and honours to managing the relationship between government and the monarch.

Anthony Bevir, who served as Appointments Secretary at No. 10 under Clement Attlee, Winston Churchill and Anthony Eden, observed a 'gradual revolution in this country' that had already taken place by the middle of the twentieth century. This 'revolution' had transformed the Prime Minister's workload: 'It has intensified his Parliamentary duties; it has increased the burden of paper; it has affected his mode of life.'[7] Bevir listed the range of duties that the role of Prime Minister had already acquired, exempting those which the Cabinet Office could assist with:

> The transaction of business with the Crown, changes of Government and appointments of Ministers, relations with Heads of Governments – either within the Empire or abroad, personal relations with other Ministers, Honours, Civil Patronage including Ecclesiastical appointments, the Civil List and funds at the Prime Minister's disposal, handling the Prime Minister's non-political affairs, e.g., representation on occasions of national importance, personal gifts, birthday congratulations and so forth. These subjects vary in importance; some of them are apparently trivial, but experience shows that a mistake in even a trivial matter may cause the Prime Minister considerable personal trouble, with which he should not be burdened. On the more important side, which may be most easily covered by the word 'constitutional', the responsibility is heavy and requires trained staff who can quickly advise and warn on precedents and past experience.[8]

John Major announces a general election to the press gathered
outside No. 10, 17 March 1997. This image captures the increasingly
public and enduringly lonely nature of the premiership.

It is true that the most apparently trivial of these duties can cause real
damage to a premiership. It is also true that Bevir's 'gradual revolution'
has continued throughout the postwar years, and the premiership has
continued to expand.

Peter Hennessy has charted key moments in the development of
the modern role, including the emergence of the Prime Minister's
right to remove ministers, the arrival of Prime Minister's Questions
and the emergence of a politically neutral Principal Private Secretary to support the Prime Minister within No. 10.[9] Comparison of
a Cabinet Office list of the core functions of the Prime Minister in
the 1940s (around twelve) with a self-produced contemporary list of
the 1990s (by then at over thirty-six) helps to chart the expansion of
the role in the postwar years. As Hennessy described, 'the mid-1990s
warehouse of Prime Ministerial functions is awesomely large'.[10] Using
the National Archives to trace the number of files that crossed the
Prime Minister's desk through recent history also provides insightful evidence as to the stretching of the job, from the 215 files on a

wide variety of topics that Attlee had to deal with in 1948, to Harold Wilson's 586 in 1965.[11]

Listing all the functions raises the question of whether the job can possibly be performed by one person alone. The breadth of duties is tremendous, and the level of responsibility is high – not to mention the incredible level of scrutiny focused on No. 10's every decision. Yet the Head of Government in the British system remains a relatively lonely position, when compared to the equivalents in other nations, in terms of the number of staff that accompany the role.

The Prime Minister's Office

The Prime Minister's Office is small and intimate. Reflecting on life at No. 10, Margaret Thatcher's former Head of the Policy Unit Ferdinand Mount described a 'tiny staff, considerably less than the staff at the disposal of the mayor of a major German city'.[12] Wilson, who thought and wrote quite extensively about the role and its realities after completing his two terms as Prime Minister, wrote that 'No. 10 is best regarded as a small village'.[13] Wilson emphasised the 'small' by contrasting the approximately 100 people who worked in No. 10 during his premiership with a reported White House staff of 2,500 under President Lyndon B. Johnson.[14] For Wilson, as for many subsequent Prime Ministers, the small scale of operations at No. 10 was invaluable to its operation, ensuring that everyone was kept in the loop and encouraging strong personal relations with staff rather than anonymity and bureaucracy. The size of No. 10's staff is therefore seen as an asset rather than a hindrance: manageable, personal and human in scale.

This personal element is hugely important in understanding how No. 10 has worked in the postwar years. As the political historians Martin Burch and Ian Holliday note, 'In the very small world of the Prime Minister's Office, where life can be frantic and work intense, personal chemistry is a crucial factor in determining precisely how things work out.'[15] The small numbers are matched by fairly cramped working conditions. In fact, it can be argued that the staffing of the Prime Minister's Office has been constrained by the nature of No. 10

itself, rather than being kept deliberately small. It is entirely reasonable to suggest that the structure and size of the Prime Minister's support staff have been shaped and dictated by the historic building in which the role has accidentally found itself, rather than purely by the requirements of the job itself.

War has been an important factor in the expansion of the staff that support the Prime Minister. The all-consuming nature of the First World War saw wartime premier David Lloyd George establish the Cabinet Office in 1916, as well as a so-called Garden Suburb of temporary offices in the gardens at Downing Street, housing additional advisers brought in to help better inform the Prime Minister's decision-making. Whilst the Garden Suburb was abolished after the war, echoes of it can be found in the Policy Unit, which was set up under Harold Wilson at the start of his second premiership, this time accommodated within No. 10 itself.

The Cabinet Office, now located next door to No. 10 in 70 Whitehall, was designed to help coordinate government policy in the complex environment of the First World War, and has arguably become an extension to No. 10, providing administrative support and coordination across government. The Cabinet Secretary has since become the most senior civil servant in the British system, sitting to the right of the Prime Minister during Cabinet, taking the minutes and ensuring the Cabinet Office is able to assist with implementing its decisions. One former occupant of the role, Burke Trend, described it as being effectively the 'Prime Minister's Permanent Secretary'.[16]

Some changes to the staffing of No. 10 have been short-lived, but others have survived. Today, over 200 people work in No. 10, performing a vast range of roles, from providing policy advice to hospitality. Whilst changing methods of counting who officially works for No. 10 have made like-for-like comparisons difficult, there is a clear pattern: in 1970, sixty-four people were counted as working in the building, rising to seventy by 1979 and 120 by 1997.[17] As the long-term Private Secretary Bevir once noted, it is a fact of life at No. 10 that 'the Office, like Topsy, "just grows".[18]

The evolving role of No. 10 Downing Street

As the role of Prime Minister has changed, the role of the building that houses it has followed. The expansion of the job has been matched by the expansion of the house – albeit on a much more limited basis. The building serves as both home and office to the modern Prime Minister, and attempts have been made throughout No. 10 to physically separate living space and working life. The gradual reduction of space for the former and expansion of accommodation for the latter has been a fairly consistent pattern of change over the centuries. Over time, the Prime Minister's personal space, which once accounted for the vast majority of the house, has slowly retreated further and further into the building's upper floors. In the 1930s, the Chamberlains began – and then the Attlees formalised – the modern arrangement whereby the Prime Minister and family live in a self-contained flat on the second floor during their stay at No. 10.

Despite these attempts to separate the working and living spaces at No. 10, it is not uncommon for Prime Ministers to find it difficult to maintain a distinction between these two main aspects of life at Downing Street. This mental challenge is reflected in the physical difficulties of separating the two functions within the house, and is illustrated by a debate around fuel expenses in the early postwar years.

An annual fuel allowance of £200, paid by the state via the Office of Works, was fixed for the official parts of No. 10 in 1938. Whilst the Prime Minister was expected to pay the costs of heating the private residence, the rest of the house was primarily used as government offices, and so the government would pay to heat them. In the postwar years, it was noted that the part of the house dedicated to the Prime Minister's personal use had become gradually smaller, retreating into the upper floors of the house. However, the costs of fuel had gone up, and so it was decided to keep the allowance the same. Tellingly, in a private note to Attlee, a Private Secretary confessed that the whole idea was far from scientific; the heating could only be turned on to heat the entire building, and it was not actually possible to work out the costs of heating the flat alone.[19] If drawing a physical boundary between the living and working quarters at No. 10 is difficult, that challenge of drawing an imaginary line between work and life is even more so.

Chapter 6 investigates the reality of 'living above the shop' in more detail.

A third, supplementary role played by No. 10, albeit one that remains very significant, is that of a place for entertaining guests. This role has increased in prominence over the years, in terms of both hosting foreign dignitaries, heads of state and heads of governments, and holding charitable and publicity events in the State Rooms or garden. This is partly connected to the freeing up of the first-floor State Rooms and State Dining Room – some of the most attractive spaces in Downing Street – when Prime Ministers ceased to use them as living quarters for themselves and their families.

It also relates to No. 10's increasing prominence in public life. Despite security issues rendering the house arguably more isolated, with the erection of barriers at the end of the street leaving it inaccessible to the general public, Downing Street is in many senses a much more public place today. Television interviews and press conferences are broadcast from inside, and Prime Ministers have for many decades addressed the nation from outside No. 10. Photographs outside the famous front door have been sought for decades, but seem to have only increased in both desirability and frequency since it has become impossible to get such a photograph without an invitation to Downing Street. Celebrities, sports personalities and philanthropists are invited to No. 10 with growing frequency, reflecting a wider societal interest in celebrity that, it can be argued, began to emerge under Wilson's first premiership in the 1960s. Business people and trade union leaders have also long angled for access to No. 10, albeit less publicly and to mixed receptions.

Over time, No. 10 has become a busier and more complicated place. Whereas a Press Office was not yet deemed necessary at the turn of the twentieth century, today's media and communications operation requires a team of staff. A greater number and range of political and non-political advisers, providing the Prime Minister with a wider range of advice on increasingly diverse issues, has also changed the building. More office space within No. 10, as well as better connectivity with the Cabinet Office next door, has been necessitated by the changing nature of the job.

No. 10 once needed to employ its own on-site tradespeople, due to its poor state of repair and the associated risks (of which more later). The maintenance of the modern building has been professionalised to a significant extent, and a Front of House team now delivers tours to guests, whilst other staff concentrate on maintaining the building's fabric much more comprehensively than has been possible in the past. Today's No. 10 is increasingly energy efficient, is connected to the internet and displays works of art chosen by a working group consisting of art specialists and No. 10 staff, rather than exclusively by Prime Ministerial fiat. It is an international tourist attraction, despite the fact that the street itself cannot be accessed.

Components

As noted earlier in this chapter, the role of Prime Minister has many different facets, from party politics and policy decisions to the personal aspects of diplomacy and leadership. The make-up of the comparatively small staff of No. 10 altered repeatedly in the postwar years, primarily with the introduction of new functions to the premiership, but the key parts of the Prime Minister's Office for the years 1945–97 can be divided into four Ps: the Private Office, Political Office, Press Office and Policy Unit.

Many other functions have been housed within and around Downing Street, as well as temporary and ad hoc positions created by different Prime Ministers according to their own personal priorities. Additionally, the small staff of Downing Street and the interconnectedness of each of the different functions of the Prime Minister's role mean that these four Ps often crossed over, with the distinct elements of the office difficult to discern. The line between the personal, political and professional elements of the premiership is a controversial topic, and a rarely subjective one. Regardless of this, the four Ps present a useful framework for understanding how both the job of Prime Minister and No. 10 itself have operated throughout the years 1945–97.

Private Office

Staffed primarily by civil servants, the Private Office has a broad, non-party political remit, succinctly described in a Downing Street memo from the mid-1970s as being 'to enable the Prime Minister to discharge his duties and conduct his business as efficiently and as conveniently as possible'.[20] The main methodology for achieving this is managing the flow of information to the Prime Minister and helping to manage their time. The Principal Private Secretary, often but not exclusively appointed from the Treasury, is responsible for overall coordination of the Private Office, and works extremely closely with the Prime Minister on a day-to-day basis. Between four and six further Private Secretaries with specialities in particular policy areas, reflected in their departmental backgrounds, also spend an average of two or three years seconded to No. 10, working in a small team. A limited number of longer-term staff are responsible for business unique to No. 10, such as managing the Prime Minister's diary, serving as duty clerks or dealing with appointments.

The existence of the contemporary Private Office began in the late 1920s, with the senior positions staying essentially the same since 1945.[21] It was Labour Prime Minister Ramsay MacDonald who established the tradition that the Private Office staff would be retained even when the government changed.[22] By the postwar years, as described by one No. 10 memo from the 1970s, it had become 'the tradition and the general (but not immutable) rule that the existing team continues in office'.[23] Tradition and precedent plays a huge role in the conduct of business at No. 10.

Prior to MacDonald's precedent, Private Secretaries to the Prime Minister were generally personal appointments, loyal to the Prime Minister and with little formal distinction between the political and the professional elements of their role. William Gladstone's first Private Secretary, Algernon West, lived in No. 10 whilst Gladstone lived at nearby Carlton House Terrace. Montagu Corry, Disraeli's Principal Private Secretary, was accused of being 'the real Prime Minister'. Private Secretaries up until the early twentieth century had broad remits, and could also be assigned political tasks, such as 'taking the temperature' of Parliament.[24] The establishment of the precedent that they would be non-partisan appointments was accompanied by an increasing distinction between their apolitical roles in assisting the Prime Minister of the day and the roles of political staff who gave assistance with the party political aspects of the premiership.[25]

The Private Office is generally staffed by civil servants, although Thatcher made her Diary Secretary a political appointment in 1979.[26] As with all roles at No. 10, and particularly that of the Prime Minister, life in the Private Office changed over time. It was the Diary Secretary's job to, for example, fix twice-weekly hairdressing appointments for Thatcher – logged under the code name 'Carmen rollers' – as Prime Minister's Questions had begun to be broadcast on television.[27] Not only did roles change over time, but the small size of No. 10's staff, as well as the extreme proximity dictated by the building itself, meant that individuals did not always strictly abide by their roles. Flexibility was key.

The role of the Private Office in providing information to the Prime Minister was summed up in a Cabinet Office document from 1976. Written to inform the Turkish Government, which was interested in restructuring its own governing arrangements, this document explained succinctly how business was transacted within No. 10 at the time. Official papers for the Prime Minister would arrive in the Private Office via the Duty Clerk, who, unless the matter was deemed so urgent that it must be run by the Prime Minister immediately, would attach any relevant past papers before passing them on to the appropriate Private Secretary. The Private Secretary would then sort them into trays, numbered from one to six:

1. Action this day
2. Action
3. Signatures
4. Immediate Information
5. Information
6. Weekend reading

The Cabinet Office noted that whilst 'these descriptions are self-explanatory [...] their interpretation clearly depends on the wishes and working methods of the Prime Minister and the Private Secretaries' experience of them'.[28]

Knowing the Prime Minister's 'wishes and working methods' is crucial to the Private Office's task of funnelling information through to them. The Principal Private Secretary is at the narrow end of this funnel. Andrew Turnbull, who served as Principal Private Secretary to Thatcher and John Major, describes the essence of the Principal Private Secretary's role as being the management of the Prime Minister's trays – a 'very important piece of kit'. The job of the Principal Private Secretary was to 'patrol that piece of kit late in the day' and perform a final 'quality control' on the information going to the Prime Minister, ensuring that they would receive the full range and choice of information necessary for swift and informed decision-making, at a minimal time cost. This included writing covering notes outlining alternative views and recommending options, as well as making a final decision as to whether something required the Prime Minister's time immediately or could be postponed.[29]

Whilst the role of paper in government business is receding with the increasing dominance of technology, this 'filtering' job remains vitally important. As the historian Anthony Seldon and the political analyst Dennis Kavanagh have described, the Private Office represents 'the key instruments filtering the world and making it manageable to [the Prime Minister;] in this sense we have a collective premiership'.[30] The Private Office must know the Prime Minister's mind: their opinions and views, but also their working style, capacity for work and potential for burnout. Managing the flow of information to a Prime Minister requires the ability to strip complex decisions down to the key facts and issues required to enable informed and balanced decision-making. But it also requires another essential component – ruthless prioritisation and avoiding overload, which can be an equally dangerous source of bad decision-making.

The management of the Prime Minister's diary – and therefore, their time – is essential in ensuring that none of the many different aspects of the role fall by the wayside. This is formally the job of the Diary Secretary, but the entire Private Office plays an important role in 'gatekeeping', with the Principal Private Secretary taking particular responsibility for guarding the Prime Minister's door against unwanted visitors. This is no easy task, and as Edward Heath recalled in his memoirs, 'The whole delicate balancing act which this entails can be thrown out of gear by an unexpected event that calls for immediate attention'.[31]

Whilst the Cabinet Secretary is a more senior civil servant, the Principal Private Secretary works more closely with the Prime Minister than any other. Harold Evans, Press Secretary to Harold Macmillan, quotes Disraeli on the intimacy of this relationship: 'Except in the marital state [...] there is none in which so great a confidence is involved, in which more forbearance ought to be exercised, or more sympathy ought to exist.'[32] Hennessy has described the job wonderfully: 'high policy adviser, honest friend and personal nanny [...] They have to be highly political animals without ever forgetting the canons of Northcote and Trevelyan. It is rather like riding two horses at high speed.'[33]

Some Prime Ministers have been initially suspicious of the Private Office upon their arrival at No. 10, perceiving Private Office staff to retain personal sympathies with the previous administration. Seldon and Kavanagh claim that this was true of Churchill in 1951 (he remarked upon his return to No. 10 that he felt the Private Office 'drenched in socialism'), Wilson in 1964 and Thatcher in 1979. However, all three 'left office enamoured of them'.[34] Churchill's Principal Private Secretary John 'Jock' Colville became so important to the Prime Minister that, alongside Churchill's Parliamentary Private Secretary and son-in-law Christopher Soames, he ended up running the country for around a month in the summer of 1953 whilst Churchill was out of action after suffering a stroke. Colville recalls this incredible situation:

> [Churchill] gave me strict orders not to let it be known that he was temporarily incapacitated and to ensure that the administration continue to function as if he were in control [...] Before the end of July the Prime Minister was sufficiently restored to take an intelligent interest in affairs of state and express his own decisive views. Christopher and I then returned to the fringes of power, having for a time been drawn perilously close to the centre. For the next two years the distance between the fringes and the Centre was far shorter than it had once been.[35]

Whilst this situation was clearly an exception rather than a rule, it demonstrates how closely senior figures in No. 10 could be expected to work with – or on behalf of – the Prime Minister.

The role of Principal Private Secretary can involve such intimacy with a Prime Minister that it is not uncommon for them, or indeed any member of the Private Office, to become widely viewed as too closely associated with a particular premier, and to therefore be deemed unsuitable to serve their successors. Macmillan's Principal Private Secretary, Tim Bligh, and Foreign Affairs Private Secretary, Philip de Zulueta, both found themselves in this situation once Macmillan left office.[36] Bligh's departure was particularly interesting, and slightly bizarre; when his successor, Derek Mitchell, was appointed the new Principal Private Secretary, Bligh refused to leave, and the two cohabited in No. 10 until the 1964 election finally saw Bligh concede his place.[37]

Despite being apolitical, the Private Office can also reflect the personality of the Prime Minister. Macmillan had a close, informal relationship with his Private Secretaries, and he introduced his friend, the aristocratic John Wyndham, into the Private Office as an unpaid adviser. Churchill insisted that Colville returned as Principal Private Secretary in his second premiership, splitting the job in an unusual joint arrangement alongside David Pitblado, the incumbent. Colville was known to be so close to Churchill that ministers would often approach him before speaking to the Prime Minister, in order to gauge what he was likely to think.[38] Colville retired alongside Churchill. Sandy Isserlis, the incumbent but recently appointed Principal Private Secretary inherited by Heath after his victory in the 1970 general election, was removed after a few short weeks in the job, deemed unsuited to Heath's personal style.

Appointments

The Appointments Team assists the Prime Minister with perhaps their most unusual role: what Hennessy describes as the 'deliciously Trollopian function' of ecclesiastical and other senior Prime Ministerial appointments. The London School of Economics (LSE) professor George Jones described Appointments Secretaries as 'heaven's talent scouts', after Anthony Bevir, the Private Secretary who took up the role from 1947–56.[39] This role may seem outdated to the contemporary observer, but it is fascinating how Bevir himself noted that it became more – rather than less – necessary as postwar Prime Ministers ceased to be drawn exclusively from the ultra-privileged social backgrounds of the eighteenth and nineteenth centuries:

> The changes through which the country has passed have led to a broadening of the field of those concerned with Government and public administration, and on the other hand the greater tendency to watertight compartments in what may be called 'society'. I mean by this that 30 years ago a Prime Minister probably knew the Arch-bishop of Canterbury, the leading Judges, leading figures in the academic world, leading artists and writers, leading ambassadors, Colonial Governors and so forth, not only from official meetings, but also either at University or in the course of public life, or at dinners and weekends.[40]

In Bevir's view, this was no longer the case. He claimed that Herbert Henry Asquith, Prime Minister from 1908–16, would have personally known the 'sort of person who would make a suitable trustee of the National Gallery, and indeed in ecclesiastical appointments', but that this had now vanished: 'I doubt if future Prime Ministers will have so wide a knowledge.'[41]

The Appointments Secretary would generally stay in post for much longer than typical Private Secretaries, providing much-valued conti-nuity within No. 10.[42] This also enabled them to get to know the 'sort of people' that were deemed appropriate for the posts that the Prime Minister appoints. Perhaps due to the limited nature of their primary job, or perhaps simply because of their comparatively great experi-ence, Appointments Secretaries would also become responsible for the maintenance and repair of Downing Street itself, alongside certain charitable functions.

Whilst Appointment Secretaries have gradually and repeatedly been relegated in the geography of power at No. 10, as we shall see in the following chapter, the post remains an important, if slightly bizarre, one. Whilst the appointments element of the premiership can appear superfluous to the role, and could be reasonably expected to be the first to be jettisoned by an overworking Prime Minister, it appears to have provided an element of pleasure to some. Alex Allan, who served as Principal Private Secretary to John Major and Tony Blair, recalls Major in particular enjoying his appointments work:

> Prime Ministers, over time, have seen it as a less important aspect of their role, and equally the units have been seen as less significant to be in No. 10. But it was interesting, because John Major, he used to get these enormous, long submissions about church appointments, you know, who was going to be the next bishop of somewhere or other. And I said to him one day, "You nearly always put tick, ok, on them. Do you really need to see them, or could I sign them off on your behalf?" And he said, "Oh, no! they're wonderful! I'll be ploughing through heavy submissions on economic policy and things like that, and then I find one of these." He loved Trollop, and they were all about people's churchmanship, and he said it was this great sort of... diversion.[43]

Heath, who wrote of the appointments aspect of the premiership in his memoirs with a degree of pride, claimed that church appointments on behalf of the Prime Minister during his time at No. 10 were 'made as a result of a selection process conducted with care and good sense'. Somewhat more controversially, he went on to claim, 'They were also often – I shall probably be excommunicated for saying this – better than they would have been had they been left entirely to the Church, with no involvement from No. 10.'[44]

The Garden Rooms

The Private Office was (and is today) supported by an administrative and secretarial staff, historically referred to as the 'Garden Room Girls', after the basement rooms that this staff, historically almost exclusively female, inhabited within No. 10. Established during the First World War, the Garden Rooms staff are often on longer-term appointments than those in the Private Office, and there is at least one member of the team in the building twenty-four hours a day, all year round. Until 1968, the Treasury would recruit Garden Room Girls from Britain's secretarial colleges; subsequently, they have been appointed from within the civil service.[45] One or two of the Garden Room staff will travel abroad with the Prime Minister when on official business, and one member of the Garden Rooms will go to Chequers on the weekend.[46]

The Garden Room staff are crucial to the smooth operation of the premiership. Their skill and experience provide rare continuity at No. 10, although they have had to be extremely adaptive. From the arrival of photocopying in the 1970s to the advent of electronic word processing in the 1980s, and from dealing with a Prime Ministerial mailbag of 12,500 letters a month in the early 1980s to over 30,000 by 1999, the job of the Garden Rooms, like much at Downing Street, has both changed and expanded immensely across the postwar years.[47] Marie Hunter, who has worked in the Garden Rooms since 1988, provides a great insight into how the role has changed over time:

> In the years I have been at No. 10, the main changes have been in technology and communication, although also in fashion. There was an unwritten rule in the 1980s that ladies didn't wear trousers while on duty, which proved a little tricky when jumping in and out of military helicopters during visits to Northern Ireland! In 1988 there were no computers or laptops in the office and therefore no emails, no BlackBerrys, and only a shared mobile phone, which really was the size of a house brick. [...] Letters and speeches were dictated and typed on Rank Xerox typewriters using carbon sheets for copies, and we were informed of unfolding events around the world by diplomatic telegrams, and of unfolding events at home by Whitehall departments – and occasionally by sneaking a look at the Reuters newsfeed tape. Our trusty shorthand notebooks became a potted history of both domestic and world affairs.[48]

The pre-computer No. 10 saw a great deal of hand-typed and hand-written paper moved around. Another anecdote from Hunter's time at Downing Street during Thatcher's third term illustrates the level of access and influence the Garden Room staff could have on the conduct of the premiership:

I famously once asked Mrs. Thatcher to resign. Spotting an error in a document, I re-submitted it to her Red Box with a covering note saying 'Prime Minister, grateful if you could please re-sign this minute'. My writing was very small and the hyphen seemingly went unnoticed, but luckily Mrs. Thatcher had a good sense of humour – and I learned to type my notes for the Box and not to handwrite them.[49]

The Garden Room Girls could work particularly closely with the Prime Minister, depending on their individual working habits. Churchill was fond of long dictation sessions, and could prove challenging to work for. During wartime, his working hours were extremely erratic, and secretaries could expect to work into the small hours. The Prime Minister then expected their attendance at his bedside in the morning to resume dictation, where it was said that they could tell what sort of day it was going to be by whether the morning papers were stacked neatly or scrunched up and thrown around the room. Churchill even dictated from the bath.[50] His second premiership was no less haphazard. As his biographer Roy Jenkins describes, 'Churchill, even at this late stage, was more than capable of original composition, but he liked doing it with an audience', and he would require a succession of Garden Room staff, on fifteen-minute rotation, to constantly type and retype his speeches.[51] Despite this erratic and somewhat demanding working style, those who worked with him still speak of him with great affection.[52]

The Garden Room Girls would have a tough time again in the early 1960s. Marcia Williams, Personal and Political Secretary to Harold Wilson, claimed that when Wilson arrived at No. 10 for his first premiership, the Garden Rooms were 'not staffed in the way one should expect in the late 1960s', being dominated by graduates of one particular 'very select and expensive secretarial college in London'. Critical of the impact this had on making No. 10 a 'closed' place, as well as the perceived tendency of the Garden Room's female staff to dress in a manner she found distasteful, Williams appears to have had some influence in changing the practices of recruitment to the Garden Rooms.[53] Arguments between the Political Office and the Garden Rooms over resources in Wilson's second term, including the use of photocopiers and Garden Room services, appear tinged with this tension.[54] This is despite the fact that, according to Williams, 'by 1970, the girls with the twin-sets and the pearls had largely gone.'[55]

Under Harold Macmillan and Alec Douglas-Home, the Garden Room Girls had attracted no such controversy. Douglas-Home's biographer D. R. Thorpe claimed that Wilson's team had proved hostile as they had 'wrongly suspected them all of being "Tory debs".'[56] Douglas-Home had no such distaste for the Garden Rooms. According to Thorpe, 'The Macmillan years had been very special for the Garden Room Girls and Alec Douglas-Home's brief tenure was the end of a particular way of working. Family informality combined with professional efficiency and a sense of happy teamwork, with Alec and Elizabeth Douglas-Home always remembering birthdays and anniversaries.'[57] The personality of a Prime Minister can significantly affect the atmosphere for working life at No. 10.

Political Office

The party-political elements of the premiership are supported at No. 10 by the Political Office. This can be argued to have been established in the late 1950s, with informal roots that stretch back as far as the premiership itself, but it was formalised in the mid-1960s.[58] The Political Office took over the Private Office's responsibility for the aspects of the Prime Minister's work that relate to the management of their party and their constituency, and its exact make-up has shifted over time, but it is generally politically appointed, smaller than the Private Office, and headed up by the Political Secretary. That role did not have an easy introduction into No. 10. Marcia Williams had run Wilson's office before he arrived at Downing Street for the first time in 1964, and was appointed Wilson's Personal and Political Secretary at No. 10, following much debate with the Private Office. The official machine was uncomfortable with her appointment, possibly due to her clear suspicion of the civil service.[59] A series of meetings between Williams and Tim Bligh, then Principal Private Secretary, in the build-up to the election had set the tone. It was during these meetings, Williams claims, that Bligh made it clear 'that the Civil Service considered that there was no place for me, or my office colleagues at No. 10.'[60]

Wilson remained somewhat resentful of the negative comments that Williams' role attracted in the press. In his estimation, Harold Macmillan's appointment of John Wyndham had been no different:

> This was not criticised by the press of the time; it was excused by the fact that, being a dollar-a-year man, he was not in receipt of public funds. [...] No member of my Political Office ever had access to classified documents. This was not the case with the appointees of Harold Macmillan or Edward Heath. Yet unremitting press comments, including unwarrantable invasions of personal and family privacy, have been addressed, uniquely, to my appointments.[61]

Regardless, the appointment of Williams would continue to cause controversy within No. 10 as well as in the outside world.

Williams saw the Principal Private Secretary's desire to keep the private and political functions separate as further evidence that the civil service was 'totally devoted to preserving the *status quo* as left by the last Conservative Government [...] the people who were personally attached to Harold's staff were made to feel like intruders and squatters, and they consequently behaved in a slightly aggressive way.'[62] However, despite a bumpy start, Wilson's successor, Edward Heath, decided to retain the Political Secretary role, appointing Douglas Hurd, and a precedent was therefore created. By the time Wilson returned to Downing Street, with his Political Secretary, Williams, now enobled as Lady Falkender, the position was part of Downing Street's fabric.[63]

The role of Parliamentary Private Secretary has historically proved a much less controversial way to maintain links with Parliament and a Prime Minister's party from within No. 10. The role is concerned primarily with keeping the Prime Minister in touch with their back-benchers, and providing a channel of communication between the warren of corridors and rooms in Downing Street and those of the Houses of Parliament. Its formal roots predate the postwar years by some decades.[64] Parliamentary Private Secretaries do not see official or confidential papers 'as of right', although the Prime Minister often decides that they want them to do so.[65] The role, like that of Political Secretary, is not entirely focused on No. 10, but rather on providing a link to the political world outside, and therefore can fluctuate in influence depending on the state of a Prime Minister's party and the wider political situation.

Press Office

Wilson, Prime Minister-turned-historian, traced the roots of the Press Office to Lloyd George's premiership, with William Sutherland the first Prime Ministerial aide 'recorded as having specific press responsibilities'.[66] Others have stated that the first internal press officer was appointed by Neville Chamberlain in 1931. Regardless, the office was not properly established until after the Second World War, only becoming a substantial unit in the latter half of the twentieth century.[67]

The Prime Minister's Press Secretary, who is often appointed from outside of the civil service, but is always a Prime Ministerial appointment, leads the Press Office. The Press Secretary is the Prime Minister's spokesperson to the media, and thus to the public. Identified in newspapers as 'sources close to the Prime Minister', the Press Secretary briefs the press lobby on at least a daily basis, a practice 'institutionalised' by Harold Evans, Press Secretary to Macmillan.[68] Donald Maitland, Heath's Press Secretary and a pioneer of the Prime Ministerial press conference, later gave the press lobby the chance to take these briefings on the record, to which the lobby voted 'no'.[69] Like the Principal Private Secretary, the Press Secretary must 'know the Prime Minister's mind' to the extent that they can speak on their behalf without any misunderstanding and without any unnecessary additional consultation with the Prime Minister. As Henry James, Thatcher's first Press Secretary, stated, the role requires the holder to be 'the alter ego of the Prime Minister, as far as the press are concerned'.[70] Like the Private Office, a member of the Press Office generally accompanies the Prime Minister whenever they travel on official business.[71]

The Press Office has grown in size, as well as importance, with the advent of changing technology and an evolving media climate. A ticker tape machine was first installed just outside the Cabinet Room in No. 10 for the 1922 General Election, to receive the results as they were declared.[72] Prime Minister Attlee resisted the use of such a machine, which was proposed by his Press Secretary, Francis Williams, in order to keep No. 10 up to date with the latest news, until Williams pointed out that it would be a good way of keeping track of cricket scores.[73] For a quiet, unglamorous Prime Minister, who described himself as 'allergic to the press', it is perhaps surprising that it was Attlee who employed the first explicitly Prime Ministerial Press Secretary, albeit initially under the title of 'Adviser on Public Relations'.[74]

Several Press Secretaries were brought in from careers in the media; Williams had previously been at the *Daily Herald*. Eden and Wilson both recruited Press Secretaries from the national newspapers, whilst Heath, James Callaghan and Major recruited from within the civil service. Thatcher's most famous Press Secretary, Bernard Ingham, had been a journalist prior to joining the civil service. Churchill began his second premiership by abolishing the Press Office at No. 10, and only reluctantly accepted a press officer being attached to the Lord Chancellor's office six months into his term, making it even more impressive that his period out of action following his stroke in 1953 was kept from the media.[75] His successor, Eden, was said to have been 'genuinely astonished, and even shocked' to find that under Churchill a small group had met regularly at No. 10 to discuss which confidential documents to leak to the press, and whom to leak them to.[76] In succeeding or failing to control the narrative of a premiership, by whatever means, the Press Office can be crucial in determining the fate of a Prime Minister.

The Policy Unit

The Policy Unit is the youngest of the four Ps that made up the Prime Minister's Office in the postwar years. The unit was established by Wilson on his return to No. 10 in 1974, under the leadership of former LSE academic Bernard Donoughue. The Policy Unit initially consisted of around eight members of staff from a mix of civil service and external backgrounds, although subsequent Prime Ministers would later expand its numbers.[77]

The Policy Unit was established to provide the Prime Minister with advice independent of that supplied by government departments. Its roots can be traced back to Lloyd George's Garden Suburb, or

Churchill's so-called Statistical Section during wartime. Most postwar Prime Ministers had made use of some form of outside advice, usually but not exclusively in the form of individual economic or scientific advisers. The Central Policy Review Staff, established by Heath in 1971 for a similar purpose and nicknamed the Think Tank, was a more recent predecessor to the Policy Unit. However, the Central Policy Review Staff sat in the Cabinet Office, and existed to serve not only the Prime Minister but also the Cabinet. Staffed by a mix of civil servants and outsiders, the Central Policy Review Staff was tasked with long-term thinking for the whole government.

The No. 10 Policy Unit, by way of contrast, was smaller and integrated into No. 10 itself, but featured a similar mix of talent. The unit was able to provide reactive policy research as well as horizon-scanning documents, and was more directly and explicitly the property of the Prime Minister. The Policy Unit's first head claimed that its main benefit was that it 'gave the Prime Minister alternative options. It meant that he could meet his Chancellor fully briefed and with critical scrutiny of the Treasury's (then often dubious) figures and arguments, and, most important in this case, to suggest alternative policy options.'[78] The Policy Unit was not limited to economic advice, however, and could equally provide the Prime Minister with advice to supplement, counter or question that of any Minister or department.

As with the Political Office, the initial introduction of the Policy Unit into No. 10 had to be managed carefully. Innovations and changes in the machinery of government at Downing Street can be greeted with some suspicion, particularly when they threaten the existing system. Donoughue made a concerted effort to bring the rest of the operation at No. 10 with him, primarily by the means of a 'concordat' signed with the Cabinet Secretary setting out details such as the unit's scope and remit, and which papers it would and would not see. For Donoughue, this approach, alongside ensuring that the unit was staffed by 'high-quality people', was crucial: 'Most insiders forecast that I would fail, because the machine wouldn't want it, and would stop me. [...] But I did it via the machine, I didn't get the Prime Minister to impose it.'[79]

Ultimately, and perhaps because of this collaborative approach, the Policy Unit proved successful, and has been retained by all subsequent Prime Ministers to date. Wilson himself claimed that the innovation attracted a great deal of interest at the 1975 Commonwealth Heads of Government Meeting in Jamaica, with several heads of government subsequently visiting the Policy Unit at No. 10 to find out how it worked.[80] This is not to say that friction with the Private Office and other elements of No. 10 vanished entirely; Seldon's biography of Major observes how the relationship still had to be carefully managed by Major's Head of the Policy Unit, Sarah Hogg, some twenty years later.[81] Whilst its influence has waxed and waned, depending upon the personalities of both the Prime Minister and the unit's head, it has become a part of the fabric at Downing Street.

The Cabinet Office

The Cabinet Secretary is the most senior civil servant in the British system. However, whilst the Cabinet Secretary works closely with the Prime Minister, the Cabinet Office is concerned with implementing Cabinet's collective decisions and helping government to function effectively at a level above that of the departments, rather than being a purely personal tool of the Prime Minister.[82]

Cabinet Secretary Robert Armstrong described the peculiarity of the Cabinet Office's position in an internal memorandum, written in preparation for an event to mark its seventieth anniversary in December 1986. Armstrong noted that the Cabinet Office had always 'seen itself and has been seen as the servant of the Cabinet and of the Government collectively'. Armstrong asserted, 'It is not a "Prime Minister's Department"', but went on to state that 'the Prime Minister is of course *primus inter pares* among those whom it serves, and the Minister responsible for it.'[83] James Callaghan made a slightly more pointed observation in his memoirs, stating, 'The conventional role of the Cabinet Office is to serve all members of the Cabinet, but if the Prime Minister chooses, as nearly all of them do, to work closely with the Secretary to the Cabinet, then it becomes an instrument to serve him above the others.'[84] As with all things at the centre of Britain's system of government, the exact nature of the Cabinet Office's role as regards No. 10 is a matter of taste and precedent, rather than a clearly defined set of black-and-white rules.

No. 10's staff has often spilled over, through the connecting door, into 70 Whitehall. But the Cabinet Office itself also supports the Prime Minister in the management of Cabinet, the business and machinery of government and the civil service. As an administrative layer sitting between the departments and the premiership, the Cabinet Office has a pivotal role; as one unnamed 'astute Whitehall observer' observed, 'Every Department is about something [...] The Cabinet Office is powerful because it is pure bureaucracy.'[85]

Continuity and change at the centre

Whilst the four Ps – the Private, Political and Press Offices and the Policy Unit – make up the majority of the Prime Minister's Office in No. 10, and the Cabinet Office offers administrative support, several other roles have supported the Prime Minister in the postwar years. Some have been temporary, highly personal and ad hoc in nature, and have not lasted the duration of the premierships of the Prime Ministers who introduced them, whereas others have outlived their initial holders and become part of the furniture at No. 10.

Some short-lived additional positions within or around No. 10 have already been mentioned. Most postwar premiers made at least one significant adjustment to the staffing of No. 10. Attlee brought Douglas Jay into Downing Street as an economic adviser for the early part of his premiership (before Jay left to become an MP), and initiated the formal establishment of a Press Office explicitly focused on No. 10. Churchill had pioneered a Statistical Section, based in Downing Street, during the Second World War, and he reintroduced it during his second premiership to provide him with economic advice, albeit on a smaller scale. He also insisted upon a joint Principal Private Secretary arrangement, so that his wartime Private Secretary, 'Jock' Colville, could return to work alongside him, and experimented with appointing what was effectively an inner cabinet of multi-departmental 'overlords'.

Eden and Douglas-Home were both only at Downing Street for a short period, but whilst the former was unusual in that he changed almost nothing about No. 10's machinery, the latter made good use of his recent predecessor's 'embryonic political office' at the Conservative Research Department. Macmillan brought the aforementioned John Wyndham into the Private Office as an unpaid political adviser. Wilson's first term saw economist Thomas Balogh recruited as economic adviser, initially based within the Cabinet Office alongside a scientific adviser, Solly Zuckerman, and a team of assistants. It also saw George Wigg take a seat within Downing Street whilst serving as Paymaster General, and the formal establishment of the Political Office under Marcia Williams. Wilson's second term saw the birth of the No. 10 Policy Unit.

As previously mentioned, between Wilson's two terms, Heath also had scientific and economic advisers, and established the Central Policy Review Staff, all based within the Cabinet Office, (although its head, Victor Rothschild, had some access to No. 10). Callaghan made great use of the innovations of his predecessors during his short premiership, although he made few of his own. Thatcher made numerous adjustments during her much longer stay at No. 10, including introducing a political Chief of Staff, David Wolfson, and a range of personal advisers over the course of her premiership, most notably her controversial economics adviser Alan Walters.

The idea of a Chief of Staff for Downing Street has long roots through No. 10's history. The title was granted to Algernon West, formerly Private Secretary to Gladstone, in 1892, upon his return to working for the Prime Minister, as that of Private Secretary was then deemed too junior.[86] However, the nature of the Private Office has altered significantly since Gladstone's time. The phrase 'Chief of Staff' was used in the postwar era by Paul Beards, Private Secretary during Attlee's premiership, to describe his Principal Private Secretary Leslie Rowan, and later by Private Secretary de Zulueta to describe Cabinet Secretary Norman Brook.[87] The Cabinet Office also described the Principal Private Secretary's job as being that of 'in effect a Chief of Staff to the Prime Minister' in an internal document produced in 1976.[88]

Establishing a formal post of Chief of Staff was considered as early as Macmillan's premiership, with Enoch Powell considered for the position, but the idea was ultimately rejected.[89] It was Thatcher who first introduced a formally monikered Chief of Staff, recruited from outside the civil service, into No. 10. Wolfson, a businessman who joined the Political Office on an unpaid basis between 1979 and 1985, had a somewhat amorphous role, which he interpreted as requiring him 'to be aware of the few things that mattered and to make sure that she saw the right people at the right time'.[90] However, others in Downing Street felt that his exact role was too unclear. In the words of one senior civil servant, 'Chief of Staff wasn't an apt description. He wasn't chief of anything and he directed no staff. His value was as a *consigliere*. It was a political job, liaison with business and particular donors. [...] And he never, ever tried to muscle in on government work.'[91] Subsequent years have seen a formal Chief of Staff position established within No. 10, separate from the Principal Private Secretary and now quite firmly embedded.

The different approaches to running No. 10 taken by each postwar Prime Minister reflect the unique political circumstances of their individual tenures. Their personalities and experience have also played a significant part in whether or not they arrived at No. 10 with plans to reform its machinery and staffing. Wilson's return to Downing Street during 1974–6, for example, saw significant innovations (such as the establishment of the Policy Unit) which were based upon his previous experience of the premiership. His first premiership had seen him contrast himself with the aristocratic Douglas-Home as a moderniser and an innovator, as well as a socialist arriving at No. 10 after over a decade of Tory rule; both of these factors influenced his approach to running No. 10. Despite his different politics and party, Heath was also part of this modernising wave, which reflected the wider social and political context running throughout Britain at that time.

To paint with a somewhat broad brush, the initial postwar years saw economic advice prioritised by successive premiers of both parties, with the 1960s and 1970s seeing an increasing focus on science and technology, as well as arguably technocratic innovations in No. 10 such as the No. 10 Policy Unit and the Central Policy Review Staff. The post-1979 era can be seen as one of increasingly diverse and numerous special advisers, an expansion of staff numbers at the centre of government in a general sense, and the increasing professionalisation of the communications functions at and around No. 10.

Keeping No. 10 going

In addition to the four main parts of the Prime Minister's Office, the Cabinet Office, the various special advisers and the Garden Rooms, several further teams helped to enable the smooth running of No. 10 as both a place of work and a household during the period studied in this book. These teams were equally essential in making the premiership possible.

The No. 10 switchboard staff – known as Switch – were housed on the third floor of No. 10 for most of the postwar period, with a brief interlude in the Cabinet Office in the 1990s. Switch had, and still have, an impressive reputation for being able to track down whoever is required, wherever they may be hiding in the more than 200 rooms of No. 10, No. 11 and No. 12 Downing Street, or across Whitehall. Switch pride themselves on being able to connect anyone on official business to anyone else anywhere around the world; the story is still told in No. 10 of an occasion when the switchboard team managed to track someone down as they travelled along the Amazon.[92] The 1980s and 1990s saw the use of the first secure Prime Ministerial mobile phone, set up within a briefcase; the installation of a direct line between No. 10 and Washington, DC; and the first video conference call, made from No. 10's Study by Prime Minister Major. Yet none of these innovations have rendered Switch obsolete.

The building itself is now protected by a team of security staff taking turns to operate as 'custodian', guarding and operating No. 10's front door twenty-four hours a day on a rota basis. Prior to 1997, however, staffing the door had been the responsibility of one individual, although this practice ended with the retirement of doorman Bob Jordan, known as 'Bob the Door'.[93] A facilities team also ensured that the building was kept in good condition and repaired when necessary, including allowing 'Clive the Clock Man' in to wind the clocks in the No. 10 flat, a job performed in buildings across Whitehall.[94] No. 10 once had on-site tradesmen, as we shall see in subsequent chapters, but an improvement in the building's physical health following its reconstruction in the early 1960s allowed them to be retired. In exchange, an in-house IT team would later be required at No. 10, a prospect unimaginable at the start of the postwar years. In a changing world, one thing remains true – keeping No. 10 operational is very much a team effort.

3

The Geography of Power at No. 10 Downing Street

The approach that a Prime Minister takes towards organising No. 10 Downing Street is revealing of the approach they intend to take towards the role itself, and therefore of their main priorities and ambitions for their premiership. The decisions taken by an incoming Prime Minister and their core team about how they will establish the geography of power at No. 10 are also intrinsically intertwined with the most important staffing decisions, and the power plays that will inevitably follow.

These decisions dictate, to a large extent, which advisers will have the most access and the most influence over the day-to-day activities of the premier – and by extension, with a little luck, over the direction of the government. Some will be left feeling that they have been stuck out in 'political Siberia', whilst others may be called upon at a moment's notice to offer their advice on the biggest issues faced by the most powerful person in the country.

However, advisers may find that the new Prime Minister's working style and personality ultimately render all previous planning irrelevant, as they adapt to the pressures and rhythms of a unique and unparalleled position at the top of the government.

A new administration rarely arrives at No. 10 without preparation. Whilst an unexpectedly rapid change in occupation at No. 10 can occur following a resignation due to ill health or dwindling support, most Prime Ministers tend to arrive following an election campaign. With a general election on the horizon, the politically neutral Private Office at No. 10 will be in touch with the opposition leadership teams, in order to plan for their arrival at Downing Street in the event of their success. Meetings between the Principal Private Secretary and

key figures in the shadow leader's team are a common feature of this
process. Crude maps of the current layout and occupants of the building can be provided to demonstrate the current setup (and perhaps to
encourage its continuation, should there be a change of government),
and on some occasions the opposition team may visit No. 10, ideally
whilst the Prime Minister is away at Chequers or in their constituency,
to get the 'lay of the land'.

Whilst precedent plays an important role in how a Prime Minister arranges their staff within No. 10 and its surrounding buildings,
nothing is prescribed or enforced. Peter Hennessy, writing on the staffing arrangements at No. 10, notes:

> One of the undoubted powers, almost an absolute one, which falls
> into the lap of a new Prime Minister on 'kissing hands' [with the
> Monarch, when forming a new administration] is the ability to
> remake, almost to reinvent, his personal machine in No. 10.[1]

In remaking the machinery of No. 10, a new Prime Minister must not
only pick the parts but assemble them accordingly. They themselves
are perhaps the engine, with the rest of No. 10 built around them.
With space so limited at No. 10, all but those deemed most essential to
the Prime Minister's work will find their proximity, and their access,
to the absolute centre extremely limited. Precedent dictates that the
most senior civil service Private Secretaries are the second most important aspect of the machine, and will therefore be granted the greatest
proximity. But even their position is not guaranteed. With the arrival
of each new Prime Minister, every place in No. 10's constrained and
unplanned geography of power is up for grabs.

Location, location, location

Having outlined the importance of the geography of power in a general
sense in this book's introduction, it is now worth considering how this
plays out, in a more specific sense, in and around No. 10. Anthony
Seldon and Dennis Kavanagh have noted how 'physical proximity
to the Prime Minister usually results in enhanced influence, which in

turn explains why battles are so keen over who occupies which office space'.[2] Seldon has also claimed that truly 'agenda-changing' premierships are extremely rare in British politics, and attributes this in part to the building itself: 'While one building cannot account for all the disappointment, its warren of small rooms – providing venues for meetings and a home to the first family – inadequately fulfils its purpose of supporting the Prime Minister.'[3]

These two quotations provide an interesting framework for looking at the geography of power at No. 10. Firstly, it is clear that physical proximity to the premier is highly desirable and sought by all who seek to influence their decisions. Margaret Thatcher's memoirs describe the first instincts of her team of advisers and other staff upon first arriving at No. 10, in a scene common to the first moments of many an incoming administration: 'We did not waste much time on conversation. They were anxious to sort out who was to go to which office.'[4] Bernard Donoughue, Head of the Policy Unit under Harold Wilson and James Callaghan, has written extensively on the importance of gaining a prime spot in the geography of power at No. 10, particularly for an outsider in a new role:

> Exercising influence on the Prime Minister in Downing Street requires above all access to his ear and, to a lesser extent, the capacity to determine who else has access to him. The press of claimants to his ear is enormous. It has to be sifted and, in many cases, resisted. Those who have access have potential influence on the levers of power.[5]

The scramble for the best office space in No. 10, and a seat as close as possible to the Prime Minister, is a common theme in the recollections of advisers and civil servants alike.

Proximity is clearly important. The Second World War threw established patterns into chaos: the conditions of total war saw Winston Churchill moving constantly between No. 10's Cabinet Room and Garden Rooms, the No. 10 Annexe above the Cabinet War Rooms (the latter now open to the public as the Churchill War Rooms), and Chequers at weekends (or Ditchley Park in Oxfordshire during a full moon, when Chequers was most easily visible from the air at night).

One Private Secretary to the Prime Minister recorded the difficulties that having Churchill spread across multiple locations engendered: 'We longed for the Prime Minister to move into his residence so that we could be closer to the scene of action.'[6] Harold Evans, Press Secretary to Harold Macmillan, observed, 'At No. 10, as in love, proximity is everything – that and the instinct that takes you to the right place at the right time.'[7]

However, as will be investigated in the following chapter, other factors can play a part in dictating influence. The movement of paper in No. 10 can have as much influence as the location of people, and differences in the working styles of individual premiers can also mean that the most influential access can be gained at times and in locations that are different to those initially anticipated. As Evans noted, it is not just the location of formal office space, but the ability to drift in and out of the right place at the right time that can be crucial in enabling an adviser to influence the Prime Minister's thinking.

The different elements of the Prime Minister's Office have differing levels of need for the best seats in the house, as whilst some are inherently involved in the day-to-day processing of paperwork and organisation of the Prime Minister's schedule, others are vulnerable to being frozen out, ignored or forgotten if they are not granted the oxygen of access to the premier. 'Insiders' generally need worry less about their physical location in the building than 'outsiders', as those who are already integrated into the established way of daily life at No. 10 are more likely to thrive in a building and a role driven by precedent.

History and precedent

There is also, of course, the question of the historic building's suitability as a home for the modern premiership. Robert Armstrong, who was Principal Private Secretary to Edward Heath and Wilson before becoming Cabinet Secretary for the majority of Thatcher's tenure, observes the role of precedent in keeping the centuries-old buildings at Downing Street essentially the same, despite their not being designed for anything like the purpose that they have since gone on to occupy:

I am sure that if you were starting from fresh, you wouldn't start with No. 10. But you aren't starting afresh. I think a conscious decision has been made – and made repeatedly – that the right thing to do is preserve No. 10 in its eighteenth-century form and live with that.[8]

The most significant point at which this 'conscious decision' was made was during the reconstruction of Downing Street and the adjacent Old Treasury buildings from 1960–3 (the subject of the fifth chapter of this book). This provided a huge opportunity for a total redesign of the home and office of the British Prime Minister, but this was ultimately rejected in favour of an essentially conservationist approach. Armstrong ultimately endorses this decision:

I think it was the right decision, because you could have gutted the house and completely redone it, but it would have changed its character. Though it might have become more efficient in some ways, part of the charm of the house is that it is what it is – what Kent and Sir George Downing created. It's got historical meaning and significance. When I was Cabinet Secretary, I had a lot to do with Ireland and Northern Ireland. As you sat at the table discussing with the Prime Minister, the Foreign Secretary and the Northern Ireland Secretary, you couldn't help being aware that subject had been discussed in that room any time in the last two hundred years, and we were just adding a chapter to the events that had taken place there.[9]

Whilst there are few who would disagree that the historic value of No. 10 is tremendous, there are plenty who would disagree that this outweighs its impracticalities. As noted in the first chapter of this book, Marcia Falkender (previously Williams), Jonathan Powell and Douglas Hurd have all expressed dissatisfaction with the use of the historic No. 10 as a place for running a modern and impactful government. However, the preservationist argument has repeatedly won the day, resulting in the arrangement of rooms and consequent geography-of-power decisions that this chapter investigates.

The centre of the centre

There is no definitive rule book on how a Prime Minister should arrange their immediate working environment at No. 10. There are historical blueprints, however, and the different setups of No. 10's geography of power tend to revolve around which room the Prime Minister decides to use as their primary office. Several Prime Ministers have elected to work at the Cabinet table, located in the ground floor Cabinet Room, straight down the corridor from No. 10's famous front door.

Despite the fact that few postwar Prime Ministers have used it for the entirety of their premierships, this can be seen as the traditional setup, with the Cabinet Room labelled 'My Lord's Study' in early floor plans from as far back as 1781. The Cabinet Room, which was extended eastwards in 1783, sits amongst a warren of smaller rooms, which can be described as the operational centre of No. 10. The offices that surround the Cabinet Room are amongst the most desirable in the building.

Many postwar Prime Ministers have decided to instead under-take their daily work in the relatively secluded first-floor Study, away from the operational centre of the house and the associated comings and goings that occur throughout a typical working day at Downing Street. The Study is located across an annexe room just off the Grand Staircase, still allowing quick access from the nerve centre around the Cabinet Room, and even the basement Garden Rooms, albeit involv-ing a brisk skip up two flights of stairs. Private Secretaries and advisers can be summoned quickly by telephone or by a buzzer system, and a short staircase just outside the Study door in the annexe room leads up to the No. 10 flat, allowing the Prime Minister to slip quietly between their key working and living spaces at No. 10.

Some Prime Ministers have alternated between both rooms, or have begun their premierships in one before changing to the other. Wher-ever it is located, the Prime Minister's Office is the pivot on which the rest of the geography of power at No. 10 turns. As Bernard Donoughue observed, No. 10 is 'unlike any other department of British central government'. The small number of staff and the nature of the job housed by No. 10 mean that 'its whole operation depends entirely on one person, the Prime Minister'.[10] The premier's location and working

The Cabinet Room in 1927, before Harold
Macmillan redesigned the Cabinet table.

style determine where the best spots and time slots can be found at No.
10, in order to gain as much meaningful access as possible.

The Cabinet Room – a history

The Cabinet Room is perhaps the most famous room in No. 10. Located
at the back of the house, on the ground floor, the Cabinet Room was
initially Robert Walpole's study and the room which he would use to
receive visitors, including hosting meetings of the Cabinet.[11] This precedent has lasted ever since, albeit with significant interludes. Several
Prime Ministers have elected to hold Cabinet meetings elsewhere, with
Robert Gascoyne-Cecil and Arthur Balfour electing to hold meetings in the more spacious and arguably more splendid Foreign Office
Cabinet Room (now known as the Grand Reception Room, part of
the building's impressive Locarno Suite). The Cabinet has also met at

several other venues including Chequers, the Prime Minister's private country residence, and the Grand Hotel in Brighton.[12] For a brief period during William Gladstone's final premiership, as well as under Henry John Temple (better known as Lord Palmerston), Cabinet met in the Pillared Room at No. 10, located on the first floor. The Pillared Room is now often used as the venue for political Cabinet meetings, which the Cabinet Secretary does not attend, and which are used to discuss party political matters. This change in venue helps to reinforce the distinction between the two meetings and their differing purposes.

Cabinet was also forced to abandon No. 10 on more than one occasion during the twentieth century. The Second World War saw it occasionally forced underground to the Cabinet War Rooms, although Churchill liked to continue holding meetings around the Cabinet table at No. 10 whenever possible. This was despite the fact that the rest of the house, with the exception of the adjacent Private Secretaries' Room, had been emptied of furniture and possessions, the contents temporarily relocated to the No. 10 Annexe at Storey's Gate. Macmillan's Cabinet was also forced to relocate to one of Admiralty House's spacious reception rooms during the reconstruction works of 1960–3. It was from Admiralty House that Macmillan sweated over the Cuban Missile Crisis, and spoke directly to President John F. Kennedy.

Yet despite repeated periods of historical respite from its primary purpose, the Cabinet Room remains the unrivalled home of collective Cabinet Government – the system of collective responsibility by which the nation is governed – in the UK. Its internal geography is as significant for the conduct of the premiership as that of the rooms and buildings around it. Dominated by the famous Cabinet table, the room connects to the Private Secretaries' Rooms via double baize doors at its eastern end, behind its twin pillars. French doors open out onto a terrace overlooking the No. 10 garden at the western end. These features are widely recognisable, with the room having been recreated with impressive accuracy in numerous films and television series including *Yes, Prime Minister* and *The Crown*. In recent years, a publicity photograph of a newly appointed Cabinet around the Cabinet table has increasingly been issued from within No.10 to accompany an announcement of a reshuffle to the national media. However, official Cabinet photographs have traditionally been taken in the Pillared

Room or outside in No. 10's garden, and photographs of historical Cabinets line the walls in the corridors of No. 10's basement.

Alongside its role as the heart of collective decision-making in the UK, the Cabinet Room also remains one of the nation's most historic rooms. Addressing the Queen at a dinner in 1985 to commemorate 250 years of No. 10's current purpose, Prime Minister Thatcher observed, 'The Cabinet Room really does know every secret – for it is there where your ministers, Ma'am, have made so many of the decisions which have shaped the future.'[13] A painting of Walpole sits behind the Prime Minister's seat, overseeing proceedings at Cabinet and reminding ministers of the great historical significance of both the room and the decisions that have been made there. Joe Haines, former Press Secretary to Wilson, observed:

[The Cabinet Room] had heard of the loss of the American colonies, plotted the downfall of Napoleon and the end of Kaiser Wilhelm as well as Hitler, and in [that room] the decision to grant India's independence was taken; how can the White House or the Kremlin compete with that?[14]

Few decisions can be said to have had more impact on Britain's fate in the twentieth century than that of May 1940, when Churchill's War Cabinet ultimately resolved to fight on alone against Hitler's Germany. This decision was made, for the most part, at numerous frequent meetings around No. 10's Cabinet table.[15] With poetic symmetry, this would go on to become the venue from which Churchill would announce to the British people, via radio, the end of the war in Europe. The image of the wartime Prime Minister dubbed the 'greatest Briton of all time' by a BBC television poll in 2002 must have often appeared in the minds of those who have subsequently sat around the Cabinet table.[16] The BBC's Christopher Jones notes:

Churchill's immense presence is still, forty years after the end of the Second World War, tangibly present in 10 Downing Street. Every Prime Minister since his day has been well aware that he or she is sitting in Churchill's seat in the Cabinet Room; staff at No. 10 who were children – or perhaps not even born – when he was

Churchill addresses the nation from the Cabinet table in No. 10, 1942.

at the height of his power speak of him with awe; it is his portrait on the staircase, in its place with his forty-seven predecessors and successors, which immediately catches the eye; a large painting of his broods over the country's most senior statesmen as they gather outside the Cabinet Room for their regular meetings.[17]

Churchill's use of the room during wartime was constrained by No. 10's vulnerability to bombing, and his second period as Prime Minister saw an increasing tendency to work from his bed. Yet it was still the Cabinet Room that he kept as his main office, pacing its length and dictating speeches furiously to exhausted secretaries into the early hours, and hosting meetings of the Cabinet whenever it was deemed safe enough to do so.

Despite Churchill's ghost still looming over the room, several other Prime Ministers have left notable and more tangible legacies in the room's appearance and layout. It was Ramsay MacDonald, the first Labour Prime Minister, who began the tradition of keeping a No. 10 library in the Cabinet Room, with books donated by Cabinet Ministers upon their departure from office and stored in book-shelves around the edges of the room.[18] The majority of the library was rehoused elsewhere in No. 10 when the building was renovated during Macmillan's premiership in order to create more space.[19] The tradition of book donations by Cabinet Ministers is still maintained, with choices ranging from ministers donating their own memoirs (as Thatcher elected to do) to Macmillan's donation of the complete works of Rudyard Kipling, resulting in a library that can be generously described as a 'curious collection'.[20]

Churchill's successor, Anthony Eden, made some alterations to the room's lighting, bringing in two chandeliers to replace the three inverted bowl pendant lights and one smaller chandelier by the pillars that had previously lit the room.[21] Prior to Eden's alterations, Churchill had used a task lamp when working at the Cabinet table, as the room's lighting was inadequate for desk work.[22] This dark, gloomy atmos-phere cannot have made for an uplifting environment for meetings of the Cabinet, although it is debatable whether the ill-fated Eden's new chandeliers brightened the mood of his Cabinet significantly.

The room's atmosphere was improved, in a literal sense, by Clement Attlee, who banned smoking in the room during his premiership, despite being a pipe smoker himself. This set a precedent that has been upheld ever since, and has had both short- and long-term rami-fications, from the reported increase in ministers finding excuses to pop out of the room for a nicotine hit during Attlee's premiership to the later appropriation of the Political Secretary's Room next door as a haven for smokers and therefore a den of political gossip during Heath's.[23] Attlee's smoking ban may have seemed ahead of its time in postwar Britain as a whole, but it actually brought No. 10 up to speed with the House of Commons, which had banned smoking in the chamber a full 250 years earlier (nevertheless, snuff is still provided for the use of Members on entry today).[24]

Eden was also approached by the Ministry of Works to make more lasting changes to the Cabinet Room. These included introducing two new portraits of former Prime Ministers – one opposite the Prime Minister's chair and one on the west wall – to keep the room's existing Walpole portrait company. Interesting early suggestions for the new portraits' subjects from within the Ministry of Works included Lord North and the Duke of Newcastle, 'who, while not in the first rank of Prime Ministers, were at any rate remarkable ones in their way'.[25] An attempt to avoid controversy saw Gladstone eliminated as a candidate over the suggestion that 'his first intervention in Debate' had been 'in defence of the slave trade',[26] and North was also knocked back by Appointments Secretary Anthony Bevir, who claimed, 'There is always a Commonwealth Relations objection to Lord North if ever one wants to hang him in a place where our touchy cousins can see him.'[27] In fact, North, most commonly associated with the loss of the American colonies, would have made for an interesting choice to join Walpole in the Cabinet Room, with the pair representing two of the earliest Prime Ministers to resign after losing the confidence of the House of Commons.

The options were eventually whittled down to five Prime Ministers. In Eden's order of preference, these were: William Pitt the Younger; William Lamb (better known as Lord Melbourne); George Canning; William Pitt the Elder (the Earl of Chatham); and The Duke of Wellington.[28] Unfortunately, Pitt the Younger was so well regarded that he was already represented elsewhere in Downing Street. Melbourne achieved fairly little as Prime Minister, and did not live at No. 10. The Earl of Chatham was only formally Prime Minister for two years, and also never lived at Downing Street. Canning was only Prime Minister for the last four months of his life. The Duke of Wellington's performance as Prime Minister is widely regarded as poor. It is interesting to note that few of the most famous and successful British Prime Ministers were thought of as uncontroversial enough to be viable options for this honour.

Eden also asked for the Cabinet's collective opinion on what should be done to the Cabinet Room. They requested only a change in the provided stationery, from notepaper headed with 'No. 10 Downing Street' to plain paper, claiming to feel 'embarrassed' by the letterhead.[29] Unfortunately, all plans to refurnish the Cabinet Room were ultimately postponed in April 1956 by Eden, who cited financial constraints.[30] The Prime Minister had already changed his mind on the introduction of new portraits into the room by this point; Eden's short-lived alternative plan to represent Pitt the Younger and Lord Melbourne in the room in the form of busts, sitting either side of the fireplace, appears to have been rejected by his Cabinet colleagues before the end of 1955.[31] Renovation of the Cabinet Room would ultimately have to wait for the upcoming wider reconstruction of Downing Street under Macmillan during 1960–3. The only Prime Minister represented by a portrait in the Cabinet Room remains Walpole, a fairly uncontroversial choice as the first holder of the office.

Heath oversaw remedial works that touched on the Cabinet Room. The introduction of lighter carpets and curtains helped to brighten up the space – which suffers from a lack of daylight due to its architecture and positioning within the building – alongside a new coat of paint.[32] Thatcher, who did not work in the room, but held hundreds of Cabinet meetings there throughout her premiership, was shocked to find on her arrival that that the Cabinet Anteroom 'looked rather like a down-at-heel Pall Mall club'. Bringing in new furniture and a portrait of Churchill, and lightening the colours in the Anteroom and the Cabinet Room itself, the Prime Minister 'changed the whole feel', reasoning in her memoirs, 'There might be some difficult times to come in the Cabinet Room itself, but there was no reason why people should be made to feel miserable while they were waiting to go in.'[33]

Macmillan made several alterations to the Cabinet Room, both trivial and significant. His legacy, whilst not as keenly felt, is much more easily observed. The first of Macmillan's alterations were short term in nature. Before he left Downing Street for Admiralty House, Macmillan 'removed the racks of writing paper from the Cabinet table, so that Ministers could not slip each other surreptitious notes', in response to the 'conspiratorial atmosphere' during Cabinet meetings under his predecessor, Eden.[34] He also introduced silver candlesticks, owned at one time by Pitt the Younger and later by Benjamin Disraeli, into the Cabinet Room.[35]

Macmillan's other changes had a more significant and longer-lasting impact on the geography of power. The first saw a small table introduced into the room, behind the pillars and next to the door to the

Private Secretaries' Room, from which his Private Secretaries could observe Cabinet meetings. As Macmillan's biographer Alistair Horne describes, the Prime Minister 'believed in the principle that his intimate staff should be kept fully "in the picture" of all that was going on'. Horne notes that Macmillan used his Private Secretaries 'as his eyes and ears, and sometimes called them his "major-generals"'.[36] However, this set a precedent for further increases in the number of 'observers' at Cabinet.

The second alteration appears to have originated in Macmillan's experience at Admiralty House during Downing Street's renovation. The Prime Minister recalled initially finding the room for Cabinet meetings at Admiralty House 'intolerably big' compared to the Cabinet Room at No. 10, and 'tried to overcome this by having a new top made for the table in the shape of a lozenge.' This allowed those at the ends of the table to better participate in discussion, as well as allowing the Prime Minister to look most of the Cabinet directly in the eye, giving the premier the best vantage point from which to eyeball ministers when they are speaking, being spoken to or being discouraged from speaking.[37] The table's design ensures that those seated just a few chairs down from the Prime Minister, on their side of the table, can still catch the Prime Minister's eye if necessary, without leaning forward in too difficult a fashion. The unusual shape has been maintained ever since, replacing the previous rectangular table, although Macmillan's description of the table top as lozenge-shaped failed to catch on; the Prime Minister's colleagues felt it more closely resembled a coffin.[38]

The geography of power plays out within the room itself. Seating arrangements at the Cabinet table are historically and symbolically important, but also have an impact upon the conduct of Cabinet Government. The Prime Minister's chair, the only one with arms, is positioned at the centre of the table with its back to the fireplace. As the house was heated by coal fire before the introduction of central heating in 1937, the Prime Minister's seat would once have also been the warmest in an otherwise cold house.[39] It is always left sitting out from the table at an angle, facing the door, enabling the Prime Minister to enter and sit immediately. Smooth and considered Prime Ministerial entrances and exits from meetings can be important as they help to set the tone of a premiership, and to project power and authority to the other attendees. As Richard Wilson (Lord Wilson of Dinton), a former Cabinet Secretary, recalled, Thatcher's exits from meetings had to be carefully stage-managed to properly project Prime Ministerial power and a serious commitment to getting on with the job:

> My first morning when I was head of the economic secretariat [at the Cabinet Office], I had a half-hour handover with my predecessor and I said to him, "Any tips for dealing with the Prime Minister?", because she had a reputation. And he thought for a moment and he said, "Well, you'll be sitting next to her and she will put her handbag down between her chair and yours, and you'll be sitting down after her. Don't get the legs of your chair mixed up with the straps of her handbag, because if you do, she, at the end of the meeting, she likes to reach down and pick up her handbag and say, 'We've got to get on with business', and if you spoil the exit because you have to unwrap it from your chair, she really won't like it!"[40]

Alongside hiring and firing ministers, the Prime Minister is responsible for establishing the order of precedence amongst Cabinet Ministers, and is also ultimately in charge of the seating plan. The only permanent positions at the Cabinet table are that of the Prime Minister and the Cabinet Secretary, who sits to the Prime Minister's immediate right, and takes the minutes of Cabinet before returning to the adjacent Cabinet Office, where they are responsible for ensuring that those minutes become actions. More senior ministers are usually clustered around the Prime Minister in the central positions, with those deemed to be less experienced, less senior in their position or simply less palatable to the Prime Minister sat towards the ends. John Campbell, biographer of both Heath and Thatcher, claimed that the former positioned the latter at the far end of his side of the Cabinet table, in a deliberate attempt to keep her as far from eye- and earshot as possible.[41] When Thatcher first attended Cabinet in the Prime Minister's chair, she responded, of course, by electing not to offer Heath a seat at the table in the first place.

The Prime Minister and the Cabinet Room

Given the Cabinet Room's long history as the space in which Prime Ministers have worked and received guests, it is unsurprising that every Prime Minister from Attlee to John Major has worked at the Cabinet table at some point. However, some have chosen to use it more than others, and others have found it completely unsuited to their needs.

Attlee used the Cabinet Room as his primary office, working on his boxes from the Prime Minister's chair at the Cabinet table, and received visitors there.[42] Churchill used the Cabinet Room as his office on occasions during the war, albeit less often from the seated position, as previously mentioned. His subsequent return to No. 10 also saw a return to the Cabinet Room, when he was not working from his bed. Reflecting on her father's time at No. 10, Churchill's daughter Mary Soames described it as 'a very convenient room [...] and I think it harmonised with his thoughts and was very conducive to pondering'.[43]

Eden's memoirs claim that he 'always' worked in the Cabinet Room, finding it 'more convenient than my study on the first floor'.[44] Macmillan liked the proximity to his Private Secretaries that the room provided, according to his biographer Horne, and also benefitted from the protection they provided him from unwanted visitors due to their location in the adjacent room.[45]

Wilson began his first premiership working at the Cabinet table, having witnessed when he was a young minister how Attlee worked there. However, in the words of Marcia Falkender, his Personal and Political Secretary:

> He always seemed a very lonely figure, sitting at the middle of the table, working away in the huge room with nothing but the melancholy portrait of Sir Robert to keep him company. It was intimidating, and uncomfortable, too, for his visitors to be received there.[46]

Wilson would ultimately decide that working at the Cabinet table did not suit him. Falkender claimed Wilson left the Cabinet Room after eighteen months, and the Prime Minister himself recalled moving offices after three years.[47] Regardless of the timeframe, it is clear that

Wilson felt he worked better in the first-floor Study, and it was to this room that he would return in his second premiership.

Callaghan described a romantic attachment to the Cabinet Room, saying, 'He would be an unfeeling man who could sit for the first time in the Prime Minister's seat at the centre of the Cabinet table in No. 10 and feel no emotion.'[48] Callaghan preferred to work in the Cabinet Room, enjoying its spaciousness and 'sense of history', and he was particularly fond of hosting visitors there.[49] In historic footage used by the film-maker Michael Cockerell for his documentary *Behind the Black Door*, Callaghan recalled using the room, the most historic and one of the grandest in Downing Street (although even the house's grandest rooms are fairly average compared to those found in the residences of other countries' Prime Ministers and Presidents) to remind guests of the power of his great office:

> That was part of the trick – if you sat in an overwhelming room, with a table twenty-five feet long, just think what the poor man who's never used it felt when he came in and sat opposite you! I won't say it was like Mussolini, who I'm told used to make you walk the whole length of his room, but it was quite an experience, obviously, for people to come into the Cabinet Room and sit there, even when the Cabinet wasn't there, and discuss things with the Prime Minister.[50]

Nigel Lawson, Chancellor of the Exchequer under Thatcher, told students of Jon Davis's 'History of the Treasury Since 1945' course at King's College London something similar. Whilst he preferred to work in his office at No. 11, Lawson liked to use the large Chancellor's Room in the Treasury, with the Chancellor's desk at one end and the entrance at the other, as a venue for meeting ministers who he wished to intimidate.[51]

Major also used the Cabinet Room as an office for the majority of his time at No. 10. Senior figures in Major's staff claim that he particularly liked the Cabinet Room's location within Downing Street, as it placed him adjacent to 'a Private Office of officials next door to shout to, chivvy and consult'.[52] The Cabinet Room was also less remote within No. 10 than the first-floor Study, something that Major's biographer

Margaret Thatcher signs letters in the Study at No. 10, 1989.

Anthony Seldon highlights as appealing to the Prime Minister, who was 'not the type who liked to work in silence'.[53]

The Prime Minister's Study

The Prime Minister's Study, looking out towards St. James's Park on the first floor of No. 10, was once the bedroom of the Prime Minister, before the residential part of No. 10 was moved up to the second floor for the Chamberlains. Clementine Churchill also used it as a bedroom during her husband's second premiership.[54] Today, it is informally known as the Thatcher Room, after the imposing portrait of the former Prime Minister that occupies its wall, painted by artist Richard Stone but, perhaps somewhat surprisingly, commissioned by Prime Minister Gordon Brown.

Most Prime Ministers used the Study at some point; it was a main office not only to Thatcher, but also to Wilson and Heath. Wilson's dislike for the Cabinet Room may have related to the geography of power around the room during his first administration. Seldon and

Kavanagh quote an unnamed official as observing, 'At one end the Private Office wanted to discuss government business with him, at the other end, Marcia [Falkender] wanted to talk over party matters.'[55] Ultimately, it seems Wilson felt that he worked better in seclusion, perhaps due to the individuals that he had appointed to work alongside him. The diaries of Richard Crossman, who held several ministerial posts during Wilson's first premiership, claim Wilson 'thought he could do all his work in the Cabinet Room. As a result, he hadn't done any writing and it's taken him four years to learn this lesson'.[56]

Despite Wilson's dependence upon his Personal and Political Secretary, Falkender, he could also find her difficult to handle. Wilson's biographer Ben Pimlott claims that, initially, Wilson chose to work at the Cabinet table not just because of the Attlee precedent, but also 'because Marcia was next door, and he found her proximity reassuring'.[57] However, this was not always the case. Bernard Donoughue, who headed up the fledgling Policy Unit under Wilson during his second premiership, claims that working in the Study not only took the Prime Minister away from Falkender's office, but also allowed for a quick (and unnoticed if necessary) getaway from No. 10:

> One purely geographical thing – Wilson could take a lift down from near the Study to go to the front door, and it brought him out near the front door. And the advantage of that was that he could do that without Marcia seeing, because it put him past her room. That was a bit of geography. We always knew that he was trying to avoid her when he took the lift down, so that she wouldn't see him go.[58]

Another intriguing point relating to Wilson's choice of office within No. 10 arose when the Prime Minister considered using the Cabinet Room for a televised interview in late 1965. Principal Private Secretary Derek Mitchell asked his predecessor, Laurence Helsby, who had been Principal Private Secretary to Attlee, for advice on the acceptability of this idea. Cabinet Secretary Burke Trend appeared surprised by this because, according to Mitchell, Trend 'regarded the Cabinet Room as his province and took the view that I should have asked him for advice'. Whilst the Prime Minister was persuaded against recording the interview in the Cabinet Room, both the current and the previous Principal Private Secretaries strongly disputed the idea that the Cabinet Secretary had 'jurisdiction over any part of No. 10'.[59]

The Study clearly suited Wilson, and it was to this room that he immediately returned when re-elected in March 1974, to begin putting together his Cabinet.[60] Wilson not only preferred the uninterrupted working environment for going through his boxes, but he also used the Study as a venue for gatherings of his closest allies, advisers and political friends, widely but loosely referred to as the kitchen cabinet, in between meetings and over a drink in the evenings. The Study was perfect for this less formal setting, being relatively out of the way within No. 10, and therefore inconspicuous, so that the room's occupants were not always known to the Private Office. Whilst the Cabinet Room doors were soundproofed,[61] the Study provided a more relaxed atmosphere, and was situated at one remove from the operational centre of the house.

Heath worked in both the Cabinet Room and the Study at points during his premiership. However, he preferred the Study, once it had been improved as part of the remedial works to address dry rot that were undertaken throughout the building during his premiership. Heath later described the renovation work in the Study as 'particularly successful', and expressed a preference for working there over the Cabinet Room, 'even though, or perhaps because, the Study was further away from the private office'.[62] Robert Armstrong, who served as Heath's Principal Private Secretary, recalled the mild inconvenience of the Study for Private Secretaries:

> There was an awful lot of going upstairs, particularly after Heath decided to use the Study instead of the Cabinet Room. But I didn't actually feel that was an inconvenience. I thought that it was perfectly reasonable for the Prime Minister to have his own study where he could sit quiet, read and so on. If that meant that I had to go upstairs, well that was what I was paid for.[63]

Callaghan occasionally worked in the Study, where Seldon and Kavanagh claim he summoned Private Secretaries from downstairs by pressing a button, which in turn activated a light in the Outer Private Secretaries' Room.[64] However, Callaghan worked primarily from the Cabinet table, describing the Study as 'claustrophobic' and claiming that using the Cabinet Room 'saves their legs'.[65] It is likely that the Cabinet Room also suited Callaghan's more formal style; as Donoughue recalled, whereas Wilson would generally call down for a visit from his Policy Unit head at least once a day, Callaghan did so much less often. Additionally, Callaghan did not welcome unexpected guests: 'With Harold, you could still drop in, but Jim was not one for dropping in on, he liked you to make appointments.'[66]

Perhaps it was this formality that appealed to Thatcher, who elected to work in the Study, rather than at the Cabinet table, when not working in the flat upstairs. The short staircase up to the private No. 10 flat, in which she not only often worked on her boxes but also insisted on regularly cooking for herself and her husband Denis, was located directly outside the door of the Study.[67] Thatcher later reminisced that climbing the stairs to the top-floor flat at No. 10 provided her with a rare opportunity for regular exercise when Prime Minister.[68]

Like Heath, Thatcher had significant changes made to the Study's décor. Finding the sage-green damask-flock wallpaper 'oppressive', the Prime Minister had the room redecorated in lighter tones at her own expense. A portrait of Horatio Nelson, better known as Lord Nelson, who Thatcher greatly admired, was also brought in at the Prime Minister's request.[69] Unfortunately, an attempt to make her successor, Major, more comfortable with working in the Study by bringing in a portrait of cricketer W. G. Grace, failed to have the same impact on him. Major reportedly felt 'alienated' by the Study's style and its distance from his staff, and he elected to work from the Cabinet Room instead.[70] Thatcher, by way of contrast, loved the room. Under Thatcher, the Study became 'a most elegant room', according to close ally Cecil Parkinson, and a venue for smaller meetings, including regular private meetings with Willie Whitelaw, her Home Secretary and *de facto* Deputy Prime Minister, before the Cabinet met downstairs.[71]

Ultimately, the room a Prime Minister chooses as their main 'base' within No. 10 can reveal a lot about their working style, and their attitude to the premiership itself. The Cabinet Room is grander, more formal, and can prove intimidating (or impressive) for visitors. But it also provides instant and direct access to the Private Office next door, with the Principal Private Secretary a shout, rather than a phone call or buzzer, away. The Study is a significant stage further into the No. 10 labyrinth from the front door than the Cabinet Room. It therefore offers more privacy both in terms of work and allowing visitors to slip in and out unmonitored. The Study can be a lonely and quiet place to work, and so whether a Prime Minister thrives in this environment depends mainly on their personality.

The Study occupies a bridging point between the working and residential parts of the building, with a short staircase up to the private No. 10 flat just outside its door, and it has its own bathroom, adding to the self-contained feel of the place. By way of contrast, the Cabinet Room is not only metaphorically shared with the entire Cabinet and the principle of collective government, but is also surrounded by an increasing range and number of staff, with the Private Office based in adjoining rooms since before 1945, the emerging Political Office at No. 10 finding a place just off of the Cabinet Anteroom in the 1960s, and the Head of the Policy Unit joining nearby in 1974.

Whilst each Prime Minister has chosen their main office for different reasons, it is interesting that more reforming, modernising premiers appear to have worked primarily in the Study, with the more traditionalist Prime Ministers choosing to work in the Cabinet Room. The Prime Ministers who made the most changes to the machinery of government at and around No. 10 between 1945 and 1997, namely Wilson, Heath and Thatcher, were also those who elected not to work at the Cabinet table. Those who have worked at the Cabinet table have tended to be more conservative in their approach to the organisation of No. 10 in general.

The 'operational centre'

Recalling his time at No. 10, Eden's Press Secretary observed that, 'All the private business was conducted in the far north end of the house, where the sun never penetrates.'[72] This was the case throughout the postwar period. Whether the Prime Minister elected to work from the Cabinet Room or the Study, the suite of historic rooms that adjoin and surround the Cabinet Room, sited in the old 'house at the back', remained the nerve centre of the Prime Minister's Office throughout.

Former Principal Private Secretary and Cabinet Secretary Robin Butler (Lord Butler of Brockwell) describes this as the 'operational centre' of No. 10. This 'centre' encompassed all of the rooms that open onto the Cabinet Room or Cabinet Anteroom, as well as those around the Grand Staircase on the ground floor, and the Garden Rooms that are located just one floor underneath. This comparatively small section of No. 10 housed those who worked most closely with the premier on a day-to-day basis throughout the postwar years.

The 'Official Suite': Private Secretaries' Rooms

The first of these important rooms is traditionally known as the Inner Private Secretaries' Room, and sits alongside the Cabinet Room, through the double doors behind the Cabinet Room's iconic pillars. Early maps show the room designated as a waiting room for what was then 'My Lord's Study' next door.[73] This adjoining room soon became the most desirable room for advisers seeking proximity to the Prime Minister.

Stanley Baldwin's Principal Private Secretary Robert Vansittart, in the late 1920s, sat in this room, from which he recalled that 'raised voices came through the double doors in chorus or duet'.[74] The doors may have been soundproofed by the twentieth century, but the room remains the closest to the Prime Minister and the Cabinet in No. 10, and represents the nerve centre of the building. As one former Principal Private Secretary described to Peter Hennessy, this room is 'the cockpit of the United Kingdom.'[75] Unlike Henry VIII's 'cock pit', the ruins of which are preserved nearby between No. 10 and the Cabinet Office, this is a room less of entertainment and rather of much serious work. In the postwar years, it has been home to the two most senior members of the Private Office: the Principal Private Secretary and the Foreign Affairs Private Secretary.

The Inner Private Secretaries' Room connects directly to the Cabinet Room, via baize-covered double doors, at one end. At the other, the room is connected to an Outer Private Secretaries' Room, which, referring back to our 1781 map, was originally designated as a dining room. Again, much like the adjacent Cabinet Room, the internal geography of the Inner Private Secretaries' Room also reflects power, with the former official granted a desk formerly belonging to Disraeli, at the Cabinet Room end, and the latter located further away, nearer to the Outer Private Secretaries' Room at the other end.[76]

In the postwar era, the Outer Private Secretaries' Room was typically home to the lower rung of three Private Secretaries, for whom direct access to the Prime Minister was deemed slightly less important, alongside a Diary Secretary and Duty Clerk. The two rooms worked extremely closely together, and they represented the final port of call for papers seeking the Prime Minister's attention, which would end up in a series of trays on the desk of the Principal Private Secretary. Proximity to the Prime Minister also ensured that, as Callaghan recalled of his time at No. 10, the Private Office could effectively act 'as a filter through which those who wish to see the Prime Minister must pass'.[77] This filtration could be exercised through the management of paper, or through control over the Prime Minister's diary; as one former Principal Private Secretary observed, 'Absolutely everybody wants a chunk of the Prime Minister's time.'[78] This gatekeeper role could also be performed in a physical sense, due to the location of the offices, as one former Principal Private Secretary recalled:

> I couldn't control people that walked into the Cabinet Room from the corridor, but not many people would do that; most people would come in through the Private Office, saying, "Is he free?" Because they wouldn't necessarily know whether he was in a big meeting with a foreign dignitary or not, so they mostly, if they wanted to raise something with him, would come through the Private Office. And so we were effectively, we could be, gatekeepers.[79]

The room was also ideally placed for quick and easy interventions into the Cabinet Room, enabling the Principal Private Secretary to drop in and pass a note or subtly signal if a meeting with the Prime Minister was running over.[80]

The Private Secretaries' Rooms benefit from being close to not only the Prime Minister, but also one another, ensuring collaborative and flexible working between the various Private Secretaries.[81] As one former Private Secretary told Seldon and Kavanagh, 'An organisation chart or assignment of fixed spheres of responsibility could not properly describe how we work.'[82] These rooms are not luxurious or particularly spacious, necessitating close working and providing little privacy or space for quiet reflection. Yet whilst they may never have represented the height of modern office working, the nature of the rooms created an intimate and exciting working environment. Their location in what is arguably No. 10's premier spot, alongside the intimacy of the offices, was highlighted by Robin Butler, who served as a Private Secretary under Heath and Wilson, and was Principal Private Secretary to Thatcher in 1982–5:

> There were few enough of us, especially as concerns the Private Secretaries, to have very direct, easy, regular access to the Prime Minister and to each other. Direct access to the Prime Minister – not going through anybody. [...] It was hard to have a private conversation, but you didn't want to. So, as you see, the whole point of it was that you could hear what was going on; you knew what meetings were being arranged.[83]

Most Prime Ministers were liable to 'wander in' to the Private Secretaries' Rooms at some point or other, although to varying frequencies and at varying times of day. As one Private Secretary told Seldon and Kavanagh, Thatcher could show up at any point, which kept them constantly on their toes:

> She would stand by your desk and rifle through your in-tray. "What is this?" she would say to us. She would flick through your papers and there'd be some stuff there you didn't particularly want her to see, so you'd be pretty careful what you put into your in-tray if you suspected she might drop in.[84]

By way of contrast, Heath's penchant for playing the piano upstairs in the White Room, located next door to the first-floor Study, provided the Private Office with a handy early warning system. The sound of the piano was not only pleasant to the ear, but also provided a welcome notification that the Prime Minister was otherwise occupied, and not about to unexpectedly drop in to the Private Office.[85]

The 'Wiggery'

The Inner and Outer Private Secretaries' Rooms are the core parts of the Official Suite at the operational centre of No. 10. However, another small suite of rooms complements them. These rooms, nearby but up for grabs, have been extremely desirable to Downing Street outsiders and political appointees in the postwar years. The suite came to be known as the Wiggery, after its Wilson-era occupant, George Wigg. The suite is easily located, and only seconds away from the operational centre. Off the Cabinet Anteroom, past the Grand Staircase and the entrances to the Inner and Outer Private Secretaries' Rooms, a corridor eventually connects No. 10 to 70 Whitehall and the Cabinet Office. Off this corridor and just before leaving No. 10, up a very short flight of stairs of less than one full floor, sat the Wiggery.

Returning to our Downing Street floor plan of 1781, the Wiggery consisted of two rooms, both up the short flight of stairs, designated 'My Lord's Gentlemen's Room' and 'Wardrobe' respectively. By the time of Attlee's arrival at No. 10, the northernmost room was allocated to the Parliamentary Private Secretary, a political role typically occupied by a backbench MP, and the adjacent room was unassigned and presumably empty, a situation that could barely be imagined in today's No. 10. The architect Raymond Erith's changes to the building during the renovation works of 1960–3 saw the suite slightly remodelled and carved into three rooms, assigned to Assistant Private Secretaries, honours staff and a typist. Parliamentary Private Secretaries continued to use the room up to Thatcher's premiership.[86] However, within a year of their 1960s remodelling, the rooms would also begin to play host to new elements introduced into No. 10.

On winning the general election of 1964, Wilson appointed his long-time associate Wigg as Paymaster General, a ministerial sinecure to which the Prime Minister attached a 'special responsibility for security'. Wigg, a former military man who had played an active role in exposing the Profumo affair, was tasked with liaison with the security services and keeping Wilson abreast of goings on within the Labour Party. Wigg was described as 'strategically placed' in the geography of power, with access to No. 10 and the Prime Minister that others such as economic adviser Thomas Balogh, stranded on the other side of the divide within 70 Whitehall, were initially denied.[87]

The well-placed Wiggery was temporarily home to the Press Secretary during Heath's premiership,[88] and was later snapped up by Bernard Donoughue, who arrived at No. 10 in 1974 eager to ensure that his new Policy Unit would be sufficiently well integrated into the No. 10 machine to survive, thrive and perhaps even outlive his tenure. Donoughue was acutely aware of the significance of geography to his success or failure at No. 10:

> In government one of the most important ingredients of power is access – access to decision-makers and access to information revealing what is going on in Whitehall. Within Number 10, that meant claiming a room close to the Prime Minister, for quick briefings, close to the private secretaries who receive all policy papers and telephone information, and close to both the Cabinet Room and the Prime Minister's Study where the most important meetings took place.[89]

When Press Secretary Joe Haines recommended that he secure the Wiggery for his offices, Donoughue jumped at the chance:

> The location was perfect. It occupied a bridge linking Number 10 with the key Cabinet Office. It gave me quick access to the action points of the house, to where the Prime Minister and his officials worked and met, and especially to the Downing Street cockpit and gossip centre, the Cabinet Room lobby where ministers and officials gather for meetings with the Prime Minister.[90]

When he first arrived, Donoughue found his chosen room occupied by Robin Haydon, a civil servant who briefly served as Heath's Press Secretary towards the end of his premiership. Haydon, accepting that his need was lesser than Donoughue's, left in a matter of days.[91]

Whilst the Wiggery rooms were not quite large enough to accommodate the entire Policy Unit, with some of the staff having to find accommodation next door in the Cabinet Office, Donoughue himself had acquired an excellent position in the geography of power at No.

Harold Wilson works at the Cabinet table, 1964. The Political Secretary's Room was located through the door to the left of the image, and the Inner Private Secretary's Room through a door at the opposite end of the Cabinet Room (behind the photographer).

10, and could therefore represent the Policy Unit from that base.[92] Access to the Prime Minister was clearly important, but for a new unit attempting to integrate seamlessly into the Downing Street machine, it was equally important to have easy, regular access to the Private Office:

> I would pop into the Private Office half a dozen times a day. After all, every time I came down the stairs, I would pass the Private Office, with the door open. Daily contact. And that way, I could sort of wander in there and look in the Prime Minister's boxes. If I only arrived occasionally, and went poking around in his boxes, they might wonder about that. If you become part of their everyday life, and they trust you, then you can look in the boxes, as part of your daily routine.[93]

The location, alongside Donoughue's personality and approach, and the quality of work produced, all combined to ensure that the Policy Unit was a success. Under Thatcher, it was Chief of Staff David Wolfson who occupied the Wiggery.[94] The Policy Unit, and its head, moved up to the first floor. Yet the unit was retained by subsequent Prime Ministers, and its influence, whilst waxing and waning as personalities changed, was not diminished overall. Donoughue had succeeded in sewing it into the fabric of No. 10.

The Political Secretary's Room

If the Private Office's rooms at No. 10 can claim to be the finest seats in the house in terms of proximity to the Prime Minister, the Political Secretary's Room, located to the south-west of the Cabinet Room and linked to it by a small door, could represent a rival for the title. The room is small but light, with two large windows and a view out onto the garden. Another small room that was once No. 10's library, and later a waiting room for visitors to the Cabinet Room, adjoins. It is also connected to an adjacent lavatory that, due to its location, can lay claim to having seen more top-level political gossip than any other in the country. This small Political Suite of rooms can be accessed from the Cabinet Anteroom, where ministers congregate before meetings of the Cabinet.

Sarah Hogg and Jonathan Hill, who both occupied prominent roles under Major, captured the essence of the Political Secretary's Room in the 1990s, as well as much of Downing Street, in their published account of life at No. 10:

> It is an office that captures the two sides of Downing Street life. High-ceilinged, with a fine cornice, a marble fireplace and some distinguished paintings, in the early 1990's it also boasted a chipboard bookcase, battered metal filing cabinet and an armchair with the springs hanging out of the bottom.[95]

This contrast between historic grandeur and modern reality is a common thread across many of the rooms and offices in No. 10

throughout this period. However, not all rooms are in quite as desirable a location.

The Political Secretary's Room was a secretary's room as far back as 1781. Gladstone's Private Secretary Algernon West worked from here in the late nineteenth century.[96] Private Secretaries under Herbert Henry Asquith and David Lloyd George also occupied these rooms. As the Private Office became more neatly defined in its role, and was staffed by more politically neutral, long-term civil servants, it found a more permanent home at the opposite end of the Cabinet Room,[97] leaving the Political Secretary's Room up for grabs – although it would go on to change purposes once more in the postwar period.

It was Marcia Falkender, Personal and Political Secretary to Wilson, who first converted the room to its new use as the home of the new Political Office. On arrival at No. 10, following Wilson's victory in 1964, Falkender (named Williams at the time) immediately set up office in the small room beside the Cabinet Room. She was shocked to find such a well-placed room occupied by No. 10 Appointments Secretary John Hewitt; her memoirs state, 'The fact that [the Appointments office staff] are there in No. 10, where space is so desperately needed, always struck me as amazing.'[98] Falkender lobbied the Prime Minister, who instructed his Principal Private Secretary to rehouse Hewitt, using the promise of an upstairs room with a stained-glass window to lure the Appointments Secretary out of his existing accommodation.[99] Falkender had come to occupy a prime slot in No. 10's geography of power.[100]

Donoughue, who published extensive reflections on his time at No. 10 as the inaugural Head of the Policy Unit under Wilson and Callaghan, reflected in 2005 on the significance of the room to Falkender and the performance of her role within Downing Street:

> Anybody from outside [...] wishing to see or talk to the Prime Minister was advised to make contact with and through her. Those who tried to gain access without first asking her permission would suffer a blackening of character and the slamming of the Prime Minister's door. [...] A similar experience faced those actually working in the entourage. This strategic position ensured her considerable power, since others had to please her in order to reach the Prime Minister.

From her critically located offices, one opening on to the Cabinet Room lobby in Number Ten, the other adjacent to the Prime Minister's room in the Commons, she acted as an impressive and effective dragon at the gate.[101]

In establishing a strong political presence in this area of No. 10, which stood between the front door and the Cabinet Room and Private Secretaries' Room, Falkender set up an alternative centre of power and influence in No. 10 that had not existed since the role of the Private Office had evolved into its modern form. Subsequent Political Secretaries, whilst changing the tone of the job significantly and making conscious efforts to improve relations with the existing No. 10 machine, would retain this key position within the geography of power until 1997.

The room was ideally located for a number of reasons, not least its proximity to the Prime Minister, should they choose to work from the Cabinet Room. Even when a premier elected to work upstairs in the Study, the room had a number of other geographical benefits; for example, Falkender's tenure saw the room provide a regular post-Cabinet meeting point for the Prime Minister and his closest allies.[102]

Douglas Hurd, Heath's Political Secretary and effectively Falkender's successor, made a particular effort to ensure that his relations with civil servants at No. 10 were much more cordial than Falkender's had been. As Richard Crossman's diaries note, Falkender's abrasive style saw her 'gradually rejected from No. 10 by the Civil Service' in Wilson's second term, performing most of her work in the House of Commons instead.[103] Hurd was determined not to follow this path. Under Hurd, the internal door between the Political Secretary's Room and the Cabinet Room was kept locked. This was a mostly symbolic move, made with the Private Office in mind, designed to show that Hurd had no intention of trying to vie with them for control of the Prime Minister's time. Hurd was happy to go through them if he needed access to Heath, and this led to a much more harmonious and integrated No. 10 operation.[104]

Hurd's collegiate approach applied to political as well as civil service colleagues at No. 10. Not only did his office open onto the Cabinet Anteroom, but any minister arriving at No. 10 for a meeting, whether in the neighbouring Cabinet Room or upstairs in the Study or private flat, would walk past the Political Secretary's Office on their way in. Hurd was wise to the benefits of such a location, describing his office as 'a place of refuge for all kinds of visitors to Number Ten, particularly those who wanted a smoke or a good grumble'.[105] In keeping his door open throughout the day, as well as operating a smoking policy, Hurd rendered the Political Secretary's Office 'a clearing house for political gossip and chat' – as Seldon and Kavanagh described it – during Heath's premiership.[106]

The primary job of the Political Secretary is to connect the Prime Minister to their party and to Parliament, and the room first chosen by Falkender, and subsequently occupied by Hurd, was perfectly placed for this purpose. Callaghan's Political Secretary Tom McNally elected to occupy the same room when he arrived at No. 10, demonstrating that a precedent had now been set.[107] Thatcher's first Political Secretary, Richard Ryder, shared the room with Ian Gow, Thatcher's Parliamentary Private Secretary, who initially thought it 'appalling' due to its lack of a refrigerator to cool alcoholic drinks. A fridge was quickly installed and filled with a fine range of beverages from Fleet Street's El Vino wine bar, which was part-owned by junior minister David Mitchell.[108] Like El Vino, the room became an excellent venue for well-lubricated gossip, continuing Hurd's trick of luring ministers into the Political Secretary's Room by providing them with an opportunity to indulge their vices.

The room's proximity to what may have been the most politically active lavatory in the country provided other, perhaps related, opportunities. Falkender claimed that Wilson's Private Secretaries would gladly follow the Prime Minister into these toilets, attempting to brief him on developments or get a decision on a paper, a move which she felt was designed to disadvantage her because of her gender:

> I could often hear their voices in there, as they reported to him, argued a point, sought to persuade him on others. It was an advantage they had on me, since they could always give him their version of an incident before I could if he happened to pop in there before looking in on me in my office.[109]

Hogg and Hill, of the Policy Unit and Political Office respectively during Major's premiership, observed that the lavatory 'is where many crucial conversations and deals take place'.[110] Hurd noted that ministers passing his room on the way from the Cabinet Room or Anteroom to use the facilities would often 'drop in for a short chat'.[111] Proximity to this particular element of the No. 10 'machinery' was, perhaps, a mixed blessing.

The Garden Rooms

No. 10's Garden Rooms are named after their view out onto the Downing Street gardens at the back of the house, below the official ground level. They are located a short flight of stairs down from No. 10's operational centre. Unusually for No. 10, the Garden Rooms have been particularly consistent in their use and function ever since the First World War, when Lloyd George established a typing pool in the basement rooms.[112] They now house No. 10's secretarial and administrative functions. During the Second World War, the Garden Rooms' ceilings were strengthened with large wooden struts, and shutters were fixed to the windows, in an attempt to make the rooms as safe as possible during air raids. Whilst they may have been the safest spot in No. 10, the building remained structurally weak and far from completely safe, should Downing Street suffer a direct hit. Yet it was in these rooms that King George VI dined with Churchill on fourteen occasions, twice having to remove to an adjacent improvised air raid shelter due to night raids.[113] To this day, a plaque is displayed in the Garden Rooms commemorating this fact.

These basement rooms were once cramped and unpleasant, with low ceilings and little natural light. Erith's revamp of No. 10 in the early 1960s improved them significantly, making them much more comfortable and pleasant to work in. The basement was not only home to the typists and secretaries that provided essential support to the rest of No. 10's operational centre, but also to two other significant and important functions at No. 10.

The first was the building's vast archives of 'confidential filing', a store containing the building's institutional memory, which could be consulted to dig out information for Prime Minister's Questions, or to search for clues as to the constitutional status or precedent for a particular Prime Ministerial decision. William Clark, Press Secretary under Eden, recalled that having to 'phone down' for files was an inconvenience of No. 10's layout. However, this was circumvented by the staff he described as the Registry, who were extremely quick and able at retrieving relevant files 'in minutes'.[114] Seldon and Kavanagh claim that it was the Duty Clerk, who sat upstairs in the Outer Private Office, who was tasked with providing a 'bridge' between the Private Office and the basement filing cabinets.[115] Physically, however, the rooms were connected by what Hogg and Hill describe as 'the kind of creaking dumb waiter that used to fuel the dining rooms under [the government offices in] Great George Street'.[116]

The other No. 10 resource found in the basement, not necessarily managed by the Garden Room Girls but arguably just as important as No. 10's filing cabinets, was the Prime Minister's wine cellar, which serviced many high-profile visits of foreign leaders, domestic politicians and business folk. It is not recorded whether the dumb waiter was ever used to deliver wine to the Private Office, nor, if so, whether it was in the service of celebration or commiseration.

The Press Office

The Press Office was housed outside the operational centre of No. 10 throughout the postwar period, but it was no less important to the running of the building. In fact, it provides an excellent example of how the best spots at No. 10 do not always relate to proximity to the Prime Minister. The Press Office's geography was important to the successful conduct of its business, despite its being housed in what was historically a different building to No. 10's operational centre.

The fledgling Press Office found its home in 1945 in what is now the bow-windowed room at the front of No. 10, facing out onto Downing Street, at the Whitehall end of the building. This site roughly corresponds with the previous site of Mr. Chicken's small home, the third house that was incorporated into No. 10 in 1735.[117] The 1781 floor plan shows that the room did not even exist in that year, and that the No. 10

laundry and the maid's bedroom were close to its eventual location, a reminder that the house's domestic functions could once be found on all of its floors. In fact, the room did not acquire its bow window until the architect Erith redesigned it in the early 1960s. Whilst he took a primarily conservationist stance, and sought to change as little as possible around No. 10's historic rooms, Erith simplified and improved the historical hodgepodge of rooms and corridors around the Press Office, eventually introducing the bow window and an adjoining room for other Press Office staff to work in.

Francis Williams, Attlee's Press Secretary, would take a short walk down the corridor from the front door to the Cabinet Room to brief the Prime Minister every morning. Given Attlee's reputation for terseness, these briefings would likely have been extremely brief. Regular access to the Prime Minister, however, is absolutely crucial to the person or people tasked with explaining the Prime Minister's thinking to the British people via the media. Otherwise, Williams was 'left to his own devices as to how he should interpret the Government to the world' from his base at the front of the house.[118] The office would take some time to find its feet. Churchill did not have a formal Press Secretary, although his Private Secretary John 'Jock' Colville recalled a press officer 'housed in a distant part of the building' during his second premiership.[119] This is likely to have been Fife Clark, a former journalist who took the title of Adviser on Public Relations from 1952.[120]

William Clark was formally appointed Press Secretary under Eden, although he suffered in the bad atmosphere of Eden's premiership, and was temporarily banned from the Private Office by the Prime Minister. Clark would eventually resign from his position over the Suez crisis.[121] The press operation at No. 10 was significantly professionalised under Eden's successor, Macmillan. Macmillan's Press Secretary, Harold Evans, 'institutionalised' the practice of holding lobby briefings at No. 10, and also brought in the editors and owners of major newspapers for meetings with the Prime Minister, as well as offering on-the-record interviews with Macmillan.[122]

Evans was no great fan of the Press Secretary's Room having a window onto publicly accessible Downing Street, feeling 'rather more vulnerable to the odd half-brick from aggrieved citizens on the Downing Street pavement' when sitting with his back to it. However, no such missile ever came through the window, 'the preferred target being the front door and the preferred weapon a milk bottle'.[123] Despite the risk of missile attack, Evans was otherwise pleased with the location of the Press Secretary's Office. The Press Office's spot at the front of the house was in fact ideal. After entering through the front door, journalists would immediately turn right to reach the office, meaning that there was no need for them to wander Downing Street's corridors or pass the Cabinet Room, minimising the likelihood of chance encounters with unprepared ministers. Evans could also monitor comings and goings in Downing Street through the window. However, the room was only 'a few seconds' from the operational centre, which helped to facilitate the access required to perform the job of Press Secretary effectively.[124]

Joe Haines, Press Secretary under Wilson, had been a journalist in the late 1950s, and so arrived at No. 10 familiar with the building's Entrance Hall and the Press Secretary's Room.[125] Donald Maitland, Haines's successor under Heath, was a Press Secretary without journalistic experience, arriving at No. 10 from a diplomatic background. Maitland wrote of the inadequacy of his small room at No. 10 for holding lobby briefings, 'The correspondents made their notes perched on the arms of chairs, or leaning against the wall, or the door if it was a busy day. This arrangement seemed to carry the British cult of amateurism to absurd lengths.' [126] Unimpressed by the lack of formality and grandeur common to much of No. 10, Maitland moved to 'a more convenient office closer to the Cabinet Room', with his deputy Henry James taking over his old office.[127]

This relocation did not last long, however, and subsequent Press Secretaries returned to the bow-windowed room at the front of the house, which, as Thatcher's biographer Charles Moore noted, 'surveys everyone who comes and goes at Downing Street'.[128] Senior advisers to Major would later highlight the lack of a 'White House–style' briefing suite as an example of how 'Number Ten is not the very model of a modern government office';[129] still, the Press Secretary remained in the same cramped den on the Downing Street side at No. 10, and the press lobby continued to have to balance their notebooks on the arms of their chairs. It wasn't until the arrival of Tony Blair that the Press Office moved into more spacious surroundings at No. 12 Downing Street, formerly the Chief Whip's Office.[130] Although located at the opposite end of Downing Street, this still had the advantage of giving the Press Office its own power base within No. 10 whilst keeping journalists away from the operational centre.

Special advisers and the Cabinet Office

The Press Office, like the Private Office and, after some initial difficulties, the Political Office, found its own distinct location within No. 10's geography of power, and it retained excellent access to the Prime Minister throughout the postwar years. Life was much more difficult for those who found themselves on the wrong side of the (initially green baize) door that separated No. 10 from the adjacent Old Treasury building (also called the Kent Treasury building), now known as 70 Whitehall, the home of the Cabinet Office from the early 1960s. Whilst this internal door connected the two buildings directly, allowing for relatively easy private passage between the Cabinet Office and No. 10 and theoretically providing extra space for the expansion of No. 10's resources, it also had huge symbolic importance.

To many Prime Ministerial advisers who found themselves based in rooms in the Cabinet Office, this internal connection to Downing Street was of little to no use. The door was kept locked, and for many years the limited copies of the key that existed were held by only a few senior civil service staff members. During the Wilson era, even the Cabinet Secretary was directly reliant upon the Principal Private Secretary for access to No. 10, despite his seniority. With the Principal Private Secretary holding the key to the interconnecting door, and the Prime Minister's diary carefully guarded, Bernard Donoughue observed an entertaining yet subtle power play between the two senior officials, which went on to become the subject of the legendary *Yes, Prime Minister* episode 'The Key'. If the Cabinet Secretary wished to see the Prime Minister, he had to telephone the Principal Private Secretary, effectively requesting permission to enter No. 10, albeit potentially to discuss something that he felt was far too secret to discuss with the Principal Private Secretary. In Donoughue's estimation, 'It was a game about territory. Some of the boundaries were clearly defined, not least by the locked green baize door between the two offices. But there was a grey area of common land which each sought to occupy.'[131] This tension was entirely navigable, but it is a curious and amusing quirk of the British system of governance. It also reveals how convention, including the physical constraints imposed by historic buildings, dictates the operation of government at the very centre.

The interconnecting door between the Cabinet Office and No. 10 is no longer covered in green baize, and passage between the two buildings has become more frequent and somewhat smoother over time. But the doorway retains great symbolic significance in dividing the two distinct functions of No. 10: the home of the Prime Minister, and the Cabinet Office, which serves the Cabinet collectively. The building known today as 70 Whitehall was historically the home of the Treasury, dating back to Walpole's time. When William Kent originally adapted No. 10, he connected the two buildings, enabling Walpole to draw on the Treasury's resources and staff to assist him in his evolving role. As the historians Andrew Blick and George Jones have noted, in the early phase of the premiership, Prime Ministers were in direct control of the Treasury, and the Secretary to the Treasury was one of the key Prime Ministerial aides.[132]

Over time, the Cabinet Secretary became the Prime Minister's closest civil service adviser outside of No. 10. The Cabinet Office was initially based in Whitehall Gardens, briefly moving to Richmond Terrace just before the Second World War. Both locations were only a short walk from Downing Street. In 1940 it transferred to Government Offices Great George Street – the grand building that stands next to the Foreign and Commonwealth Office on the opposite side to Downing Street – alongside the Treasury staff, some of whom were formerly housed adjacent to No. 10, at the Old Treasury.

It was Macmillan, after the Second World War, who decided to take the opportunity provided by the reconstruction of Downing Street and the Old Treasury to move the Cabinet Office out of Government Offices Great George Street and bring it next door to No. 10. The Old Treasury building had a long association with the department after which it was named, and contained Conference Room A, the historic meeting room of the Treasury Commission and home to a throne formerly used by George III. But its historic role as home to Treasury officials was now at an end.

The Treasury had hoped to return to the Old Treasury building at some point in the postwar years, but Macmillan concluded that it was in fact the Cabinet Office – and the Cabinet Secretary – that he wanted nearby. The Prime Minister was also very hostile to suggestions that the Foreign Office should be moved elsewhere, as it was noted that 'the Prime Minister attaches great importance to the Foreign Secretary being close at hand'.[133] Macmillan informed his Chancellor of the Exchequer Derick Heathcote-Amory that he had 'made bold' his plan to move the Cabinet Office to the Old Treasury on 7 July 1958. The Prime Minister indicated that this was to be undertaken on a temporary basis, as the Old Treasury would not be large enough for the entire Treasury unless adjacent buildings were also taken over, and this would not be possible for several years.[134] In his response, the Chancellor raised no objections to this suggestion but indicated that he hoped that the Treasury would eventually return to the Old Treasury.[135] However, as No. 10 Appointments Secretary David Stephens noted when looking over a draft of Macmillan's note to the Treasury, 'The Treasury may hope this but I don't think the Prime Minister hopes anything of the kind.'[136]

This change represented a significant promotion in the geography of power for the Cabinet Office and the Cabinet Secretary. Former Cabinet Secretary Robert Armstrong keenly emphasises its significance:

> Before that point, the Secretary of the Cabinet, if he wanted to go see the Prime Minister, had to go across Whitehall or walk from Great George Street [but after that point] the Secretary of the Cabinet was ensconced in 70 Whitehall. And though it is called 70 Whitehall, his office is in the Old Treasury building – he is less than a minute's walk from the Prime Minister. [...] I think it is crucially important in the history of the Cabinet Office, and to some extent in the history of No. 10, that the arrival of the Cabinet Office in that building, and the immediacy of the connection, really meant that the Prime Minister looked first of all, apart from his private office, to the Secretary of the Cabinet next door [...] It's more than symbolic. It was practically – hugely – significant.[137]

Despite the proximity of the two buildings, the physical divide between them held important symbolic and constitutional significance. Another former Cabinet Secretary, Robin Butler, felt the locked door served as a reminder of his role:

> I regard it as symbolic. When I became Cabinet Secretary – first of all I had a department, and secondly I had a responsibility not just to the Prime Minister but to the Cabinet as a whole. Although the Prime Minister is my main boss, and because I had a key to that door, I could come in and out whenever I liked, but nonetheless there was a locked door between that indicated the greater separateness of the Cabinet Secretary from the Prime Minister.[138]

Not all Cabinet Secretaries were so keen to highlight the 'separateness' that the locked door between No. 10 and 70 Whitehall represented. Andrew Turnbull took the view that it was more important to emphasise the unity of the two, to discourage the Prime Minister from seeking to make No. 10 too 'self-sufficient', stocking the building with advisers and neglecting to 'go next door as often as [they] should do'.[139] The balance between the separation and cohesion of the Cabinet Office and No. 10 has long been the subject of academic debate.

However, for the Prime Ministerial adviser finding themselves housed in an office in the Cabinet Office building, with a locked door between themselves and the premier, for which they were not permitted a key, their separateness from No. 10 could hardly have been clearer. Thomas Balogh, economic adviser to Wilson, was one such figure. As Wilson's biographer Pimlott observed, following Wilson's arrival at Downing Street in October 1964, Balogh 'failed to forestall a Whitehall move to contain his influence by putting him in the Cabinet Office on the wrong side of the connecting door to No. 10.' The key to this locked door, in Pimlott's description, was 'a melancholy symbol of his exile'.[140]

Wilson's Personal and Political Secretary, Falkender, recalled that, despite having thrice-weekly appointments with the Prime Minister, supplemented by occasional informal chats over drinks, Balogh was too isolated to have day-to-day influence on Prime Ministerial decision-making.[141] Balogh and his small team had neither access to Cabinet papers nor any direct control over the contents of the Prime Minister's boxes. However, this did not stop the adviser acquiring a reputation to the opposite effect in the outside world, as Falkender recalls:

> The story was that Thomas somehow dominated No. 10 and Harold's economic thinking in a sinister, Rasputin-like fashion. It was true that his contribution to economic thinking at No. 10 was invaluable and his analyses were extremely accurate. But what is equally true is that Thomas was never as fully integrated in the team surrounding the Prime Minister as people imagine he was. Quite the reverse.[142]

In fact, it has been claimed that Wilson deliberately allowed Balogh to be ushered next door, reportedly telling his Principal Private Secretary, Derek Mitchell, 'I do not want him popping in every few minutes.'[143] By 1966, with the relocation of the Appointments Secretary within No. 10, space was found for Balogh on the 'right' side of the door, but he never managed to gain a central place in the geography of power.

It was not just advisers, but ministers too who found the locked door between No. 10 and the Cabinet Office virtually impenetrable. Richard Crossman complained to his diary of 'the trouble it takes to go to the 120 yards from my office through the back passages into No. 10', which required tracking down two separate sets of keys to unlock internal doors. Crossman was clearly frustrated by this 'infernal' waste of time. 'Civil servants are allowed keys; I'm not. It shows you how Whitehall is run for the convenience of civil servants and not for the Ministers who are supposed to be in command.'[144]

Donoughue, in contrast to Balogh, realised the importance of geography to the conduct of his role as head of the new Downing Street Policy Unit. Donoughue has since written of the attempts of Falkender, Wilson's Personal and Political Secretary and a key rival for the Prime Minister's ear with whom Donoughue's relations became increasingly strained, to force him out to 'a remote part of the Cabinet Office'. Donoughue resisted strongly. His memoir states, 'There I would be cut off from direct access to and influence over the Prime Minister. I would also lack access to the crucial information which flows through No. 10 relevant to all the policy issues concerning him.' This, Donoughue believed, would mean that both he and Haines, Press Secretary and close ally, would be 'neutered' and 'unable to do our job'.[145]

It appears that Donoughue was right to resist relocation. The Central Policy Review Staff would suffer from its Cabinet Office location until its abolition by Thatcher in 1983. Thatcher did not rate the Central Policy Review Staff highly, partly because she found its papers too lengthy but also, as Thatcher's biographer Charles Moore has written, because it was 'attached by the rules and by Whitehall geography to the Cabinet Office, rather than to the Prime Minister. It was structurally incapable of working fast to a political agenda'.[146]

Overall, the connection between No. 10 and 70 Whitehall provided the Prime Minister's small office with access to a substantial support staff, but also drew a clear dividing line between the constitutional functions of each building and those who worked there. It also allowed quiet, undetected passage between the two buildings, as Cecil Parkinson, Conservative Party Chairman and close ally of Thatcher, discovered during the Falklands War. Parkinson found that his membership of Thatcher's War Cabinet remained undiscovered by the press throughout the conflict, due to his passing between the Cabinet Office and No. 10 via the internal door. Parkinson insisted that this was not deliberate, but more of a practical security decision ensuring that his papers never left the building, highlighting another factor of the connection's usefulness.[147]

Rooms upstairs

Whilst the Head of the Policy Unit at No. 10 has normally been able to stake a reasonable claim on a prime slot within the geography of power at No. 10 (starting in the aforementioned ground-floor Wiggery, and moving up into a first-floor room above the front door shortly after),[148] the rest of the unit has generally been consigned to its upper reaches, far from the operational centre. David Willetts, who worked in the Policy Unit under Thatcher from 1984–6, recalled that the second-floor rooms occupied by the unit had previously been part of the No. 10 flat, a historical legacy meaning that 'a serious discussion of a tricky point of policy may take place against the incongruous background of flowery 1950s wallpaper and domestic curtains'.[149]

Sarah Hogg, Head of the Policy Unit under Major, was also acutely aware of the historic nature of her room on the first floor at No. 10, describing it as 'not so much part of the kitchen cabinet as the nursery region of Number 10, [once] inhabited by the children and grand-children of Prime Ministers'.[150] The upper-floor rooms themselves, although remodelled and improved by the architect Erith's reconstruc-tion of Downing Street during Macmillan's premiership, remained somewhat inconvenient. Later in Wilson's premiership, Marcia Falk-ender's Political Office moved up into rooms on the second floor, near the Prime Minister's private flat and on the Downing Street side of the building. Falkender recalled hot, cramped and noisy conditions, which intensified the stress of life at Downing Street, particularly in the hours immediately before Wilson's departure from No. 10 in 1970. She wrote, 'As the temperature rose outside, the pressure mounted inside [and] this discomfort was heightened by the noise and atmos-phere of the crowd outside.'[151]

Sarah Hogg also found the Policy Unit's upstairs rooms far from relaxing, with life at No. 10 being 'made hideous' by noisy repair works being performed on the Foreign and Commonwealth Office, just across Downing Street. Hogg wrote that the noise was such that she thought the sound of an IRA mortar bomb exploding in No. 10's garden on 7 February 1991 was 'merely an extra large pole hitting the ground [although] Michael Heseltine, like [Defence Secretary] Tom King, knew better. "I didn't think the poll tax was quite such an explo-sive subject," he said.'[152]

The rooms allocated to the Policy Unit can be far from ideal, then. As Hennessy observed in *Whitehall*, the unit's staff are far outnum-bered by 'the more cautious regulars' at No. 10, and disadvantaged by 'tradition, continuity and the geography of power'.[153] However, with its office space lying inside No. 10's boundaries, and the Head of the Policy Unit generally taking up an advantageous position, it is fair to say that the Policy Unit has acquired a status that is the envy of many outside Downing Street. A room on the upper floors of No. 10 still necessitates entry via the building's lower floors, puts the unit's staff no more than a couple of minutes' notice away from the Prime Minister, and substantially increases the likelihood of chance encounters and informal meetings with other key Downing Street staff. Access from within the building is infinitely better than from outside.

Downing Street, as seen from Whitehall, 1947.

The Geography of Whitehall – and Geography Subverted

Two further elements affect the geography of power at No. 10: the arrangement of the buildings that surround it, and the non-geographical factors that can influence power at Downing Street. The position of No. 10 itself, with such close proximity to the Chancellor's residence, the Foreign and Commonwealth Office and the House of Commons, has as much of an effect on the conduct of business as the internal layout of the building itself. The first half of this chapter investigates this aspect of No. 10. The second half demonstrates that, should an official or political adviser manage to find themselves stationed in a prime location within No. 10, there are still several factors that can alter their position and even render it irrelevant, from the Prime Minister's working style to membership of unofficial kitchen cabinets and even the forced relocation of No. 10's operations during its periodic emergency renovations.

No. 11 and the geography of Whitehall

The geography of power in Whitehall, as opposed to merely within No. 10, is equally revealing of the history and workings of government in this period. The title of First Lord of the Treasury – one of several official titles that accompany the role of Prime Minister – adorns the letterbox of No. 10. The Chancellor of the Exchequer, who has lived at No. 11 throughout this period, is the Second Lord of the Treasury, the second most senior position on the Treasury Board that historically (but no longer practically) oversees national expenditure on behalf of the monarch. The proximity of the living arrangements and office space of the Prime Minister and Chancellor are both symbolically and practically important, reflecting the fact that these are the two most senior roles in British government.

No. 10 and No. 11 may have separate addresses, but they are internally linked, and it is often unclear whether a room, corridor or staircase is within one or the other of the two properties. The integrated nature of the buildings embodies and enables the extremely close working relationship that a Prime Minister and Chancellor are expected, and required by their jobs, to enjoy. As Edmund Dell, a former Trade Secretary and a historian of postwar Chancellors, has observed, 'few things are more important to the Second Lord than his relations with the First'.[1] The inverse can be equally true.

The Chancellor of the Exchequer ultimately controls the nation's purse strings, and has the power to enable or disable all other ministers' policy initiatives and projects. This gives the Chancellor great power within the Cabinet. However, the Chancellor can be overruled by the Cabinet should it turn on him or her collectively, and only the Prime Minister has the power to hire and fire members of the Cabinet. This apparently simple dynamic lies at the centre of the relationship between the two positions at the pinnacle of British governmental power.

The internal geography of No. 10 and No. 11 is revealing. Denis Healey, Chancellor during Harold Wilson's second premiership as well as under James Callaghan, stressed that he took care to keep his Prime Ministers informed throughout his time at No. 11. He did so in private meetings, 'but also by dropping in to see him whenever it seemed useful. The Chancellor is the only minister who can do this without alerting the press-men who hang around Downing Street.'[2]

Wilson claimed to have been told by Hugh Dalton, Chancellor of the Exchequer under Clement Attlee from 1945–7, that the status of the connecting door between No. 10 and No. 11 was a good indicator of a happy or distressed ministry. A locked or closed door between the two properties would reflect unusually strained relations between the Prime Minister and Chancellor, and was a particularly worrying sign for the present administration. Wilson claimed that, during his time as Prime Minister at No. 10, 'it was a freeway [...] and it was used for two-way traffic'.[3]

Whilst the internal doors between No. 10 and No. 11 are rarely locked, there are other ways that a Prime Minister can use the geography of Downing Street to assert their authority upon their Chancellor. Margaret Thatcher was well aware that it was No. 10, and not No. 11, that housed the role of First Lord of the Treasury, and she was reportedly quite happy to remind her Chancellors that it was she who held that position and not they.[4] Robin Butler, formerly Principal Private Secretary and later Cabinet Secretary under Thatcher, recalls the Prime Minister using the occasion of a change in Chancellor as an opportunity for a land grab for No. 10. The Prime Minister had noted that some rooms on the top floor, at that time allocated to No. 11's flat, would be handy for No. 10's use:

> On the day of the 1983 election, she had secretly given instructions that a partition should be constructed to cut off the staircase from Number Eleven to the top floor so that Number Ten had whole access to it. And between [Geoffrey] Howe stopping being Chancellor and Nigel Lawson arriving, we put this partition in place so that when Nigel Lawson arrived and came to view his premises at Number Eleven, he supposed that the partition had always been there.[5]

Nigel Lawson's memoirs reveal that this mission was slightly less than top secret. He recalls that when Thatcher first suggested promoting him to that post in 1983, she immediately added that she would need part of his private flat to house her staff from No. 10. 'At the time,' Lawson recalled drily, 'I was scarcely in a position to object.'[6] Over time, Thatcher's increasing reliance on advisers in No. 10, such as her economic adviser Alan Walters, at the expense of her relationship with Lawson would give Lawson more cause to object, and would play a part in her downfall. Perhaps there is a lesson here in geography *and* power.

The Treasury is still based near to No. 10, at Government Offices Great George Street (originally known as the New Public Offices), just down Whitehall, beyond the imposing Foreign and Commonwealth

Office building, which stands tall on the opposite side of Downing Street to No. 10 and No. 11. Designed by the architect George Gilbert Scott, the impressive Foreign and Commonwealth Office building was opened in 1868. With an architectural style that references the Roman Empire, chosen at a time when Britain was approaching the peak of its own imperial power, the building was designed to reflect and project Britain's global might. The Locarno Suite of rooms, named after the Locarno Treaties of 1925 that sought to maintain peace following the First World War, are amongst the most impressive in Whitehall. The contrast with the humble No. 10 could not be more stark.

Access to the Foreign and Commonwealth Office building was historically gained via Downing Street, reiterating the close relationship between the Prime Minister and the Foreign Secretary, particularly at the peak of the British Empire. Whilst it could be argued that the role of Foreign Secretary has diminished alongside Britain's place in the world, it remains one of the four biggest jobs in British politics. The Foreign Secretary is granted a grace-and-favour country house at Chevening in Kent, alongside an apartment at Carlton House Terrace, less than ten minutes' stroll from Downing Street. Their office in the Foreign and Commonwealth Office building is moments away from No. 10, just across Downing Street. This puts them close to the centre of power at No. 10, although they have much less direct and regular access to the Prime Minister than the Chancellor of the Exchequer.

When first opened, Scott's building also incorporated the Colonial Office, the India Office (which had an even more ornate interior, due to the involvement of private finance via the East India Company) and the Home Office, which was located at the Whitehall end. The Home Office was subsequently moved out to 50 Queen Anne's Gate in 1977, receiving another demotion in the geography of power, although what Peter Hennessy's *Whitehall* termed the 'geography of administration' is somewhat less influential when it comes to entire departments of officials, for whom direct access to the Prime Minister is much less relevant. However, it is no coincidence that until the late 1970s, the offices of the Prime Minister, Chancellor of the Exchequer, Foreign Secretary, Home Secretary and Cabinet Secretary were all within a few minutes' walk of one another. Interestingly, Britain's bright red telephone boxes – such as those that stand on Whitehall alongside what is now the Foreign and Commonwealth Office, perhaps the most photographed telephone boxes in London – were designed by Giles Gilbert Scott, grandson of the architect that designed the Foreign and Commonwealth Office building.[7]

Channels of information

Geography clearly matters, particularly to outsiders coming into No. 10. The allocation of office space at No. 10 remains a source of much excitement and controversy, even today. For newcomers at No. 10 – such as Bernard Donoughue or Marcia Falkender, who arrived at Downing Street (as Marcia Williams) effectively tasked with establishing and formalising a new function for the Prime Minister's Office – the position that they are to take in the geography of power has the potential to make or break their new roles. A good position, with access to both the Prime Minister and the existing machine at No. 10, is crucial to ensuring that a newcomer becomes embedded into the fabric of the office.

For long-established parts of the Prime Ministerial support team, geography can be less important. The Private Office, for example, has a well-secured position in the geography of power, directly alongside the Cabinet Room, the historic and traditional office of the Prime Minister. However, even though Prime Ministers made increasing use of the first-floor Study as their office in the postwar years, the location of the Private Office stayed the same – and yet it remains just as desirable. In part, this is a result of the room still providing easy and quick access to the Prime Minister's Office, albeit up one short flight of stairs. But it is also because physical proximity is in this case trumped by procedural proximity in the flow of information to the premier.

Between 1945 and 1997, information, communication and decision-making were managed almost entirely on paper. Ideas and information arrived at the No. 10 Private Office from across Whitehall, in the medium of carefully drafted documents, for the consideration of the Prime Minister. Views and ideas from within No. 10 (for example, from the Policy Unit after 1974) or from the Cabinet Office next door (such as from the Cabinet Secretary, the Central Policy Review Staff during 1971–83 or other advisers) would also arrive in the form of further documents, often at a later stage in the process. The management of this information was one of the primary responsibilities of the Private Office staff, who were tasked with making it clear, manageable and easy to digest for the Prime Minister. It was their job to sort through and refine the various papers in their in-trays, to perhaps add a cover note or their own advice, and to place the refined end product into the Prime Minister's boxes. Decision-making at No. 10 was ultimately driven by this process. The task of working through these boxes, whether of an evening or first thing in the morning, annotating the notes contained in their boxes, making decisions and keeping up to date with events across the government, was at the heart of the Prime Minister's job. As the final gatekeepers of the Prime Ministerial paper chain, the Private Office therefore had the final say on what information reached the Prime Minister and when, and in what form it was presented.

This gave the Private Office great power, and great responsibility. However, the fact that something was declared important enough to be included in the Prime Minister's boxes didn't automatically mean that it would be read in detail. On occasion, even the Private Office would have to use subtle tricks to ensure that important issues gained the attention that they warranted. When serving as Edward Heath's Principal Private Secretary, Robert Armstrong was responsible for the introduction to the Prime Minister's desk of a new locked box for top-secret documents, painted red with a blue stripe. The appeal of the secretive box to the premiers provided an excellent opportunity for getting their attention:

> It was a box to which only the Prime Minister and I had a key – so I put the really private stuff into this box. The Prime Minister knew perfectly well that the juicy stuff was in that box; they all went to it first. If there was something you particularly wanted done, you could always sneak it through into this box. [...] And when Mr. Wilson arrived and found this had been one of the changes that had been made [whilst he was out of office], he was very pleased. He called it "Old Stripey".[8]

When asked whether any Prime Minister wised up to this tactic,

Armstrong said, 'I expect they did. But provided you didn't abuse it, it suited everybody.' [9]

Andrew Turnbull, who was Principal Private Secretary to both Thatcher and John Major, stated that geographical proximity was less important than being the last to view and control the flow of information to the Prime Minister:

> You want to position yourself so that you are the last person in the chain, so to speak. The person who passes information over last has an influence, because they can have the last word, add something to the dossier or delay a submission until some further information or view can be added. [10]

Robin Butler, also formerly Principal Private Secretary at No. 10, felt that 'the flow of government business is such that you are not seeking access, you just have to have access. There will be other people in the building – like the Head of the Policy Unit – who might have to compete a bit more for access. But Private Secretaries don't.' [11]

Marcia Falkender, formerly one such newcomer to Downing Street, took a highly critical view of those longer established elements at No. 10:

> The permanents, the civil servants who are sometimes there for many years, become deeply attached to it. They think the system is splendid and they have an almost proprietorial attitude to what they come to believe is their building. To an extent that belief is right. In many ways No. 10 does belong to them. [12]

Given the Private Office's position in the geography of power, the longstanding nature of its role and its penultimate position in the flow of paper to the Prime Minister, it is easy to see why outsiders could view its staff as the 'owners' of No. 10.

Falkender's comments in part reflect her particularly disparaging view of the civil servants she encountered at No. 10, whom she perceived to be a conservative blocking force against the Labour government. However, not all No. 10 outsiders took such a confrontational stance towards the established No. 10 machine. Bernard Donoughue, a peer and fellow outsider, took the opposite approach and worked closely with the Private Office, as outlined in the previous chapter. Donoughue noted that the internal geography of No. 10 mattered much less to the Private Office, as 'most of their real access is on paper, through the Prime Minister's boxes'. Geography, he said, 'matters much more to us "pirates" – that is to say, political advisers'.[13] Once Donoughue had secured a key location for himself within No. 10's geography of power, he then sought to integrate the Policy Unit into the flow of information. This was partly achieved by regular informal communication with the Private Office, aided by the proximity of the two offices. Geography also played a role in ensuring that Donoughue was able to influence the flow of paper to the Prime Minister:

> I used to go down and look in the box in the late afternoon, and place my papers in the box. I would often wait until after the Private Secretaries had gone home, or the Cabinet Secretary's paper had come in, and I would read it, and then put in my paper. I was well placed to get the last word in. So [the geography] helped me to live with [the paper system]. And also, remember, the Cabinet Secretary, if he came through, or when his end-of-the-day paper came in, it came through the green baize door beside my office, so I knew when that was happening.[14]

The advantage of having a well-placed office, in this case, meant that the traditional flow of information to the Prime Minister could be monitored, influenced and perhaps even subverted on occasion.

Working habits

The working style of a Prime Minister can also negate the influence of the geography of power at No. 10. In an environment as complex as No. 10, with all activity ultimately centred around the Prime Minister, there is a great deal that can serve to disrupt organised patterns of work. Whilst the work of the Prime Minister's Office can be generally be divided into the four Ps outlined in previous chapters, the organisation of the office is wholly dependent upon the Prime Minister themself.

In the close environment of No. 10, personality matters a great deal. The small size of the building and the correspondingly small number of staff who work there make for a very intimate working environment, which directly reflects the character of the Prime Minister. The working style of a Prime Minister also impacts strongly on how No. 10 works. And the premiership is ultimately, as Liberal Prime Minister of 1908–16 Herbert Henry Asquith said, 'what the holder chooses and is able to make of it'.[15] Whose advice is most regularly heard and taken; the location, timing and attendance of big decisions; working hours at No. 10; and the amount of time and effort spent on particular issues – all these are ultimately dictated by the Prime Minister's personal traits more than anything else.

Working from bed

In such a personalised office, the geography of power can easily be subverted by Prime Ministerial working habits. During Winston Churchill's second premiership, his personal secretaries, Jane Portal and Elizabeth Gilliat, were given the room next to the Prime Minister's, in the Chamberlains' converted self-contained flat on the second floor.[16] This reflected Churchill's penchant for working from his bed or bath, dictating speeches to his secretaries, as well as his increasingly informal working style and erratic working hours.

In the famous words of the biographer Roy Jenkins, by his second premiership, Churchill was 'gloriously unfit for office'.[17] Yet his eager successor, Anthony Eden, acquired similar working habits, despite arriving with a very different reputation. According to William Clark, Eden's Press Secretary, the Prime Minister's preference from working from his bed, surprisingly not primarily due to his ill health, could cause a range of difficulties for those tasked with supporting him:

> We used to have little troubles like finding that the most secret telegrams had been made into his bed. One inconvenience of this room [the Prime Minister's bedroom in the self-contained flat], which was like a large bed-sitter, was that it had no filing cabinets – and nor had the Cabinet Room – so that if you wanted to get a file

you had to phone down for it. Fortunately, the Registry, housed in long-tunnels under No. 10 and No. 11, was superbly efficient, able to retrieve a file in minutes. A good deal of business was done in the mornings while the Prime Minister was having his bath.[18]

This habit of working from the living quarters at No. 10 rather than the official parts of the house certainly made the work of supporting the Prime Minister less practical and less convenient. When combined with the events of the Suez crisis, alongside Eden's personal temperament (of which more later), this could make life at No. 10 erratic and stressful.

Harold Macmillan would also begin the day with a meeting in his personal quarters, which Harold Evans, his Press Secretary, described as a 'bedside audience'. Macmillan's approach to the premiership was generally more businesslike than Churchill's. As biographer D. R. Thorpe observed, despite often working and rising late, Macmillan avoided Churchill's habit of late-night meetings and working from bed until midday, 'with a cat as a hot-water bottle'.[19] However, Macmillan still elected to begin his day by working on his boxes from bed. Evans would arrive at No. 10 at 9 am, before anyone else, and phone up to Macmillan to seek a gossip-heavy audience with the Prime Minister in his bedroom before the formal working day began, thus subverting his own notional place in the geography of power, in the Press Office at the front of No. 10.[20]

Kitchen cabinets

An out-of-hours private audience with the Prime Minister can make all the difference at Downing Street. Wilson was accused particularly of running a kitchen cabinet of informal but allegedly influential advisers, outside of formal processes at No. 10. The Cabinet met once a week, downstairs in the Cabinet Room. The kitchen cabinet, however – which consisted primarily of political advisers such as Marcia Falkender, George Wigg, Peter Shore and Harold Davies – met much more regularly, with its 'main forum' being Falkender's Political Office Room.[21] It also convened in the Prime Minister's private flat, or in the first-floor Study, where advisers formal and informal could meet and reflect over drinks, poured and proposed by Wilson with increasing frequency, particularly as his second premiership progressed.[22]

This practice has historically been much more commonplace than is widely acknowledged. As Anthony King observed, 'Churchill, Macmillan and Harold Wilson all had friends and cronies – people they liked to drink with after hours – but Brendan Bracken, John Wyndham and Williams were not central to running the government.'[23] During wartime, Churchill had a close but informal group of ministerial and civil service advisers that he referred to as his 'Secret Circle'.[24] However, no postwar Prime Minister acquired a reputation for taking private advice above that of officials and the Cabinet more than Wilson and his kitchen cabinet of advisers.

The degree to which this group exerted influence over the Prime Minister is highly debatable. But the soft power it provided was certainly of some use to advisers. Donoughue, Head of the Policy Unit during Wilson's second premiership, recalled that making himself available for informal, impromptu meetings with the Prime Minister was one of the most time-consuming but also productive tasks that his role involved. At a moment's notice, he could be called to join Wilson in his Study:

> [We would] banter cheerfully about politics, football, gossip, or whatever interested him that day, however trivial. This was fun and gave me useful insights into the character of this very complex man. It also helpfully gave me constant access to the Prime Minister to raise serious policy issues.[25]

Wilson's enthusiasm for gossip and discussion was not limited to political advisers, though. Armstrong, formerly Private Secretary to Wilson, recalled similar experiences to those described by Donoughue:

> The afternoons when Wilson was not asking questions in the House, he would go upstairs to the Study. There would be a call on the telephone and he would say, "Bring me up a box of papers to work on." So I would bring him a box of papers. But he never worked on it, we just gossiped! About everything that was on his mind... It was very good for business.[26]

Wilson's successor to the premiership, Callaghan, favoured a much more disciplined and organised working day, and actively discouraged unexpected guests. Donoughue observed:

> [Callaghan] needed a lot of time and space for his working process. He did not like a crowd of advisers around him, preferring them to approach him singly, by prior arrangement and having sent in a paper in advance so that he could prepare mentally.[27]

Callaghan was therefore less inclined towards maintaining a kitchen cabinet, the alleged existence of which had met with widespread derision and suspicion during his predecessor's reign.[28] This meant that the traditional geography of power and channels of information had more of a direct influence on Callaghan's decision-making process.

Can a kitchen cabinet meet in the Study?

Informal and out-of-hours meetings can provide the opportunity for useful and influential access, even for Prime Ministers who preferred a more disciplined and regimented working day. Tim Kitson, MP for Richmond in Yorkshire and Parliamentary Private Secretary to Heath, was granted an office on the upper floors of No. 10, opposite the private flat. This proved a good location in the after-hours geography of power, and Kitson is said to have become 'a regular late-night confidant and conversation partner for Heath'.[29] Victor Rothschild, first head of the Central Policy Review Staff, did not let his unit's isolation in the neighbouring Cabinet Office prevent him from networking extensively out of hours within No. 10, serving 'cider cup' (cider laced with strong liquors) to loosen tongues.[30]

Heath's working style was generally more formal than Wilson's, and he did not attract a reputation for shadowy, behind-closed-doors decision-making in the manner of his Labour rival. However, the Conservative Prime Minister had his own, albeit less political, version of the kitchen cabinet. Robert Armstrong recalls how the Prime Minister, who lived alone at No. 10 throughout his tenure, liked to hold informal advisory sessions to help develop his thinking on key issues:

He liked to sit down, upstairs in the drawing room, with a team –
me and one or two of my colleagues, Donald Maitland from the
Press Office, [Douglas] Hurd from the Political Office – and we
would throw a subject around, discussing the various aspects of it.
And I remember Mr. Heath would sit there looking sphinx-like.
Very often he would not say anything himself, but after he would
have made up his mind what he thought about it. That was the way
in which he came to a decision. [...] But it didn't replace the official
machine. It was the process by which the Prime Minister decided
where he was coming from. [...] It was never as highly organised
as sofa government and kitchen cabinet. It was a collection of the
people who were on the job.[31]

The diverse nature of such a grouping, not explicitly or exclusively
political in its nature, and its related awareness of the need to avoid
subverting the official machinery and processes of No. 10, suggest a
clear distinction from the more overtly political and seemingly clandes-
tine activities of Wilson's kitchen cabinet. However, Heath's unofficial
'drawing room cabinet' highlights the fact that most Prime Ministers
do take advice outside of office hours in some form or another. Contemporary debates rage around various forms of 'sofa government' (a
phrase popularised during Tony Blair's premiership), the perceived
increasing 'presidentialisation' of the British Prime Minister, and the
associated conduct of government by bilaterals rather than through
'traditional' Cabinet Government and collective responsibility. But
these debates can fail to acknowledge the degree to which all Prime
Ministers fall somewhere on a sliding scale between the two extremes,
rather than operating at either end.

Informal access to the Prime Minister not only provides advisers
with the opportunity to influence decisions, but can also help them
to keep informed on the Prime Minister's thinking, which in turn
increases their power within the network of official and political advisers and aides within Downing Street. Under Thatcher, an equivalent
of Wilson and Heath's informal advice group would gather to work on
the Prime Minister's major set-piece speeches in the first-floor Study
at No. 10, retiring to the upstairs flat in the not-infrequent event that
speech-writing was not completed by dinner time. John Redwood,

head of Thatcher's Policy Unit during 1983–5, recalled how Thatcher's slightly obsessive approach to speech-writing provided him with a vital opportunity for discussions regarding strategy, policy ideas and getting to understand the Prime Minister's thinking:

> I spent most time with her when she was supervising the production of a large speech for Party Conference or the Mansion House. She personally spent many hours going over the drafts we produced and arguing with us over what she wanted to say. I joined in because it was important to make a double use of her time when she was spending so much time on it. I was able to test out her views and thoughts on a wide range of issues, and introduce new ideas of what she might want to do, so they became policy sessions as well as speech-writing sessions. The sessions were mainly in the evening and might continue till 2 or 3 am, with food in the flat to keep us going. It meant I could then do my day job knowing exactly what the PM thought about a given topic and what she wanted to achieve. If Whitehall queried it, I was confident I knew her mind and they could check if they must.[32]

This is not to say that there were not significant differences between these 'kitchen', 'drawing room' and 'study/private flat' cabinets. The membership of these informal groupings varied from the political to the official, and this was significant in itself. The degree to which they influenced individual Prime Ministers also depended entirely on the personalities of the Prime Ministers concerned, their working styles, their attitudes towards Cabinet and their openness to taking advice on board in the first place. However, it is worth noting that most postwar Prime Ministers could be accused of having some form of alternative advice to the traditional civil service and Cabinet Government.

Wandering

Both Thatcher and Major were great daytime explorers of No. 10, another factor that could occasionally subvert the traditional way of doing things in the Prime Minister's Office. Sarah Hogg and Jonathan

Hill recalled that Major 'always liked to work off his restlessness by wandering the building, picking through people's in-trays, discovering for himself what his staff were up to'.[33] Major himself recalled deliberately making informal visits to the Policy Unit 'whenever I had a spare moment. This, I soon learned, was almost unheard of, but it soon became a familiar pattern. Our formal and informal discussions soon bore fruit'.[34] Thatcher would also occasionally wander through No. 10's offices, including the Garden Rooms, where she could be spotted rifling nosily through correspondence. On one such excursion, as recorded by Thatcher's biographer Charles Moore, the Prime Minister came across a letter from a florist in Wandsworth, who had written to express his distress at his business being undercut by cheaper supermarket retailers. From that point on, the Prime Minister made a point of ensuring that all of her orders for flowers went to the florist in question.[35]

Living (and working) elsewhere

There have been rare occasions in the postwar years where the geography of power at No. 10 has been dismantled by the Prime Minister's forced relocation from No. 10 to another building. Macmillan was forced to relocate to Admiralty House, located a short walk along Whitehall, for a sizeable chunk of his premiership (1960–3) whilst the Downing Street houses underwent serious, essential and much-delayed renovation. The Prime Minister was reluctant to leave historic No. 10, despite the fact that Admiralty House had plenty of history of its own, with Churchill having lived there as First Lord of the Admiralty from 1911–15 and 1939–40. Macmillan's biographer D. R. Thorpe claimed that the Prime Minister soon grew to love Admiralty House, preferring the sizeable rooms and flowing connections of the residence to 'the higgledy-piggledy nature' of No. 10.[36] (However, Admiralty House was not universally liked: Healey and his family moved there after his appointment as Defence Secretary in 1964, and found living arrangements 'highly inconvenient'.)[37]

Unfortunately, the more orderly layout of Admiralty House did not lead to a more orderly government for Macmillan. It was from

Admiralty House that the Prime Minister plotted his controversial 'night of the long knives', sacking a third of his Cabinet in one fell swoop.[38] The orderliness of the building also failed to help Major organise his thoughts, or his colleagues, into a successful response to the Black Wednesday exchange rate crisis of September 1992, after he had been forced out of No. 10 by renovations following the 1991 IRA mortar attack. A lack of adequate communications technology at Admiralty House hampered the Prime Minister's ability to respond to the fast-changing crisis as the pound plummeted and Britain was forced to fall out of the European Exchange Rate Mechanism. Major later admitted that 'we didn't have all the familiar immediate information' during the crisis. However, he insisted that Admiralty House's facilities did not have a serious impact on the government's response to the crisis, saying, 'We were not seriously out of date [...] We didn't have a market screen but we had officials coming in and out.'[39]

Ken Clarke, then Home Secretary and part of Major's inner circle that assembled at Admiralty House to deal with the crisis as it unfolded, paints a different picture. Clarke recalled waiting for the group's third emergency meeting of the day in a 'pleasant sunny room' in the Prime Minister's temporary new digs, making small talk to pass the time, because, in Clarke's words, 'stuck in our antechamber at Admiralty House, with no radio, TV, market screens, ticker tape or information source of any kind, we were the most out of touch people in London'.[40] Clarke may have exaggerated slightly, but it is certainly known that communications at Admiralty House were 'much more disorganised'.[41] The opposite was true during the Cuban Missile Crisis, which saw Macmillan connected directly to President John F. Kennedy via transatlantic telephone link, rendering the Prime Minister one of the most 'in touch' people in the world during that crisis – albeit with debatable influence over events.

Admiralty House may have provided more space and a more traditional layout than then labyrinthine No. 10, but it also brought disadvantages. For all of its flaws, No. 10 has a long history of functioning in a particular manner, and disruption to this long-established way of working can prove challenging to those tasked with aiding the premier. Alex Allan, Principal Private Secretary to Major, noted that the experience of operating in Admiralty House 'made us all realise that the tight-knit community here, where you maybe were on top of each other a little bit, was actually an advantage.'[42]

No. 10's geography, as well as its long history of successfully hosting the office of Prime Minister and those that support it, appear to be clear advantages of the building. However, for those of a superstitious bent, the examples given here suggest that Admiralty House is to be avoided at all costs for Prime Ministers. Whilst the relative merits of the architecture and the various rooms in the two buildings can be debated, it could certainly be argued that Admiralty House attracts disaster, with an alarmingly high ratio of Prime Ministerial time spent there to number of major crises occurring. On the other hand, Downing Street has hosted its fair share of disasters, from the loss of the American colonies to the fall of France in the Second World War, and from the Suez crisis to Britain's humiliating application to the International Monetary Fund in 1976. Ultimately, for Prime Ministers, there is no escaping a crisis.

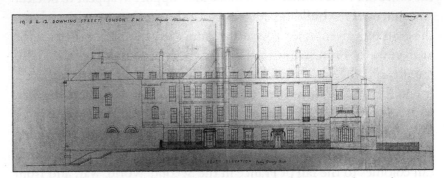

Drawing showing proposed alterations and additions to the south elevation of No. 10, No. 11 and No. 12 Downing Street, 1958.

Reconstructing No. 10 Downing Street

We have seen how the geography of power at No. 10 Downing Street can shape the decision-making process at the centre of the British system. And yet only once in recent history has the design and layout of the Downing Street houses been seriously reconsidered. This occurred during Harold Macmillan's premiership of 1957–63, when No. 10 was redesigned, vacated and rebuilt alongside No. 11, No. 12 and part of the adjacent Old Treasury building (now home to the Cabinet Office). The story of this reconstruction has its own implications for No. 10 and the office of Prime Minister in the postwar years.

Time to rebuild

No. 10 survived the Blitz, but in March 1955, just short of ten years after the end of the war in Europe, the building was in an appalling state. Ministry of Works surveys of No. 10 performed over the Christmas recess and the previous summer had found problems with the building's foundations, serious issues with dry rot and wood-boring beetles, uneven flooring, poorly laid-out and ageing plumbing and cracked brickwork throughout. The Downing Street frontage wall bent outwards as far as 7½" from vertical. Whilst it was predicted that five years could pass 'without grave risk of major damage or of collapse', the investigation also concluded, 'On the other hand, the longer we leave things the more difficult and expensive restoration will be.'[1]

In its report, the ministry outlined two options: the continuation of 'extraordinary first aid repairs' as and when needed, 'accepting the risks until a major collapse occurs'; or acknowledging that 'the [Downing

Street] houses have reached the end of their useful life' and rebuilding them almost entirely, either to a new or replica layout.[2] With almost £750,000 (in 1957 prices) estimated to have been spent on renovating and improving No. 10 alone from 1720–1957, the Ministry of Works decided that it was time to try a new approach.[3]

A major reconstruction job was anticipated, but restoration was thought preferable to the more straightforward task of simply knocking down the Downing Street buildings and starting again. Despite the potential benefits of redesigning a new and potentially much more suitable building for the Prime Minister's home and office, the Ministry of Works claimed that 'the houses in Downing Street are deeply embedded in our history. To destroy them would be an act of impiety'.[4] These arguments ultimately won the day, although it would take two further Prime Ministers before any action was to be taken.

Winston Churchill's reunion with Downing Street upon the advent of this second premiership in 1951 had been a joyous one, described by his daughter Mary Soames as 'like a bird returning to its nest'.[5] The two-time Prime Minister's pleasure at being back in No. 10, coupled with his condition of health at that time, mean it is perhaps unsurprising that the planned major disruption to life at No. 10 was passed over. The aforementioned Ministry of Works report of March 1955 was not considered until after Churchill's retirement on 5 April 1955.

When the report on the Downing Street houses was finally considered in Cabinet on 21 June, Prime Minister Anthony Eden and his Chancellor of the Exchequer, Rab Butler, both accepted the need to proceed with detailed plans for the rebuilding of Downing Street, but pushed the works back until the middle of 1958.[6] The fact that substantial rebuilding would require both figures, their families and their private offices to move out of Downing Street and into temporary accommodation for the duration of the works, which would take several years, cannot have failed to play a part in the decision to postpone as long as possible.

After Eden's brief premiership ended shortly following the Suez Canal crisis of late 1956, the responsibility was passed on to Macmillan, Prime Minister from 1957–63.

Macmillan arrives at No. 10

Macmillan arrived at No. 10 on 10 January 1957 determined to intro-
duce an air of calm to the building. No. 10 had become a fractured
place under his predecessor, Eden, even before the trauma of the 1956
Suez crisis.[7] Events in Suez increased the 'temperature' in the house
significantly. Clarissa Eden, who thought Downing Street 'the nicest
house you could possibly wish to live in', also famously claimed during
the crisis that she had 'felt as if the Suez Canal was flowing through my
drawing room'.[8] Prime Minister Eden's subsequent decline served as a
stark warning to his successor.

Macmillan's contrasting approach was captured by a sign he hung
on the Cabinet Room door, which bore a quotation from Gilbert and
Sullivan's *The Gondoliers*: 'Quiet, calm deliberation disentangles every
knot.'[9] Whilst the Prime Minister himself was often privately prone
to nervousness over political matters, a sense of calm and a much-
reported 'family atmosphere' would develop as key features of the new
No. 10; Macmillan's grandchildren had such free reign to play in the
building that he found it necessary to impose a ban on riding tricycles
and bicycles in the front hall on Cabinet days.[10]

Despite this, at the time of Macmillan's arrival, the deteriorating
condition of No. 10, No. 11 and No. 12 Downing Street was becoming
critical. It was becoming impossible to postpone serious renovation
works any longer. However, Macmillan was conscious that the general
public could react negatively to a Prime Minister apparently electing
to spend a large sum of public money on his own house. He told the
Ministry of Works in June 1957:

> As the present tenant of this great house and as an interested party,
> I find myself in some difficulty in trying to decide what is best to do.
> [...] We are all interested parties and before we decide to spend £1
> million of public money upon reconstructing Downing Street I am
> sure that we must fortify ourselves with some independent advice.[11]

Macmillan announced the appointment of a small independent committee, chaired by the Earl of Crawford, the following month. The
Crawford Committee met five times between July and November

1957, and was tasked with considering and interrogating the Ministry of Works' 1955 report into the state of Downing Street, making its own enquiries and recommending a course of action to the Prime Minister. Its final report was published in June 1958.[12]

The Crawford Committee

The Crawford Committee found that the condition of the Downing Street houses had deteriorated even since the Ministry of Works had conducted its surveys in 1954–5. The house now posed a severe fire risk, and representatives of the Ministry of Works told the Committee that there was now 'serious risk of collapse of parts of the building [...] possibly not for twenty years, possibly at any moment'.[13]

The floor of the Cabinet Room was a particular concern. Large wooden struts underneath the floor, initially installed to provide air-raid protection for the Garden Rooms below as they were used by Churchill during the war, had been retained 'lest the floor of the Cabinet Room collapse'. The State Rooms on the first floor, where prominent guests were received and high-profile events were held, required careful management during events; members of the Downing Street staff were circulated to prevent too many guests congregating in any one room, in case they caused a collapse of the floor or supporting walls. The possibility of the full Cabinet falling through the floor mid-meeting, or a group of international dignitaries suffering a similar fate whilst being entertained upstairs, made an upgrade of No. 10 a priority.[14]

The Crawford Committee concurred with the Ministry of Works' findings and suggestions, and concluded that a substantial rebuild of Downing Street was required. However, the Committee decided that the construction of an entirely new building should be rejected, despite the potential benefits of starting from scratch. Its final report stated:

> A completely new building would have many advantages, notably that the layout and services could be specifically designed to suit the purposes for which the houses are used. [...] However, we do

not recommend this course. The houses, and especially No. 10, have many historical associations and we should deplore their demolition.[15]

The Committee decided that it was vital to preserve 'something that has figured so prominently in public life over nearly three centuries and which has become such a familiar feature of the London scene', and noted that, despite the 'patchwork' nature of the building, Downing Street still contained 'features of great architectural importance' that should be retained.[16]

It was recommended that the Downing Street houses undergo underpinning and grouting to make them structurally sound, but that 'rooms and features of historic or architectural importance should be preserved'. This included the Cabinet Room and the rest of No. 10's operational centre. The State Rooms on the first floor, which had once been the private quarters of the Prime Minister and their family but were now primarily used for ceremonial purposes, should also be preserved. The majority of the houses' external features should be retained, although the fire-damaged No. 12 could be rebuilt to its original height, and some alterations could be made to the upper floors of No. 10. The Royal Fine Arts Commission were to be consulted on any changes to No. 10's external appearance.[17]

The view from No. 10

Ultimately, the Crawford Committee's recommendations endorsed the Ministry of Works' original plans, and recommended that an independent architect be appointed to lead the work. Meeting only five times, including one visit to Downing Street on 15 August 1957, the Crawford Committee essentially offered an independent check on the plans. Importantly, however, the Prime Minister's Private Office had also been consulted about these plans throughout their development.

A 1956 note from David Pitblado, then Principal Private Secretary to Eden, provides an excellent insider's perspective on the challenges faced in reconstructing Downing Street, and the needs of the Prime Minister's Office. The note observed that the Prime Minister's Office was 'both a Private Office and a small Department'. Whilst a normal Private Office could rely upon its department for records and services, in this case most such work had to be performed within No. 10. In a sense, the work of the Prime Minister's Office was 'wider in scope and greater in amount than a normal Minister's Private Office.' In addition, the office had been operating on a twenty-four-hour basis since the Second World War.[18] Despite this heavy workload, the relatively tiny team that supported the Prime Minister in his or her various functions had changed little in size or structure for several years, and Pitblado predicted that it was 'unlikely to be modified fundamentally' in the future. Whilst it was acknowledged that special advisers had been brought in to No. 10 'from time to time', and that at present there was little room to accommodate such additions, the current structure was 'certainly the necessary basis of any plans prepared now for the future'.[19]

The arrangement of the rooms around the Cabinet Room kept the small team of Private Secretaries very close together, and close to the Prime Minister. The layout of these rooms also provided a waiting room for the Prime Minister's guests, an anteroom for Cabinet Ministers to congregate in before meetings and easy access to the stairs leading down to the Garden Rooms, where confidential filing, typing and other administrative support functions were housed. Cautious not to lose an arrangement that the officials felt essentially worked, and with the Cabinet Room suite thought to be of particular historical value, it was proposed that this layout should be retained. Any capacity for future expansion, special advisers or rehousing the No. 10 staff currently based in the adjacent Old Treasury buildings would have to be found elsewhere, further away from the 'core' of No. 10.[20]

Pitblado's note acknowledged that the current arrangements at No. 10's operational centre around the Cabinet Room were flawed, but warned against attempting to alter them. In his view, this part of No. 10 was 'indeed on analysis surprisingly convenient – whatever other defects it may have – since the rooms were certainly not designed as office rooms'.[21] However, much of the rest of No. 10 was far less convenient:

The Official staff in No. 10, apart from the Private Office, is housed in accommodation not originally designed for office work. Indeed some of it would be considered quite unsuitable on ordinary standards. But it works adequately and people are reasonably content. Any improvements that can be made on rebuilding would obviously be desirable.[22]

It is worth noting that the Cabinet Room itself was not originally designed for its purpose, and had been adapted and extended over time. Yet despite the present arrangement having been arrived at essentially by chance, there was little appetite for radically rethinking No. 10's core layout to suit the changing needs of the premiership. This decision was reflected in both the choice of architect and the brief given to him.

The architect's view

Raymond Erith, a rare but prominent classical architect in a prevailingly modernist climate, was chosen to lead the works on Downing Street. Erith saw his role as primarily to renovate and preserve the building's history, rather than to put his own imprint on it. Erith's persona is captured in correspondence held in his personal archives at the Royal Institute of British Architects. In late 1958, the *Architects' Journal* chose him as its Man of the Year, and contacted the architect for a quotation and profile for their announcement. Erith advised that 'you could not have picked on anyone about whom there is less to say', adding that 'certainly I have built practically nothing that is of architectural interest'. On the Downing Street job, Erith claimed, 'I owe that to Fortune and am very conscious of being in Fortune's debt: it is still a long way from being an achievement.'[23]

Erith's approach to his work on Downing Street was equally unassuming. The architect stated before the works, 'I do not intend to leave my mark on the additions in Downing Street, nor on No. 12: I attach no importance at all to originality or modernity.' Erith's main objectives were, in his own words, 'improving vertical and horizontal communications, letting in light, and generally tidying up the mess left by a hundred years of piecemeal additions'. However, some provision for the expansion of the Prime Minister's staff was also included. New office space was provided on the second and third floors, once the decision was made to 'push the Chancellor as much as possible into No. 12 in order to make room for the expansion of No. 10'.[24]

This new office space was not near to the Cabinet Room and therefore the Prime Minister, but Erith viewed this as a positive. After speaking to the current occupants of No. 10, the architect was reinforced in his view that discouraging the expansion of the Prime Minister's Private Office, which thrived on being a small and intimate team, was a positive thing. He said, 'If the Private Office got bigger it would not be possible for everyone to know what everyone else is doing, and soon the Prime Minister would not know what he was doing either.' Erith noted that he was unsure who would actually use the new space – 'Advisers? People more or less apart from the Private Office.'[25] Those who were assigned rooms in the newly converted offices were therefore consigned to work without the benefit of proximity to the centre of activity in No. 10, although this was still preferable to being housed elsewhere in Whitehall, as had previously been the only option.

Additionally, after investigating and speaking to the staff of the Garden Rooms in the basement, Erith decided that there could be no better location for them, despite their sometimes-dingy surroundings. Work was undertaken to enlarge the rooms and let more light in. The Garden Rooms provided quick and easy access to the core of No. 10, and Erith found the clerks and typists who occupied them 'devoted' to their location by the garden:

> They told me, with feeling, that it would break their hearts if they had to go. My sympathies are entirely with them: there are not many offices in London where one can look through an unobstructed window into a garden, and the Prime Minister's garden at that, nor many rooms with more history: nor are there any other rooms at all that are under the Cabinet Room.[26]

It was not uncommon for Erith to be told, when speaking to the current staff of No. 10 about his work, that the existing occupants liked their accommodation very much, but that they would not want 'to stand in the way of the general good by sticking to this room'. Erith clearly found this slightly frustrating, and eventually elected to 'put everyone back where he was before in the room he is used to and likes, and hope I will be forgiven for lack of puritanical zeal in seeing that everyone suffers for everyone's well being.'[27]

The Prime Minister and No. 10's rebuilding

In commissioning the Crawford Committee, Prime Minister Macmillan had reverted to what he called the 'politician's natural instinct [for] passing the buck'.[28] Consulting an external body was considered crucial in deciding whether to undertake the costly works,[29] and the Prime Minister claimed to have been disappointed when the Committee reported back that a major structural overhaul of the buildings was indeed required during his premiership.[30] The Committee's recommendations were to be implemented from 1960–3.

Despite the independent nature of the Crawford Committee's advice, however, Macmillan was unable to resist attempting to influence the redesigning of the buildings. By virtue of inheriting No. 10 at the point that its renovation became unavoidable, Macmillan had the opportunity to make a significant and lasting impact upon the physical centre of British government. In some of these interventions, he was successful. Others were opposed by the civil service, or by Erith. But each case reveals a great deal about the evolution of No. 10, and how the future operation of British government was physically shaped in this period.

A place for sleeping or a place of work?

Macmillan's attempts to influence the internal reconfiguration of No. 10 itself met with less success. An early intervention by the Prime Minister concerned the number of staff to be housed in No. 10. In this case, civil servants at No. 10 gently pushed back against the Prime Minister, and navigated around an idea that would have altered No. 10 significantly. In mid-1958, shortly after Cabinet had given the revamp of Downing Street the go-ahead, Macmillan suggested that he would like to see as many staff moved out of Downing Street as possible, with the building used primarily for domestic purposes. However, Macmillan's Principal Private Secretary Freddie Bishop, alongside his Appointments Secretary David Stephens, who had represented No. 10 at a hearing of the Crawford Committee, believed the exact opposite to be desirable.

Bishop and Stephens had advised the Crawford Committee that No. 10 was just about adequate for its present purposes. However, its staff had spilt over into five rooms in the Old Treasury building – an arrangement born of necessity rather than design, and one that the Treasury was less than pleased with. The No. 10 staffers cautioned that 'another Prime Minister might well wish for an increased staff with, possibly, a number of special advisers, in which case the present accommodation would be quite inadequate'.[31] In their view, it was clearly desirable that as many staff as possible should be accommodated in office space within No. 10 itself, and that room for further expansion should also be provided.[32]

The Garden Rooms in the basement of No. 10 were at the centre of this debate. These rooms were then poorly lit and cramped with low ceilings. It was widely accepted that they were far from ideal for their use. Macmillan was inclined to turn the rooms over to confidential filing and move their occupants out of the building entirely. The Prime Minister suggested that only his small Private Office team, presumably including his Political and Personal Private Secretary John Wyndham, should be retained within No. 10 itself.

By the beginning of July, Bishop and Stephens became aware that the Prime Minister's thinking had 'diverged' from theirs. They privately advocated instead for the expansion and improvement of the basement rooms, noting that 'quite a lot of it could, we believe, be made habitable for office staff and there is none too much space in No. 10 for the staff that we need to have here'.[33] The two were cautious in their attempts to change the Prime Minister's mind. Waiting until they were asked to draft a minute to the Ministry of Works on his behalf, they collaborated with the Cabinet Secretary in preparing a note that advocated for expansion rather than contraction of the office space at Downing Street. Stephens stated privately to Bishop that, when the draft note came back from the Cabinet Secretary, it was possible that it would 'contain things that will, at first, be unpalatable to the Prime Minister. But we must deal with this when it arrives'.[34] A few days later, the Principal Private Secretary wrote directly to the Prime Minister. Stephens informed Macmillan somewhat diplomatically that his draft of the note had diverged from the Prime Minister's view significantly:

> I have been anxious lest we may have departed too far from your conception that No. 10 should be primarily domestic and should in future house the <u>minimum</u> of office staff. But if we have departed too far the reason is that if you have your Private Secretaries grouped around the Cabinet Room, as you clearly must, it is essential that the supporting staff, typists, confidential filers, Parliamentary Questions section, and so forth, should not be too far away.[35]

Stephens went on to explain that using the basement Garden Rooms only for storage would push a great deal of staff out into the further reaches of the Old Treasury building, causing 'great practical difficulties for office working'. With the Ministry of Works already informed, the Cabinet Secretary on side and the note already written, the Prime Minister accepted the new line in one handwritten word: 'Yes.'[36]

Admiralty House

The Prime Minister had initially been very sceptical of Admiralty House as a temporary home and office whilst the Downing Street renovation was undertaken.[37] However, he soon warmed to the place. In September 1961, No. 10 Appointments Secretary Stephens recorded that the Prime Minister had become quite taken by the 'fine open room' at Admiralty House that he had been using as a stand-in Cabinet Room. No. 10's Cabinet Room, the Prime Minister had indicated, would now 'give him some feelings of claustrophobia' by comparison. Adding that he 'had never liked the pillars' in No. 10's Cabinet Room, Macmillan sought advice as to whether they could be removed – a self-described 'somewhat radical suggestion'.[38] In response, Erith conceded that the columns did not appear to be necessary to support the roof. They did not bear any substantial weight, and seemed to have been erected by architect Robert Taylor in 1783 for aesthetic rather than practical reasons. However, Erith was strongly attached to them, claiming that if they were removed the Cabinet Room would 'look a bit too much like the lounge of a Trust House'.[39] Macmillan accepted this argument shortly afterwards, telling his Appointments Secretary on 6 October 1961, 'I expect the Architect is right.'[40] However, just three days later, the Prime Minister wrote directly to Erith to tell him he had had 'second thoughts'. Macmillan claimed that 'distinguished visitors' found themselves 'much impeded' by the pillars when visiting – 'and so do I'.[41]

Macmillan was also acutely aware that, in his own words, 'Modern Cabinets seem to get larger and larger'. The Prime Minister had just announced a Cabinet of twenty-one members, saying, 'This might easily become twenty-two.'[42] The spacious and comfortable room at Admiralty House may have been a catalyst for the original thought, but Macmillan was concerned that future Cabinets could continue to expand in size (a prediction that would prove to be mostly accurate), and that the room at No. 10 would not accommodate such expansion.[43]

Erith ultimately won this argument, and the Cabinet Room's pillars were retained. Once again, the future expansion of operations at No. 10 had been considered, and once again it was provided for only in a strictly limited capacity. Just as office space on the upper floors of No. 10 was improved, and slightly pushed out into No. 11, the Cabinet Room was enlarged only by the removal of the historic library. Conservation was seen as key, and alteration was limited, ultimately restraining future expansion as much as it accommodated it.

A 'rather sudden' decision

Following the Crawford Committee's endorsement of their recommendations in June 1958, the Ministry of Works selected construction firm Mowlem as the contractor for the renovation of Downing Street. The ministry was pleased to note that Mowlem's tender was not only the cheapest received, but in fact appeared to be so low in cost as to be 'evidently loss making'.[44] The prestige of the job, it seems, was reward enough for Mowlem, and as the Prime Minister was informed by the

Architect Raymond Erith inspects progress on a hollowed-out No. 10, 1962.

Minister of Works, John Hope, the next best tender was expected to cost £10,500 more.[45] The price ultimately took precedence over concerns on the parts of both the architect Erith and the Prime Minister that the firm lacked experience.[46]

Erith dispatched an assistant to perform limited surveys of the Downing Street houses to assess their condition in the winter of

1958–9.[47] The extent of these surveys was restricted, however, by the Prime Minister's reluctance to move out whilst they were undertaken. The upcoming renovation of the houses was then estimated to cost £464,000, based upon what little was then known about the condition of the buildings. The decision to go ahead was described by the Ministry of Works as a 'rather sudden' one, and the Macmillans moved out of Downing Street and into Admiralty House in August 1960. The Prime Minister was eager to return to No. 10 as soon as possible, however, and was influential in setting a target of August 1962 for his return.[48] However, as Macmillan's biographer Alistair Horne describes, the optimism of this ambition could have been foreseen by 'anyone with Macmillan's experience of British building methods' – after all, this was the man who, as Housing Minister under Churchill, oversaw the building of 300,000 houses a year in Britain.[49]

Unpleasant surprises

It soon became clear that the houses at Downing Street were in much worse condition than had first been indicated. A team of ex-miners, sent down to reconstruct the houses' timber foundations, found them shallow and severely water damaged, rotted and crumbling.[50] The walls of Downing Street's superstructure were found to consist of rubble with timber rather than proper brickwork, creating the ideal conditions for dry rot. Many were also suffering from insect damage. Wartime strengthening work on several of No. 10's floors, performed alongside the construction of an air raid shelter in the basement, had proved inadequate, leaving several rooms unstable.[51] Many of the deficient walls were also significantly 'out of true' (that is, not properly aligned) and structurally unsound; the BBC's Christopher Jones recorded that in some cases, 'apparently solid walls were held up only by the plaster covering them'.[52]

Ultimately, more than half of the existing fabric of the building had to be renewed, with the foundations being substantially underpinned, the main brick walls grouted or reconstructed entirely, all roofs and most floors replaced, and modern services installed, alongside the planned structural alterations designed to expand and improve No.

10's working spaces.[53] A great deal of wood treatment was required throughout to try and prevent future deterioration; in some cases, repairs on internal doors became so intricate that they ended up costing two or three times the value of a new door.[54]

As early as April 1961, it became clear that the original anticipated completion date for the Downing Street houses had already become unachievable. A letter from Mowlem to Erith struck a pessimistic tone:

> We have felt rather concerned during the last few months about the many problems arising on the work at Nos. 10 and 11 Downing Street. We think you will agree that as the pulling down has proceeded, it has been found that far more complete restoration work will be necessary than may have been envisaged before work started, owing to the state of the existing buildings.[55]

The letter also cited the high quality of the services, decorations and details demanded by the building – and by Erith himself – as an additional cause for delay. Noting that Downing Street was the home and office of the British Prime Minister, and not simply 'a very plain office type of building', the contractors expected that more time would be required to complete it.[56] Unfortunately, further delays were just around the corner.

The importance of tea breaks

It is perhaps appropriate that work on such an iconic British building was disrupted by a dispute over another British icon: cups of tea. On 2 October 1961, tools were downed at Downing Street, amongst a number of other sites across London, in response to a new industry ruling which saw weekly working hours reduced, but with the caveat that tea breaks would no longer be paid. A strike began unofficially, but was declared official on 4 October by the Amalgamated Society of Painters and Decorators. Most affiliated unions followed the next day. The Minister of Works now considered the target for completion of August 1962 as increasingly unlikely, noting that a fortnight's ideal weather had been lost. A suggested compromise – bringing tea out to the men without a formal break, in what was described as a 'free tea' solution – was rejected.[57]

In November 1961, it had been reported that the Downing Street programme was three months behind, although much of this delay was attributed to the unexpectedly high level of refurbishment work required, rather than the strikes.[58] A revised estimate predicted that the works on Downing Street would cost £100,000 more than first envisaged. By November 1962, this figure had risen once more, to £300,000. As well as structural problems with the buildings continuing to drive up costs, a series of strikes over the preceding twelve months – including a plumbers' strike from May–August 1962 that had shut down the site completely – were taking their toll.[59]

Erith was becoming increasingly panicked by events at Downing Street. As early as May 1962, the architect wrote to the Ministry of Works:

> As you know I have for some time been worried about the state of affairs at Downing Street. So far as I can see the plumbers' strike is no nearer to a settlement than it ever was. The labour force is out of balance, the men appear to be doing next to nothing, and the contractor seems to be helpless.

The architect stated that it was not his business, or his decision to make, but urged the government to intervene and make a substantial change in the existing arrangements, because 'money is so obviously being wasted'.[60] Erith was also critical of the contractors themselves. He wrote, 'I think everyone is far too ready to see Mowlem's difficulties and cannot help feeling that what is really wanted is a good kick in the pants all round.'[61] The architect claimed that the contractors had 'somehow managed to infect almost everyone else on the site with a defeatist attitude' that made delays inevitable, and also complained about 'red tape' from the Ministry of Works holding up decisions.[62] For their part, the contractors found it difficult to work with Erith, citing his fixation on detail and tendency to change his mind at the last minute.[63]

The anticipated deadline for completion was extended further, and set at August 1963 for Downing Street and October of the same year for William Kent's Treasury building. A bonus system was brought in to incentivise rapid completion of the works, and the Ministry of Works noted with some concern that Parliament had shown 'considerable interest' in the lack of progress on Downing Street.[64]

Macmillan's caution

One further factor complicated the works on Downing Street. Macmillan had been acutely aware of public perceptions from the start of the process, with the appointment of the Crawford Committee designed as a counter to accusations that the Prime Minister was spending public money on improving Downing Street at his own volition. This concern continued throughout the process. A member of Erith's office staff told the historian Anthony Seldon, 'The principal point Macmillan impressed on Erith was that the rebuilding should not look expensive.'[65] However, Erith's vision for No. 10 did not sit easily alongside this advice.

A letter to a ministry official from the final stages of the project in December 1962 reveals the depths of Erith's anguish over the Prime Minister's insistence that the decoration to finish Downing Street's interiors be as plain and unpretentious as possible:

> I ought to have written to you sooner but after I saw you I felt too despondent to say anything [...] For the last 4½ years most of my time and thought has been spent on Downing Street. Now, when the time has come for the final effort needed to set the whole thing off I am told in effect that the house is to be virtually undecorated [...] The only way to justify what we have done is by making the place look as if it was worth keeping [...] At the end of this job I want people to say, "My word, this house is something, of course they were right to keep it."[66]

Continued and expensive delays to construction at Downing Street also led the Ministry of Works to insist on economies being made in the finishing of the house wherever possible. Erith stated with regret that he now feared the press would greet the reconstructed Downing Street with disappointment and criticism, and ask, 'Is this all we get for £900,000?'[67]

In addition, Erith complained that both of the Macmillans seemed not to trust his judgement. The architect appeared on the verge of resigning over the finishing of No. 10, and particularly the historic Cabinet Room, which the Macmillans were insisting on decorating as plainly as possible, as Erith conveyed in his letter:

> The P.M. thinks what I shall do will look extravagant, and probably both he and Lady Dorothy think that anything but cream or pastel shades might look out of place or ridiculous in some way or other. [...] If the Prime Minister and Lady Dorothy have no confidence in me I hope they will find someone else who could do the job properly and who they trust.[68]

Erith asked the Ministry of Works to convey his displeasure to the Prime Minister, 'without being so tactful that he does not know what it is about'.[69] Ministry officials replied, perhaps unsurprisingly, that the present Prime Minister was ultimately in charge of the works, and that his 'personal tastes' had to be accepted.[70]

Despite his personal feelings on the matter, Erith was obliged to carry out the Prime Minister's wishes. But, as a biography of the architect notes, he was 'heartbroken'.[71] Erith was a classicist, seeking to accurately restore the historic buildings to their former glory. He appears to have regarded the public sector's 'economy campaign' as philistine, confiding to a friend, 'They are talking about using good modern furniture. I asked if bad modern would not be cheaper still. They said, quite seriously, no they didn't think so. I despair.'[72]

Not quite finished…

The Prime Minister moved back into Downing Street in September 1963, more than a year later than had first been anticipated. As Alistair Horne surmises, 'Despite the greater space and finer rooms of Admiralty House, he was glad to be back; the "atmosphere of its historic past" doubtless made it all the harder to contemplate leaving, and he thought the architect and builders had "certainly done a good job" at No. 10.'[73] The Old Treasury, now home to the Cabinet Office, would be ready for occupation the following year.

The Downing Street part of the contracted works, estimated at £400,000 when the initial decision was taken to rebuild, and then at £464,000 following a limited survey in the winter of 1958–9, had ended up costing £1.15 million. Strikes were blamed for an estimated £208,000 of the Downing Street expenditure.[74] The unexpectedly poor condition of the houses, and the high quality of the work that Erith demanded, accounted for the remainder. Unfortunately, however, expenditure on the reconstruction of No. 10 was not yet complete.

In 1964, dry rot was discovered in the State Dining Room, in the second-floor toilet and under the Cabinet Room patio. The following year, it was found in the Pillared Room.[75] Prime Minister Harold Wilson initially tried to keep the problem quiet, since it came so soon after the renovations that had been branded a full overhaul of No. 10.[76] Wilson ordered a full investigation to be performed before news of the issue became public.

Erith ultimately accepted blame for the oversight, but claimed that the only way of avoiding the possibility of dry rot 'would have been to raze the building to the ground and start afresh'. It was possible that the dry rot had been 'activated' by a leak from a pipe accidentally burst by Mowlem during restorative works on the house. Regardless, the problem was attributed to a 'technical, rather than a political' error, which had occurred against a background of spiralling costs, and was seen as understandable if inconvenient for the Prime Minister to explain to the public.[77] Wilson finally accepted the need for repairs to be undertaken in 1966, although the serious disruption caused by this work led to its being terminated before the Ministry of Works felt that it was fully complete.[78]

By 1969, discolouration was found on the walls in the White Room, making it almost certain that dry rot was also present there. Whilst No. 10's occupants were reported to be in a state of denial regarding the extent of the problem, the Ministry of Works regarded this as 'wishful thinking', with potentially serious consequences. It stated that 'the most alarming aspect is the (admittedly slight) possibility of collapse;

the concrete ceilings are held up only by low grade brickwork, powdering mortar and rotting timber'.[79] Prime Minister Edward Heath eventually had to accept that even more disruptive work was required and unavoidable, and the work was finally completed by 1973, ten years after Erith's initial revamp of Downing Street had come to its end.[80]

Was it all worth it?

Not all agreed that restoring No. 10 had been the correct choice. In a note to Prime Minister Wilson explaining the need for 1966's dry rot works at Downing Street, the Minister of Public Building and Works analysed the building's recent reconstruction, in an attempt to glean some lessons from the No. 10 experience. Considering that the cost of No. 10's reconstruction under Macmillan had more than doubled the original estimate, without including the additional dry rot treatment that was later required under Wilson and Heath, he concluded:

> If this first estimate had been realistic, the course followed was prudent, but for the final cost, we could probably have rebuilt the house completely. [...] My conclusion is that all that has gone here is a risk inherent where selection between one part and another has to be made in the rehabilitation of an old building.[81]

Noting how intrusive the post-1963 works to repair dry rot had been to the operation of No. 10, Appointments Secretary John Hewitt was reported to have said in 1971 that 'the terms of reference of the Crawford Committee were misconceived and that No. 10 should have been pulled down'. In addition, Hewitt 'still believed that this would be the best policy if the PM was going to be upset every two or three years [by further remedial works]'.[82]

However, it is worth reminding ourselves of the Crawford Committee's conclusions. Ultimately, after considering all the available options, the Downing Street houses were thought to have such national and historical significance that the Committee stated that it would 'deplore their demolition'.[83] Whilst it was possible (but equally far from certain) that an entirely new building could have been

Harold Macmillan hosts US President Dwight Eisenhower at No.
10 for a televised 'fireside chat', 1959. The building, like the role
that it houses, has seen its public role increase over the years.

constructed for a similar or even lower cost, the decision had been
taken that the hundreds of years of history contained within the short
row of terraced houses in Downing Street were worth preserving.

Prior to Erith's rebuilding, No. 10 was in an intolerable state, and
had become an unsuitable base for the modern premiership. The
extent to which it had become unfit for purpose was illustrated during
US President Dwight Eisenhower's famous televised 'fireside chat' at
No. 10 with Macmillan, in the run-up to the 1959 general election.
The President of the United States, visiting for an unprecedented and
historic live television broadcast with the Prime Minister, was said to
have been concerned that the floor could give way under the weight of
the television cameramen and their equipment.[84]

The substantial rebuilding that Macmillan finally sanctioned, after
successive Prime Ministers had stalled or avoided the disruption,

saw him uprooted and housed in temporary accommodation for almost half of his premiership. However, these works meant that the Downing Street houses were made more robust than they had been for over 200 years, with the historic first-floor State Rooms and Cabinet suite of rooms preserved for posterity, and the building's capacity for both living and working vastly improved.

Downing Street was also made a much more effective home and office for the British Prime Minister. To start with, the houses no longer posed a fire risk, and for the first time in many years, it was no longer necessary to employ an industrial fireman to watch over the building full-time.[85] With the building's foundations strengthened, there was also no need for the permanent on-site carpenter, who had previously been retained to constantly adjust No. 10's windows and doors as they moved in and out of true.[86] Modern services were installed, and some degree of sense was made of the building's mishmash of hundreds of years of architectural adjustments.

No. 10 was expanded, with the Chancellor pushed out towards No. 12 Downing Street, which was rebuilt to its former height in red brick (No. 10 and No. 11 had their brickwork painted black, to mimic the sooty appearance they had before renovation). This 'land grab' for No. 10 reflected the increasing importance and breadth of the premiership. Additional office space was opened up on the upper floors, and the building's capacity was expanded as well as improved in quality. So, whilst preserving the building's history was a clear priority, No. 10 was also, in a very British way, gently and subtly modernised to suit the changing role of the British Prime Minister.

6

Living Above the Shop

Arriving at No. 10 Downing Street as a newly appointed Prime Minister can be an intimidating experience. The changeover with the previous occupant is swift and relatively unceremonious; the new premier is greeted with important decisions from the moment they arrive fresh from 'kissing hands' with the monarch at the palace. There is an official staff to meet, a Cabinet to appoint and, in modern times, a 'letter of last resort' to write, instructing the captains of Britain's nuclear submarines what to do should the Prime Minister and the Government be destroyed in a nuclear attack.

The weight of this awesome power and responsibility, suddenly placed on the shoulders of a new premier, is surely offset somewhat by the adrenaline and excitement of arriving at No. 10, passing cheering crowds, making a speech on that famous doorstep and feeling the thrill of the opportunity to change the country for the better. However, on a human level, the experience is a strange one. Arrival at No. 10 sees the removal of the previous occupant not only from office but from his or her home. A passage from the author Charles E. Pascoe's 1908 reflections on Downing Street is evocative of the transient nature of living at No. 10:

> The outgoing tenant has taken away all his kindly wares – his household goods, pictures, personal belongings, and other evidences of home; and the incoming tenant has brought in apparently as few as need be of his own domestic idols; not knowing how long he may tarry. The State is the landlord.[1]

Arriving at Downing Street must be a somewhat claustrophobic experience. Home and office are no longer to be distinct, and all privacy vanishes – or is at least compromised – immediately.

A new Prime Minister arrives at No. 10 unsure of how long they will stay, with the imprint of their predecessor often visible throughout the house. Over time, should they remain in power for long enough to occupy No. 10 during a necessary periodic renovation, they will have an opportunity to shape the building into their own mould. They can decorate and customise here and there to reflect their personality and vision of what the office of Prime Minister should be, but there are also limits to the scope of their ability to do so in a building that is never theirs alone. Some Prime Ministers take to this unusual live-work arrangement with great ease; others find it unnatural, intrusive or inconvenient. Some relish their time away from Downing Street more than their time there. All premierships are affected by the relevant Prime Minister's ability to 'live above the shop', to borrow Margaret Thatcher's famous phrase, which referred to her own childhood experience of living above her father's grocery shop in Grantham. How Prime Ministers have responded to life at No. 10 is fascinating and revealing, but it also has real consequences on the conduct of government at the centre, effective or otherwise.

The Prime Minister's living quarters

The history of No. 10 as a building reflects the story of the premiership that it houses. As the role itself has expanded, acquiring more functions and responsibilities and necessitating increasing numbers of staff to assist in its conduct, the amount of space in the building dedicated to private life has gradually receded. Over hundreds of years, the residential part of the house has gradually retreated from the official part, moving further from the front door and up successive flights of stairs into the upper reaches of the building. A clearer distinction between the private and official spaces has also developed, and by the postwar years, private living arrangements for Prime Ministers and their families were generally confined to a self-contained flat on the second floor.

Robert Walpole, as the first Prime Minister, slept on the first floor in one of the suite of rooms now referred to as the State Rooms, above

the Cabinet Room.[2] Floor plans from 1781 demonstrate the extent
to which residential functions dominated even the ground floor of
the house: aside from 'My Lord's Study' (today's Cabinet Room), an
adjacent waiting room (later the Inner Private Secretaries' Room)
and a 'Secretary's Room' (later the Political Secretary's Office), the
ground floor was otherwise primarily a part of the domestic residence.
A laundry, 'wardrobe', porters' room, maid's bedroom, dining room,
library and 'My Lord's gentlemen's room' all occupied space that had
become home to offices and workspaces by the postwar years.

The first floor of No. 10 was almost entirely residential all the way
up to the 1930s. The first-floor rooms just off of the Grand Staircase,
today known as the State Rooms and the Prime Minister's Study, were
once used as the bedrooms and living quarters of Prime Ministers and
their wives. The Small Dining Room was used by Prime Ministers
for private dining with their families. Second-floor rooms were used
on the occasion of an incumbent with a large family, such as Spencer
Perceval, whose six daughters and six sons all stayed in second-floor
rooms, with No. 10's numerous cooks and other servants presumed to
have slept in the basement due to a lack of space.[3]

However, the Prime Minister and his or her partner were soon to be
forced up to another floor, one more step removed from the working
and official parts of the house. It was during Neville Chamberlain's
premiership from 1937–40 that the Prime Minister's living quarters
moved up to the second floor, at the behest of his wife, Anne Chamberlain. The first-floor rooms alongside the State Rooms were converted into offices, with the room now known as the Study acquiring
its modern purpose. A great deal of renovation was performed alongside this work, taking around ten months, costing £25,000 and including the raising of some ceilings and the provision of new windows.
The Chamberlains therefore did not move straight into No. 10 when
Chamberlain became Prime Minister, but instead remained at No.11
Downing Street until the renovations were complete.[4]

It was at this point that the White Room, today one of the State
Rooms and historically used by Prime Ministers as their bedroom,
became an extra drawing room (although Clementine Churchill
returned to using it as a bedroom during her husband's second premiership). The White Room was painted yellow at the time, and

used as a personal study/drawing room by Anne Chamberlain. The adjacent middle State Drawing Room was painted red (although it too has subsequently changed colour, first to blue, and now to the shade that makes it known as the Terracotta Room). The third State Room was larger and distinguished by its two pillars, and fortunately for historians, it has been referred to fairly consistently as the Pillared Room. The anteroom to the State Rooms, which lies just off of the Grand Staircase, was no longer used as a bedroom itself, but rebuilt as a passageway, with a short staircase incorporated up to the new living quarters.[5]

With the exception of the Churchills in the Prime Minister's second term, the Baldwins were therefore the last family to live in the State Rooms.[6] The rooms were subsequently repurposed for entertaining, an increasingly important function of No. 10. Winston Churchill took over the premiership from Chamberlain in May 1940, but he encouraged the Chamberlains to remain at Downing Street until June, enabling the former Prime Minister the time and space for a leisurely move. The Churchills then moved into rooms on the second floor.[7] However, neither Winston nor Clementine Churchill would spend a great deal of time at Downing Street during the war, with No. 10 judged unsafe during the Blitz.

The repair of bomb damage was partly responsible for the Attlees also taking their time to move into No. 10, after Clement Attlee won a landslide victory in the first postwar general election, on 5 July 1945. Further adaptations were also made to the living quarters, developing a truly self-contained flat in No. 10 for the first time.[8] Whilst this work was performed in order for the Attlees to inhabit the flat, it had been undertaken at Clementine Churchill's recommendation, and whilst it was completed the Attlees stayed in Churchill's old room in the No. 10 Annexe underneath Government Offices Great George Street.[9]

Despite Clementine Churchill's involvement in the development of the self-contained flat at No. 10, her husband's return to the premiership did not see her use it. Whilst the Prime Minister and his secretaries lived in the second-floor flat, Clementine Churchill instead elected to use the Prime Minister's Study on the first floor as her bedroom, and the adjacent White Room as a study.[10] Churchill would make his way up to his room in the self-contained flat via the lift, which had by then fortunately – given the Prime Minister's deteriorating physical condition – been installed in the corridor from No. 10's front door.[11]

Following Churchill's eventual reluctant departure from No. 10, the Edens moved into the second-floor flat together.[12] The Macmillans did the same until Harold Macmillan was forced to relocate to Admiralty House whilst No. 10 was renovated, although Dorothy Macmillan took the first-floor White Room for her own use.[13] Subsequent Prime Ministers and their families would all live in the self-contained second-floor flat at No. 10, with the exception of Harold Wilson during his second term, when the Wilsons elected to live outside of No. 10 at Lord North Street, just a short walk away, with Harold commuting in by car every morning. The arrival of Tony Blair's relatively large family (at least in comparison to then-Chancellor Gordon Brown's) at Downing Street saw the Prime Minister move into the more spacious flat above No. 11, a trend that has continued ever since. In Downing Street, as in the British political system in general, precedents, once set, tend to stick – at least, until they are replaced by new ones.

Family atmosphere?

No. 10's dual role as the home and office of the Prime Minister, alongside its intimate geography and small group of staff, means that the atmosphere inside the building is particularly reliant on the particular Prime Minister and family that inhabit it. During the Victorian era, Prime Ministers and their families lived at No. 10 sporadically at best. This was due to a combination of the decline of the area around Downing Street and the tendency of Victorian premiers to be from aristocratic backgrounds, preferring to live at their own much grander properties elsewhere.[14] However, throughout the twentieth century, the domestic presence of Prime Ministers and their families has consistently influenced the working environment at No. 10.

Not all premiers have found it easy to live at No. 10. Ramsay MacDonald, the first Labour Prime Minister, arrived at Downing Street a widower, relatively poor compared to his predecessors and reliant upon one of his daughters, Ishbel MacDonald, to purchase linen and furnishings to fill the house. His youngest daughter, Sheila Lochhead, described 'a completely unfamily house'.[15] MacDonald was unused to having servants, and ill at ease in No. 10.

Others took to life at No. 10 much more easily. Whilst working life at No. 10 could be chaotic during Churchill's second premiership, the Churchills had already spent time at the house, and were comfortable with domestic arrangements at Downing Street. Anthony Eden should have been equally comfortable when arriving at No. 10; Eden's wife was Churchill's niece, and the couple had been married at No. 10 in August 1952.[16] According to Eden's biographer Robert Rhodes-James, Anthony and Clarissa Eden 'were unusual in that they both loved the house, for which many Prime Ministers and their wives have developed a considerable dislike'.[17] The Edens arrived at No. 10 full of enthusiasm for their new home, and the Prime Minister gladly entertained an impressive succession of world leaders at Downing Street.[18] However, the atmosphere at No. 10 during Eden's premiership would soon sour, as the Prime Minister's temper and the crisis of Suez tainted the air. Randolph Churchill, a relation but not an ally of Eden's, described his premiership as 'the Eden terror', with Downing Street 'supposedly a Forsterian world of telegrams and anger'.[19]

Eden's successor, Macmillan, made a conscious effort to cool the temperature of No. 10. The Macmillans brought an air of comparative calm into No. 10, as well as a family atmosphere. The Prime Minister would later claim of his wife Dorothy:

> She filled [No. 10] with children and all their paraphernalia; she filled it with flowers. But above all she made it seem like a family gathering in a country house with guests continually coming and going, with a large number of children's parties and with a sense of friendliness among all the staff and servants who worked long hours with cheerful willingness.[20]

The constant presence of children and grandchildren, alongside Dorothy Macmillan's friendly attitude towards the domestic and political staff at No. 10, made for a warm and pleasant working environment. As D. R. Thorpe notes, 'For an "official" house, No. 10 Downing Street, in Macmillan's time, was a very "lived in" building, and consequently welcoming in an informal way to all kinds of visitors.'[21]

It can be argued that the Macmillans, like their successors, the Douglas-Homes, were so at ease with life at No. 10 and so beloved by their staff because they were used to living amongst those who worked for them. An excerpt from Ben Pimlott's biography of Alec Douglas-Home's successor, Wilson, offers a possible explanation for the ease with which the Douglas-Homes took to life at No. 10:

"You might say they knew how to handle servants," says one official whose spell at No. 10 spanned the transition. "As the election results came in, lots of the garden room girls were in tears at the thought of losing two very nice people."[22]

Having a range of servants, including cooks, drivers, a door man, security and domestic help, would prove an unfamiliar and perhaps uncomfortable experience for some Prime Ministers. However, the Macmillans and the Douglas-Homes both found the experience an easy and pleasurable one.

Elizabeth Douglas-Home was particularly close to the Garden Room Girls, the secretariat based in the basement of the building, and gave them chocolates and chatted to them in coffee breaks. Douglas-Home's biographer Thorpe observed:

The Macmillan years had been very special for the Garden Room Girls and Alec [Douglas-]Home's brief tenure was the end of a particular way of working. Family informality combined with professional efficiency and a sense of happy teamwork, with Alec and Elizabeth Home always remembering birthdays and anniversaries. Elizabeth was very much part of the team, making sure that things worked and thinking nothing of driving up to the Hirsel and back over a weekend with Angela Bowlby, Alec Home's personal secretary, to bring things back that were needed.[23]

Pimlott has noted that the Douglas-Homes, like the Macmillans, 'spread the influence of their personalities through the passages and State Rooms, providing the feeling of a busy private residence, and encouraging civil servants who worked there to regard themselves as treasured family retainers.'[24]

Alec and Elizabeth Douglas-Home in the White Room. The
Douglas-Homes were at ease with domestic arrangements at No.
10, in contrast to their successors Harold and Mary Wilson.

This atmosphere at No. 10, that of a gentle, aristocratic country
home, would change quite substantially under Wilson. The Wilsons –
consisting of Harold and Mary, plus two children, a dog called Paddy
and a cat called Nemo – moved into the self-contained second-floor
flat at No. 10 from their home in Hampstead Garden Suburb.[25] The
Wilsons tried to make the No. 10 flat as homely as possible, but they
found it difficult to live with the frequent disturbances by officials.[26]

Mary Wilson found moving into the flat particularly unappealing.
Some felt that she held a deep suspicion of the officials at the house,
and reported that at Downing Street she cut a lonely, despondent
figure, highly uncomfortable with the lack of privacy that living in her
husband's place of work entailed.[27] Mary Wilson also insisted on the
installation of a doorbell for the self-contained flat on No. 10's second
floor, to discourage officials from walking straight in unannounced to

see the Prime Minister.[28] Ultimately, as Pimlott summarised, for the Wilsons, No. 10 'was an office, never a home'.[29]

Other Prime Ministerial families managed, but still found their personal lives slightly strained by the unusual experience of 'living above the shop'. Attlee described life at No. 10 as 'very comfortable', and noted that he was able to see more of his family than in any previous job, where he had lost time commuting back to the family home in Stanmore at the end of each day.[30] He also enjoyed walking his dog Megan in St. James's Park in the mornings.[31] However, whilst the Prime Minister found life at No. 10 convenient and relatively relaxing, Violet Attlee found the intrusiveness of the premiership much more problematic. Anthony Seldon claims that Violet Attlee was 'jealous of the time others spent with her husband', and found life at No. 10 'overwhelming [...] her illnesses seemed to his secretaries as much mental as physical'.[32]

James Callaghan, who, like Attlee, was well liked and widely thought of as temperamentally suited to the premiership, did not have an entirely straightforward experience of No. 10 either. Callaghan had originally sought to retain and use his grace-and-favour residence at nearby Carlton Gardens instead of moving into Downing Street, 'adamant that he was not prepared to inflict upon his wife the discomforts of living at No. 10'.[33] This was despite – or perhaps because of – the fact that he had never been able to occupy the property during his time as Foreign and Commonwealth Secretary, due to essential repair works.[34] The Prime Minister considered living permanently at his private flat in Kennington Park Road, once officials had managed to convince him to free up the property at Carlton Gardens for the use of his Foreign Secretary, Anthony Crosland.[35] Callaghan may have been nervous of repeating Wilson's domestic difficulties at No. 10, but in the event a fairly happy balance was found. After living at the Kennington flat for the first three months of his premiership, the Prime Minister and his wife moved into No. 10, and found it much more pleasant than expected.[36] Callaghan ultimately felt secure living there, and his supportive wife, Audrey Callaghan, was described as 'the first Labour Prime Minister's wife to actually enjoy being at No. 10'.[37] A much better atmosphere developed within the building, with a Prime Minister who was comfortable with the job and a Prime Ministerial

James Callaghan inspects the gardens at No. 10 with gardener Len Hobbs, 1978.

couple who were happy there.[38] However, the Callaghans would often stay in their South London flat or spend weekends at their Sussex farmhouse.[39] This could prove challenging for the Prime Minister's security, but it perhaps accounts for the relatively happy atmosphere at No. 10 when the Callaghans did stay there.

On several occasions, the 'family atmosphere' at No. 10 has meant something quite different, as there has been no traditional 'family' living there. In the case of Edward Heath, a bachelor without pets, the atmosphere at No. 10 became 'a little more formal'.[40] Heath, however, thought very highly of the aides, civil servants and political staff who provided him not only with advice, but also with companionship, throughout:

I had complete confidence in their intellectual abilities, their competence, their commitment, their loyalty and their discretion. No Prime Minister can ask for a better or more agreeable team to support him in No. 10. [...] They were not just colleagues but friends, and to me, on my own as I was, a kind of extended family.[41]

Heath's time at No. 10 had an unusual atmosphere, then, but not necessarily a bad one. In fact, for officials, Heath's willingness to allow his
personal and professional life to blend, and his openness to bringing
work into the living space within the building and allow interruptions
whenever necessary, was ideal for the conduct of the premiership.
Robin Butler recalls how much work was performed and discussed
with officials in the private flat, by way of contrast to Wilson:

> In the evening, Heath would go up to the flat – when the Study
> wasn't being used. He would be in his sitting room. When there
> were issues that had to be dealt with in the evening – and there fre-
> quently were – the Private Secretary who was on duty would go up
> to his flat and put issues to him there, where he would be sitting
> playing music extremely loudly. And he wouldn't turn it down.
> I remember one of the first times I had to do this, you would go
> up the stairs, a little breathless, the music would be playing loudly
> and you would try and explain [the issue] to the Prime Minister.
> He looked at you – and Ted Heath had this blank stare – and you
> wouldn't know whether he heard you or not. Then there would be
> a long silence. So I'd start again, only to be interrupted by him and
> for him to tell me what it was he wanted to say about it. Also, Heath
> used to have his lunch up there in the flat – and we would prepare
> for Prime Minister's Questions there. So there was quite a lot up
> there in the flat. At times things happened overnight – sometimes
> you had to shout through the bathroom door, or into his bedroom.
> There was a feeling of intimacy.[42]

It was in the private, self-contained flat that Heath chose to celebrate
the greatest moment of his premiership: Britain's entry into the European Economic Community. Robert Armstrong, who worked closely
with Heath as his Principal Private Secretary, recalled a moment that
encapsulated the Heath persona perfectly:

> I do remember being up in the private sitting room on the evening
> when the House of Commons passed the vote on our entry into
> the European Economic Community. Of course, that was a great
> evening – October 1971. For Mr. Heath that was one of the real

triumphant moments. And of course there was party after party to go to. But he came back to the house, went up to the flat where his father and his brother and his wife were, and one or two other people, and he sat down with his little clavichord and he played the first prelude from Johann Sebastian Bach's *Well-Tempered Clavier* on the clavichord. It made a very small sound as these small instruments do. But we were all listening very intently; the sound filled the room. I've often thought about it – that was the way in which he marked his deep satisfaction at having got us into Europe, to sit down and play that bit of music on his clavichord. I felt that he was claiming Europe, as it were, for Britain. It was an amazing moment. Then he went to all the parties. He felt about it very deeply I think.[43]

This quiet and intimate celebration in the flat, with European classical music, could not have better encapsulated Heath.

John Major, despite being a married man when arriving at No. 10, was also described as cutting a lonely figure during his stay at the building. His wife, Norma Major, initially lived at their private residence near Huntingdon during the week, with their two young children. This kept the family out of the media's glare fairly successfully, but left the Prime Minister alone at No. 10 during the weeks.[44] Major's biographer Anthony Seldon paints a lonely picture of his working week at No. 10:

> At night, after the security guards had gone round and closed the wooden shutters in Number Ten, the building became a cavernous place. If Major had no engagements, he would wander down from working on his boxes in the flat, and call in on the Private Office, or invite them for a drink or chat. Even in his first few months, he was often a loner as Prime Minister.[45]

However, Major's Principal Private Secretary Alex Allan offers a slightly different perspective:

> Norma was here quite a lot. I always got in very early, and John Major worked out that I got in early, and used to ring down and say could I please come up to the flat for something or other... and so then I'd have to start getting in even earlier, and eventually I had to

tell the switchboard that they weren't allowed to admit I was there until half past seven, or something like that. But yes, quite often I'd go up to the flat and Norma would be there [...] You don't have much chance to get lonely given the amount of work you have to do. I mean, if he was here on his own on a weekday, by and large we'd have meetings and things here until quite late, and then he'd have boxes of work to go through, and that is to say nothing of the fact that he often had to go out for dinners and so forth and get back, so I don't think there was much time to get lonely, really.[46]

But the atmosphere at No. 10 was clearly different under Major than it had been under Macmillan, for example. One of the stewards from Chequers was summoned to cook for Major at No. 10 on those week-nights that he was home, as his family was living elsewhere. It has been claimed that the Prime Minister 'brought out the protective side in people. They worried about his solitary late-evening existence in No. 10 [...] and the unhealthy junk food he would have brought in, if he ate at all'.[47] However, in his Principal Private Secretary's view, it was ultimately 'a bit of a caricature to say he was lonely'.[48] Whilst staff at No. 10 clearly felt warmly towards him, the atmosphere whilst Major was Prime Minister differed from that of his predecessor.

Thatcher was said to have found life at No. 10 particularly agreeable, and enjoyed very positive relations with the staff there. Her memoirs describe 'almost a family atmosphere' at Downing Street.[49] This senti-ment was echoed by Janice Richards, head of the Garden Room Girls under Thatcher, in an interview for the Strand Group.[50] The Prime Minister was said to have taken a great interest in the lives and fami-lies of the staff at No. 10. She also found that life at No. 10 suited her. Despite this, the Prime Minister was keen to get away from No. 10 at weekends, as most Prime Ministers have been, telling the BBC's Christopher Jones that during the weekend 'somehow the whole place [No. 10] is a morgue. It's so terribly quiet'.[51] When at Downing Street, Thatcher not only took a keen interest in her staff, but also pre-sided over a welcoming, comparatively friendly atmosphere amongst senior advisers. Robin Butler, Principal Private Secretary to Thatcher, described a less formal atmosphere, with more blurring of the lines between the personal and official spaces in No. 10:

[One had to] be careful not to go up when she was in her curlers; but it was much more relaxed, people knocking on the door and coming in. I remember her sitting in the sitting room with her legs curled up on the settee with her red boxes. She would spend evenings up there. We'd go up to the flat to see her.[52]

No. 10 has long been the home to family pets, which have come and gone with Prime Ministers and their families. Today, Larry the cat occupies a civil service–style non-partisan role as Chief Mouser at No. 10, and has served alongside three different Prime Ministers (at the time of publication). The Churchills left several cats at No. 10, although Winston took his favourite, named Nelson, with him when he departed. The cats helped to deal with the long-standing rat problem at Downing Street, but Clarissa Eden eventually arranged to have the cats relocated to Churchill's home in Hyde Park Gate after several months.[53] Churchill's famous poodle, Rufus, also departed Downing Street with him, as Wilson's dog and cat team did with him some years later.

A proper predecessor for Larry can be found in Humphrey, the No. 10 cat described by Seldon as the 'Pitt, Churchill or Gladstone of the late twentieth century', who served under three successive Prime Ministers (Thatcher, Major and Blair).[54] Whilst the keeping of domestic pets at No. 10 may be tempting, providing an uplift in atmosphere and potential for stress relief, it involves risks. The Government was considering putting in a clause to make owners responsible for any animal-initiated damage to property at No. 10 as early as 1947.[55] Responsibility for damage to clothing caused by budgerigar droppings, as seen during Churchill's second premiership, remained a grey area.

Dark clouds at No. 10

The unusual live-work arrangement at No. 10, alongside the building's historic intimacy and small staff, can make for a wonderful collegiate working atmosphere. However, the nature of life at No. 10 means that when things aren't going quite as well, it can be felt throughout the house. Eden's premiership, increasingly consumed by events surrounding the Suez Canal, provides an example. The No. 10 historian Christopher Jones described how both family and working life at Downing Street during the Suez crisis became increasingly disrupted and stressful:

> It was very tense [...] and also it was never-ending. It went on all through the night; private secretaries were rushing in and out of the bedroom with papers. Crises were developing every night. Meals were regularly three hours late. Nobody knew where they were going to be.[56]

Those present during the collapse of Prime Ministerial power often describe an eerie feeling in the building. Bernard Donoughue, Head of the Policy Unit under Wilson and Callaghan, described being at No. 10 during the Winter of Discontent of 1978–9. Outside Downing Street, the Government appeared to be losing control of the country, amidst industrial unrest that saw rubbish bags piling up on Trafalgar Square and bodies going unburied in Liverpool due to a gravediggers' strike. Donoughue described life in No. 10 as 'like being on an Atlantic liner when all the engines had stopped'. Whereas the building was 'often cathedral-y calm [...] It now had the calm of the morgue.'[57]

Cecil Parkinson, a close ally of Thatcher's, described a similar scene at No. 10 during the final few days of her premiership. Interviewed by Sue Cameron for the Strand Group's *Thatcher and Number 10* video histories project, Parkinson recalled his final visit to the building to see the soon-to-depart Prime Minister:

> I'd decided that I didn't want to work with John Major and John Major's government. I felt that the cabinet had really let her down, and I just didn't want to be involved. So, on the Monday – the final vote was on the Tuesday – I came here to say to her, 'Look, you appointed me. I would like to resign to you, and leave with you.' And I came in here, and so an appointment was made. I came in, and it was the most eerie experience, because every corridor and all the staircases were lined with flowers. There were literally thousands of bouquets of flowers, and they went right up the stairs right to the door of the Study. I went in there, and she was sitting behind the

desk with four or five papers to sign, and there was the most... I'd been in a similar situation before, but you had the feeling that all power had gone. You know, this was the most powerful person in the land – one of the most – until a few hours earlier, and the power had been stripped away. The only other time I had experienced that was when Ted Heath, in '74, he came into the whip's office when he'd called the election – I was a whip then, and we had a drink, and we drank champagne – and then he came a few days later, when we'd lost, after the election, and he'd been trying to put a coalition together. He came back into the whip's office, the opposition... and all the power had gone from him. All the authority. And it was exactly the same feeling in No. 10 that night.[58]

Descriptions of this kind are commonplace amongst those who have been at No. 10 when power has left the building. It is as if the building's great history does not sit easily alongside those who are unable to command the respect that it feels that it deserves.

Work-life balance

In a building that serves dual roles as both home and office, it can be challenging for a Prime Minister to achieve a balance between the demands of their role and their personal or family life. A Prime Minister is necessarily never truly 'off', even when asleep or on holiday, and their leisure time can be interrupted suddenly and unexpectedly should the situation demand. Leaving their work at the office is even more challenging when the office is also their home. The job can be all-consuming, and managing its pressures and strains successfully is one of its greatest challenges. Those Prime Ministers who discovered they were temperamentally unsuited to the role, becoming overwhelmed or consumed by its demands, tend to dominate the lower echelons of historical league tables. The ability to maintain a degree of separation between work and personal life, and to occasionally find respite from the incredible seriousness and responsibility of the job, is absolutely crucial to survival at No. 10.

Attlee provides a good example. Attlee's daughter Felicity Harwood claimed that he would always finish his work (generally meaning working through his boxes) in its entirety before he came up from the Cabinet Room to the self-contained No. 10 flat.[59] Attlee's lifestyle, like his approach to work, remained disciplined, and he even found time for regular morning walks in St. James's Park, sometimes accompanied by his wife Violet Attlee, and always followed discreetly by a detective.[60]

Other Prime Ministers have also found life at No. 10 relatively easy. Callaghan claimed to have felt that the premiership left plenty of time for other things. Callaghan observed that, having been Chancellor, Home Secretary and Foreign Secretary before his premiership, he found life at No. 10 a task of 'relative idleness'.[61] Callaghan later observed that a Prime Minister 'need not be the hardest worked member of his Government':

> To an extent the Prime Minister makes his own pace. It is the Prime Minister himself who takes the initiatives, who pokes about where he chooses and creates his own waves. Ideally he should keep enough time to stand back a little from the Cabinet's day-to-day work, to keep touch with Parliamentary and outside opinion, and to view the scene as a whole, knowing full well that periods of crisis will occur when this will be impossible.[62]

However, the amount of time the Prime Minister has to spend on making decisions or working through their boxes is irrelevant if the individual premier is unable to draw a line between their work and their home life at No. 10. Eden fell victim to this problem during the difficult days of the Suez crisis. Clarissa Eden, his wife, tried to protect the Prime Minister from the all-consuming nature of crisis, and reportedly 'kept the door like a tiger, rarely allowing anyone but true and staunch friends to see him.'[63] Eden himself would later write of life at No. 10 during Suez, 'During these days private life ceased to exist. It was useless to fix engagements and unwise to invite guests to meals. Luncheon could be at any hour and dinner was often not eaten until far into the night.'[64] The Prime Minister was said by others to have been of a better temperament following a weekend out of No. 10, whether at Chequers or at his personal residence, Rose Bower. Otherwise, Eden

The highs: John and Norma Major look out the window
of No. 10 the day after election victory, 1992.

could be consumed by anxieties relating to his work, and his inces-
sant phone calls could irritate 'even so relaxed and calm a man as [Alec
Douglas-]Home', according to Eden's biographer Rhodes-James.[65]

Temperament is a crucial factor in making or breaking a Prime
Minister, and the working atmosphere at No. 10 is invariably affected
accordingly. Heath worked at becoming particularly good at relaxing at the weekends; his sailing trips sometimes rendered him almost
uncontactable.[66]

The end

Whilst each Prime Minister can take a very different approach to
the job, they all have one thing in common: their premierships will
eventually end. Most end suddenly, unexpectedly and at the hands of

others. If the decision to eject an occupant of No. 10 has been made by the public or the Prime Minister's political party, rather than by the premier themselves, things move at a brutal pace. There is no such thing as a 'lame duck' Prime Minister, and – unlike in the United States – once a decision is made that a change in premier is required, the existing occupants are often thrown out with very little ceremony, and the new occupants are thrust head first into the most powerful job in British politics. For a newly arriving Prime Minister, propelled into the most powerful role in the country with relatively little real notice, it can be a whirlwind.

Wilson recalled arriving at No. 10, after beating Douglas-Home in the general election of 1964, and wandering the corridor that runs from the front door to the Cabinet Room, 'a little bewildered, more than a little lonely, but above all else conscious of our small majority and the utter unpredictability of even the immediate future'.[67] Within minutes, he was informed that the Chinese had exploded their first nuclear weapon the previous day. He wrote, 'It was a stormy welcome.'[68]

If Wilson was shocked by the rapidity of his change in circumstances, his predecessor had even more cause to be unsettled. The Douglas-Homes were kicked out of Downing Street with alarming speed. The Wilsons arrived at No. 10 before the Douglas-Homes had vacated the property, forcing the former occupants to flee from the back of the house via the garden. So rushed was the evacuation, which took place on Friday 16 October 1964, that Elizabeth Douglas-Home had to return after the weekend to finish packing.[69] The Douglas-Homes then stayed in a penthouse suite in Claridges until they found a permanent place to stay. Both Wilson and Douglas-Home subsequently thought that the Leader of the Opposition should be granted a residence of their own, 'to minimise the indignities of sudden eviction from Downing Street'.[70] Likewise, Heath initially had nowhere to go when he was ejected from No. 10. In 1985, the Thatchers bought a house to ensure that they would avoid the same fate should the Prime Minister be suddenly evicted from No. 10.[71]

Prime Ministerial departures are often sudden, and can be emotional occasions for all involved. It is tradition for a departing Prime Minister and their family to be 'clapped out' by No. 10's staff – whether personal, political or official – as they leave. The building's occupants line

And the lows: Margaret Thatcher peeks out of the
window on the last day of her premiership, 1990.

its corridors and Entrance Hall for the premier's exit. Those present
are aware that a Prime Minister is being forced to leave not only their
job but also their home, and it is not uncommon for the next Prime
Minister, arriving shortly afterwards, to find fresh tears on the faces of
the staff who greet them on arrival.

Thatcher's departure from No. 10 was famously emotional. Removed
against her will, feeling her party had betrayed her, the newly former
Prime Minister was pictured with damp eyes as she departed Downing
Street by car. When her successor, Major, departed Downing Street in
1997, he asked No. 10's staff not to clap him out. Major feared that the
emotion of the moment would leave him unable to compose himself
and deliver his final speech outside the famous front door:

> Leaving was very painful. [...] I knew our farewell would be a highly
> charged emotional moment, and I could not face it immediately
> before emerging to present a stoical face to the press assembled
> outside. I asked Alex Allan to arrange for me to say farewell to the
> staff in the State Rooms on the first floor. [...] There were wet eyes

all around the room – sometimes to my surprise. [...] I went upstairs to the flat for one last gesture: I left a bottle of champagne for Tony and Cherie Blair with a brief note saying, 'It's a great job – enjoy it.'[72]

Major felt the emotional connection to the building that had been his home and office for six-and-a-half years so keenly that he pledged in his memoirs, 'I will never go back. It is a building for government, not memories.'[73]

7

Hosting the World

Let me entertain you

No. 10 Downing Street serves three main functions. It is firstly the home and secondly the office of the Prime Minister of the United Kingdom. As illustrated in the previous chapter, these two roles have been reflected in No. 10's physical development across the postwar years. Its office space has gradually increased, mirroring the expansion of the premiership itself, and its domestic function has become increasingly enclosed and withdrawn to the upper reaches of the building. The third function of No. 10, as a place for hosting and entertaining guests, has been particularly affected by the evolution of the second. With the upwards retreat of the Prime Ministerial residence into a self-contained flat, the first-floor State Rooms once used as bedrooms and private spaces have become increasingly formalised as venues for visits, events, photo opportunities and Prime Ministerial announcements.

Entertaining visitors, both domestic and international, has long been an important activity within No. 10. It has also become an increasingly prominent element of the premiership, with the arrival of television leading to interviews and public announcements being made from No. 10 in the postwar years. Whether the Prime Minister is seeking to cement an important international relationship, demonstrate support for a particular charitable cause or take advantage of a visit from a well-regarded celebrity or sports personality, No. 10's role in deploying 'soft power' is significant. A photograph outside the famous front door, an invitation to a reception or a diplomatic visit can have a tremendous impact on currying favour at home and abroad. Of No. 10's multiple personalities, it is its role in 'hosting the world' that has evolved to the greatest extent throughout the postwar years.

The Government Hospitality Fund was established in 1908 to provide food and drink to functions for foreign and domestic guests. According to Anthony Seldon, the fund, which was wound up in 1999, kept samples of its food for two weeks after it was served, for testing in case guests reported food poisoning.[1] The wine used for functions at Downing Street came from a cellar underneath Lancaster House, near Buckingham Palace, and was (and still is) selected by the Government Wine Committee, established in 1922. This committee still meets three or four times a year, and consists of a chair and four members. All are unpaid and all members are Masters of Wine, holding a UK-issued qualification held by only a few hundred wine experts.[2] In 1990, it was estimated that in a typical year 9,000–10,000 bottles were consumed at functions across the Government.[3]

Functions are mostly hosted in the State Rooms on the first floor of No. 10, with the majority taking place in the Pillared Room. Formal dinners generally take place in the State Dining Room, the grandest room in No. 10. The large State Dining Room has its own geography of power, of course: despite the relatively cramped conditions, the Prime Minister is able to engage with around ten guests maximum when dinners are held there. Gaining one of the best seats in the house can make all the difference between a pleasant evening and the opportunity to influence the most powerful politician in the country.

Harold Macmillan was the first Prime Minister to invite television cameras into No. 10 – but entertaining at No. 10 came with the territory long before Macmillan's time. Some Prime Ministers hosted at Downing Street more than others. With repairs required throughout his premiership, as well as adaptations including developing the self-contained flat, Clement Attlee entertained relatively rarely during his premiership. The first-floor rooms that had historically been used as bedrooms and living quarters went almost unused, in what was a fairly austere period for No. 10, which also saw the Prime Minister cut the number of staff involved in running the building itself from six to two.[4]

Attlee was not famous for his enthusiasm for small talk. When his Private Secretary John 'Jock' Colville suggested Attlee's potential membership of the Other Club, a political dining club, to its joint founder Winston Churchill, Churchill declined, branding Attlee 'an admirable character, but not a man with whom it is agreeable to dine'.[5] Churchill himself could be a much more gregarious host, but lost his enthusiasm for receptions and parties in his second premiership. In fact, it was whilst hosting the Italian Prime Minister Alcide De Gasperi in No. 10's Pillared Room on 23 June 1953 that the Prime Minister was seen to visibly slump after suffering a stroke. Guests were swiftly ushered out of No. 10, and so began one of the most impressive known cover-ups in British history.

Clementine Churchill was a more enthusiastic host, as was Clarissa Eden, her successor. Clarissa Eden organised the catering and took an active interest in the menu for dinners at No. 10, reportedly taking great joy from an incident in which US Secretary of State John Foster Dulles was overheard betting his dining neighbour that he knew exactly what would be served for dinner – a bet he lost.[6] However, even her key organisational role did not guarantee her a seat at the table; it was felt, according to the historian Christopher Jones, that 'the presence of women at the table would [...] hinder the important conversation of the men, so she had to stay in her "harem"'.[7] Being the Prime Minister's spouse, particularly in the 1950s, could be a thankless task.

The Macmillans seem to have arrived at No. 10 eager to entertain; during her husband's chancellorship, Dorothy Macmillan had been keenly investigating the upper limits of the number of guests she could host for dancing at No. 11 (200 for ballroom, 100 for square dancing).[8] However, as outlined previously, No. 10 was only very briefly in an adequate state for the Macmillans to host large gatherings, with a strict limit on the number of guests who could be held in the first-floor State Rooms at any one time, for fear of the floor giving way under the weight.[9]

The renovation of Downing Street was completed – albeit with a legacy of undiscovered dry rot – by the time Harold Wilson displaced the Douglas-Homes from No. 10 in 1964. A Downing Street doorkeeper during the Wilson era kept a tally of how many times the famous front door was opened and shut for visitors: in just one day, the door was attended to 945 times between the hours of 6 am and 11 pm.[10] The Prime Minister was not quite as good at entertaining visitors in his second premiership as he had been during his first, with his aides becoming increasingly nervous that Wilson would talk about

Anthony Eden, then Foreign Secretary, and Clarissa Eden celebrate
their wedding in the garden at No. 10, alongside Prime Minister
Winston Churchill and Clementine Churchill, 1952.

whatever was on his mind rather than picking up on the interests of
his guests, or would focus exclusively on the Labour Party people in
the room.[11]

Still, receptions were held in the first-floor State Rooms, as they
had been since the Prime Ministerial living space had moved upstairs
under Neville Chamberlain and become self-contained under Attlee.
At these receptions, Wilson's Press Secretary Joe Haines recalled,
'Philistines regularly grind their cigarette butts under their heels on
the Persian carpet without any apparent lasting effect.'[12] John Major
would later host nearly 2,000 receptions for British and overseas visitors during his premiership, not far short of an average of one a day.[13]

All around the world

Who comes to No. 10, and how does the building shape their experience? Visitors have ranged from Benito Mussolini, who visited in December 1922 for a conference of European ministers, to Nelson Mandela in 1990.[14] Anthony Eden's premiership provides an excellent example of the range of visitors from around the globe that could be hosted at No. 10. As a former Foreign Secretary and widely acknowledged international statesman, Eden hosted dinner guests including US President Dwight Eisenhower; US Secretary of State Dulles; German Chancellor Konrad Adenauer; French Prime Minister Guy Mollet; King Hussein of Jordan; King Feisal II of Iraq and his Prime Minister Nuri al-Said; and Plaek Phibunsongkhram, the Prime Minister of Thailand – to name but a few.[15]

Gifts from leaders around the world remain at No. 10, a reminder of the building's long and international history. A large wooden globe, so large that it had to be cut in half to enter the building, where it was reassembled, sits at the bottom of the Grand Staircase. This gift from

Clement Attlee and his Foreign Secretary Ernest Bevin meet
French Prime Minister René Pleven and French Foreign
Minister Robert Schuman at No. 10 in 1950.

French President François Mitterrand to Prime Minister Margaret Thatcher has remained in the same location ever since, perhaps due to the physical challenge of moving it. This is despite the Falkland Islands being subtly labelled 'Islas Malvinas', the Spanish name for the islands used by the Argentinians.

Small segments of moon rock were mounted and presented to Wilson by US President Richard Nixon, following the Apollo 11 mission in 1969. These have been displayed again recently, following some time languishing in a cupboard upstairs for several years; it appears that no one knew what else to do with them.[16] The clash between eminent figures and mundane concerns is normal at Downing Street, due to its dual purposes; former Principal Private Secretary Robin Butler recalled being forced to stop storing his bicycle downstairs at No. 10 after Indian Prime Minister Indira Gandhi snagged her sari on its pedal.[17]

No. 10 speaks

Different Prime Ministers have used No. 10 to send a message to their international guests in ways that reflect their individual personalities and political styles. Contrasting the approaches of Attlee and Thatcher, the two great 'weather-maker' Prime Ministers of the postwar era, helps to illustrate this point.

Attlee would generally host dinners in the State Dining Room, on the rare occasions that he did entertain foreign guests. Visits from the French and the Danish were given particular consideration, as the former Prime Minister told the historian R. J. Minney:

> When we were entertaining members of the French Government I had to pause and think for a moment. "No, don't sit there, take this chair," I said, for I felt it would be embarrassing for them to face the portrait of either Wellington or Nelson. With the Danes only Nelson was involved because he had bombarded Copenhagen. But they smiled as I placed them with their backs to the picture, and one of them said: "We don't mind. It happened a long time ago." When we entertained the Russians it was so much easier. I told them to

sit anywhere they liked as they were not likely to find a Crimean General in that room.[18]

Attention to these seemingly trivial details could help to set the tone for meetings, sending a message to the Prime Minister's international counterparts from the outset. Attlee's story may be lighthearted, but it demonstrates how No. 10 as a building can be used to project an atmosphere of friendly cooperation, or to create unease or even offence.

The portrait of the Duke of Wellington referred to by Attlee continued to intrude on international politics from Downing Street long after Attlee's premiership. Robert Armstrong recalled how Wellington's image interjected itself into diplomacy some years later, during his time as Cabinet Secretary:

> In the State Dining Room, when Heath and Wilson were there, there were copies of portraits of the Duke of Wellington and Lord Nelson, but they were only copies and Thatcher wanted originals. She kicked them out and got two eighteenth-century portraits in instead. I took the Duke of Wellington into my room in the Cabinet Office. I always had a great admiration for the Duke. When we were negotiating an Anglo-Irish agreement in the 1980s, I used to have meetings with our Irish counterpart in that room. One day, when the meeting had gone well – he and I became very good friends – I pointed up at the picture and said, "You see, I have an Irishman hanging on my wall." Of course, the Duke of Wellington was born in Dublin. And [Secretary to the Irish Government] Dermot Nally looked up at the picture and said, "Not everything that is born in a stable is a horse."[19]

Thatcher decided that No. 10 should send a different message to the world than Attlee had once intended. Her memoirs reveal a stauncher approach to the impact of No. 10's decoration on her guests:

> I felt strongly that when foreign visitors came to Downing Street they should see something of Britain's cultural heritage [...] On my foreign visits I quickly found that many of our embassies had superb works of art which added greatly to the impression people had of

Britain. I wanted foreign visitors to be similarly impressed. [...] I also had some fine portraits hung of the nation's heroes; through them you could feel the continuity of British history. I recall on one occasion watching President [Valéry] Giscard d'Estaing gazing at two portraits in the dining room – one of the young Nelson and the other of Wellington. He remarked on the irony. I replied that it was no less ironic that I should have to look at portraits of Napoleon on my visits to Paris. In retrospect, I can see that this was not quite a parallel. Napoleon lost.[20]

That Thatcher took a more confrontational stance should not be surprising, but the comparison demonstrates how Prime Ministers can use the decoration of No. 10 to project their personalities in the presence of guests.

On other occasions, the relative lack of pretension and grandeur provided by No. 10 could put guests at ease and make for more informal meetings. However, Charles Powell (Lord Powell of Bayswater), close aide to Thatcher, recalled how the welcoming atmosphere did not necessarily prevent the Prime Minister from being somewhat hostile:

Because No. 10 has this air, of something of a private house, it was actually rather a good place to have meetings and it doesn't have the stuffy formality of the Élysée Palace in Paris or even the White House. It's much more a place where you sit on sofas and armchairs and therefore the nature of the discussion can be more relaxed and more informal, and therefore very often more productive. An extraordinary range of people did come through, some of them rather unusual. I remember the Foreign [and Commonwealth] Office insisted on her seeing the president of the then French Congo, a notorious Marxist. I advised very strongly against this, I said I didn't think this would be a meeting of minds but, "Oh we're so pleased that we persuaded her to come here," and I said, "Well, I don't think this is going to work out but we'll try." He arrived with his interpreter and sat down on the sofa obviously at Margaret Thatcher, who remarks, "I hate communists." The African interpreter to his great credit, related this in French to the president as, "Madam the prime minister says that on the whole, in her long experience of politics, [she] has found that she rarely agrees with the doctrines of Karl Marx." And I thought the interpreter probably saved his life but he certainly deserved a medal![21]

No. 10 was not always such a confrontational place. In fact, the building has played a powerful diplomatic role in the past. The symbolism of an invite to Downing Street can be a powerful asset. Edward Heath's memoirs reveal the impact that the building had during the tripartite negotiations leading up to the 1973 Sunningdale Agreement. Heath used No. 10 for a 'change of scene' when the talks became difficult, claiming that it 'was soon evident that No. 10 had never hosted such a gathering before'.[22] Following a successful dinner, all involved sung Irish songs together late into the night. Heath recalled John Hume, representative of the Social Democratic and Labour Party at the meeting, telling the Prime Minister:

> We never expected to be inside Number 10. The last time we came here, we were lying on the pavement opposite in a protest demonstration and no one as much as offered us a cup of tea. What's more, it rained all night so we packed it in first thing in the morning.

Heath believed – at least at the time – that the trip to No. 10 played a part in ensuring that the Irish and Northern Irish alike departed with spirits lifted, and feeling more inclined to engage constructively with Britain.[23]

No. 10 is an enduring, stoic constant in the nation's history. It has seen war and conflict, the rise and fall of the British Empire, the Troubles and the peace process. Twenty years after the Sunningdale negotiations, No. 10 would play a central role in another key moment in the Northern Ireland peace process, lending its name to the Downing Street Declaration, announced at No. 10 by Major and the Irish Taoiseach Albert Reynolds on 15 December 1993. Years later, former Cabinet Secretary Richard Wilson observed a seemingly ordinary scene demonstrating how radically the situation had transformed:

> I was talking to my Private Secretary in the room outside just in the Cabinet Office and looking out in the garden of Number Ten, and

Mr. Blair's children were playing skateboarding. They had a plank on a barrel and they were going up the plank and it would tip and go down the other side. And there was [the Sinn Féin leaders] Gerry Adams and Martin McGuinness watching them and then Gerry Adams saying, "Let me have a go," and actually falling quite badly.[24]

Wilson described an amusing scene, but one that is loaded with incredible historical and political significance. This juxtaposition of the everyday and the remarkable is typical of No. 10, a humble and relatively ordinary house that has been at the heart of the most extraordinary events in British history.

Reflecting the Prime Minister

Prime Ministers have long used the decoration of No. 10 to reflect and project their personalities in different ways. The tradition of decorating the building with great works of art began with the building's first occupant, Robert Walpole, whose private collection included impressive works by Nicolas Poussin and Carlo Maratti. However, it was Labour Prime Minister Ramsay MacDonald, who did not have his own private collection of expensive paintings when he arrived at Downing Street, who introduced the tradition of No. 10 borrowing works of art from the National Gallery. Now about half of the art in No. 10 belongs to the Government Art Collection, which is used to decorate government buildings across the UK and British embassies around the globe.[25] Today, the art displayed in No. 10 is chosen by committee, with No. 10 staff both political and non-political playing a role in picking what is displayed. However, although the Prime Minister is not *primus inter pares* in the official decision-making process of the Government Art Collection, a premier's extreme disliking of a particular piece could still see it disappear to another location and be replaced with something more to their taste. The BBC's Jones, interviewing Thatcher as Prime Minister, commented that it must be delightful to view and choose works of art from one of the most impressive collections in the country. Thatcher replied, 'Oh, they will not let me have the best [...] They hide it when you go round!'[26] Nevertheless, as previously mentioned, Thatcher was still able to emphasise the tone of her premiership in the minds of guests and visitors through her choice of art. Equally, when her successor, Major, entered No. 10, small changes in decoration, bringing in more modern art, helped to change the tone of the building to reflect the new regime.[27]

More lasting changes

On occasion, more substantial renovation and redecoration give the sitting Prime Minister and their family scope to shape No. 10 in a more lasting way. However, a free rein is rarely provided, and circumstances often constrain the premier's ability to truly transform the historic building. The Edens, arriving at No. 10 already well familiarised with the building, provide a particularly relevant example of how this can play out. Clarissa Eden entered No. 10 with a vision of restoring its historic glory. She even visited Houghton Hall, the country residence of the first Prime Minister, Walpole, to view the work of No. 10's early architect William Kent for inspiration.[28] Clarissa Eden described No. 10 as 'the nicest house in London [...] It was the nicest house you could possibly wish to live in'. Yet she believed it could be even more splendid, and planned to restore the building's reception rooms back to the original Kent style, with the State Dining Room and Small Dining Room restored to the colours indicated in John Soane's original plans.[29] However, economic concerns were to lay waste to these plans. In April 1956, the Minister of Works wrote to Clarissa Eden to inform her that the planned refurbishments must be postponed due to budget cuts, but suggested, 'Perhaps in my capacity as Minister of Works I could take some of Harold [Macmillan, then Chancellor of the Exchequer]'s premium bonds, and if lucky devote the proceeds to buying furniture: thus saving and spending at the same time!'[30]

This sort of work may have had a more lasting effect on the appearance of No. 10 than the mere placement of portraits and other works of art. As we have seen in Chapter 5, the Macmillans had a rare opportunity to seriously influence the reconstruction of Downing Street, with long-term implications for the building's look, feel and functionality. However, Macmillan's approach was relatively conservative, and the bulk of the 'new' No. 10 constructed in the early 1960s was altered very little.

Edward Heath

It would be left to later Conservative Prime Ministers to truly redesign the place. Heath, Prime Minister from 1970 to 1974, began a process of making No. 10 a more attractive residence. Heath described No. 10 as 'a splendid house with great traditions', but thought it 'dowdy and seedy'.[31] Whilst visitors tended to like the 'intimacy' of the place, Heath felt that it was 'necessary to get away from the old shoddy things and really have lovely things at No. 10'.[32] The Prime Minister had the State Rooms lightened up and renovated, had the Entrance Hall and Grand Staircase refreshed, brought his piano into the White Room (as William Gladstone had done in the nineteenth century) and 'borrowed treasure from friends' to make No. 10 more attractive – or, rather, more attractive to the Prime Minister's own eye; as Heath's memoirs reveal, his alterations were not universally popular:

Edward Heath's piano arrives at No. 10, 2 July 1970.

Once all the work was complete, I held a dinner party in celebration. Harold and Mary Wilson came and, although Mary took great interest in all of my innovations, she made it clear at once that, if Harold ever became Prime Minister again, she would get rid of the whole lot – and bring back her own decorations, including the copies of paintings, and her celebrated enamel swans alongside the main fireplace.[33]

Mary Wilson was already familiar with undoing the decorative decisions of previous occupants of No. 10, having originally arrived to discover that the portraits of past Prime Ministers that traditionally line the Grand Staircase had been moved into a corridor by Dorothy Macmillan.[34] They were immediately moved back.

Heath's changes were substantial. Returning to No. 10 in 1974, Marcia Falkender (formerly Marcia Williams) observed that 'Every part of the building seemed to have been redecorated, with the exception of only my room – in Heath's day Douglas Hurd's room – on the ground floor, which did not appear to be touched.'[35] The colour scheme of the other rooms around the Cabinet Room, and even the room itself, had been radically altered, and generally lightened, to suit Heath's personal tastes. To Falkender, 'it all felt elegant and co-ordinated, but I felt a touch of nostalgia for those dark and serious colours, shabby though the room had become, that seemed to underline the weightiness of office'.[36]

If these redecorations seem relatively trivial, reflecting only the Prime Minister's personal tastes, perhaps slightly more could be read into the choice of art that Heath selected to adorn the walls of No. 10. Arguably the most Europhile Prime Minister of the postwar era, Heath 'ruffled some patriotic feathers' by bringing into No. 10 French paintings from the National Gallery and two Renoirs on loan from a private collector, in place of the portraits of English statesmen that preceded them.[37] Falkender certainly perceived the Prime Minister's decorative preferences as representing 'another facet of Heath's pro-French, pro–Common Market policy', and Wilson subsequently ensured that they were replaced with paintings of the Duke of Wellington and the Whig politician Charles James Fox.[38]

Margaret Thatcher

Thatcher shared Heath's enthusiasm for lightening up No. 10's décor, even if the two Prime Ministers had little else in common aside from their political party and their relatively humble backgrounds. Attempts to lighten the dingy building, whose relatively small windows allow little natural light in, have been made throughout history. Yet Thatcher was not afforded the opportunity of a building redesign. The Prime Minister changed the colour of the carpets, replaced and lightened the wallpaper in the Study at her own expense and removed dark baize from downstairs doors and throughout No. 10, in what the BBC's Christopher Jones described as an 'anti-baize campaign'.[39]

Thatcher paid great attention to the building's appearance, ordering a revamp of the Cabinet Anteroom shortly before arrival. She stated in her memoirs, 'There might be some difficult times to come in the Cabinet Room itself, but there was no reason why people should be made to feel miserable while they were waiting to go in.'[40] The Prime Minister also had a strong magpie tendency, regularly relocating to No. 10 any furniture and works of art from other government buildings that took her fancy.[41] The Prime Minister's tendency to acquire desirable decorations was primarily a consequence of her view that No. 10 should reflect the status of the office it housed, as close ally Cecil Parkinson recalled:

> She was very proud of No. 10, and she really wanted to make it an elegant place as well as a working place. So she loved the history of the house, and the idea that she could perfect it, and beautify it, and improve it. [...] It was her home upstairs, but downstairs it was the home of the Prime Minister of the United Kingdom, and she wanted people to see it at its best.[42]

Thatcher specifically brought British works of art into No. 10, including a Henry Moore statue that remains in the corridor leading from the Entrance Hall to the Cabinet Room to this day. The sculpture joined several Turners and a painting by Churchill in the White Room upstairs. Portraits of historic British actors including Ellen Terry, David Garrick and Sarah Siddons surrounded the Moore sculpture

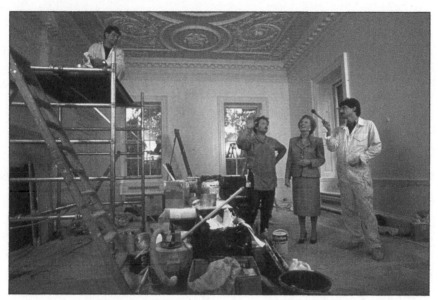

Margaret Thatcher chats with workers renovating the White Room, 1989.

during Thatcher's premiership, in one of several locations in No. 10 dedicated to displaying the historic 'best of British' in different arenas.[43] Upstairs, the Small Dining Room was decorated with portraits of significant British scientists including Joseph Priestley, Humphry Davy and Edmond Halley, alongside a bust of Isaac Newton.[44]

If this British theme to the decoration of No. 10 was intended to inspire and celebrate historic achievements by Brits throughout history, Thatcher's deliberate featuring of military leaders added a less subtle reminder of the nation's historic might. In her own words, the Prime Minister chose portraits of Lord Nelson (a personal hero) and the Duke of Wellington to 'get more strength into the whole place'.[45] Thatcher was at No. 10 for longer than any Prime Minister in this period, and her approach to decorating and adapting the house provides a perfect example of the interaction between building and occupant. The Prime Minister came to feel deep affection for the building and its place in Britain's long story. She said, 'This place seeps into your blood [...] It becomes part of your life. It is, above all, a home – and it is a house of history.'[46]

Quinlan Terry and the State Rooms

Thatcher's greatest legacy at No. 10 can be seen in the first-floor State Rooms, used primarily for hosting and entertaining, which line up in a row alongside the Study. In 1988–9, with the rooms requiring a periodic redecoration, the architect Quinlan Terry – a former mentee of Raymond Erith – was summoned to lead the work. The subsequent redecoration rapidly escalated into a complete revamp, as Terry, with the Prime Minister's encouragement, sought to return the rooms to the former glory of the Kent era. Unlike Erith, however, Terry was no stickler for tradition, and was more than willing to indulge Thatcher's grander tastes. For Terry, perhaps unlike his predecessor, 'Classicism is a living language [...] It has to adapt to changing times.'[47] As a result, ornate plasterwork and gold leaf now adorn the previously plain ceilings, giving the rooms an almost regal feel. In the White Room, the ceilings feature an intricate design. In the Terracotta Room, beneath a similarly impressive ceiling, a small sculpted character resides over the door leading to the Pillared Room. On closer inspection, the figure can be seen to be carrying reeds in a bag on its back, whilst climbing onto a roof. It is said that the Prime Minister asked Terry to incorporate this detail, so that there would always be a 'thatcher' in No. 10.

The renovation of the State Rooms saw a clash between conservatism and radicalism that has recurred throughout No. 10's history. For Thatcher, and by extension for Terry, No. 10's appearance should reflect the power of the office and the history of a great empire, as the architect told the historian Anthony Seldon:

> I was not, in truth, very interested in historical precedent. I was interested in doing something that was architecturally fairly lively – especially because so much of Downing Street was rightfully restrained. She [Thatcher] thought the rooms were boring. The best of the three was the Pillared Room, and she wanted the rooms to be more imposing. She wanted pictures of achievers, like Nelson, Wellington, and she felt that, after the Falklands War, the time had come to do something mildly triumphalist and confident.[48]

However, No. 10's senior civil servants were naturally more cautious

John Major enjoys himself in the impressive State Dining Room, 1993.

about appearing too triumphalist, as Thatcher's former Principal Private Secretary recalled:

> Up until that point, everything had been plain white. [...] I had an argument with the architect, Quinlan Terry, who said, "Much more gold! There would have been much more gold in William Kent's design." And I had a row with him. "Look, any more gold than what you are putting in now would be really quite over the top. Although it would be historically accurate, people would think of it as delusions of grandeur." [...] If you are Prime Minister, and at one moment it is white and austere, and the next there is loads of gold, people will think, 'Who does this person think she is?'[49]

This clash between visions touches on a recurring debate around No. 10. To some, its relative ordinariness is an asset, a particularly British reminder that the Prime Minister is not a president, nor the sovereign, but rather *primus inter pares*. To others, No. 10 is a building of incredible history, and should project a power commensurate to that of the role that it houses.

No. 10 is ultimately a balancing act between these two elements. The State Dining Room, probably the grandest room in the house, is dark, is not exceptionally large, can be cramped at formal dinners and is nowhere near as ornately decorated as the Foreign and Commonwealth Office's Locarno Suite, for example. No. 10 is not a palace, and its power, like that of the British Prime Minister, is subtle, not ostentatious. The building's most famous feature remains its most ordinary: its iconic front door. So powerful is the draw of this extraordinarily unspectacular feature that No. 10's switchboard operators, forced to temporarily relocate to the Cabinet Office during renovations following the IRA mortar attack of February 1991, still elected to enter by No. 10's front door every day, transferring to the other building internally.[50] No. 10 has a power and a symbolism that runs much deeper than its physical appearance.

8

No. 10 Under Attack

The premiership: a risky business

The security of No. 10 Downing Street has been a concern since before it was home to the British Prime Minister. In 1654, Oliver Cromwell moved from the 'house at the back' to the Palace of Whitehall, where he was reported to have changed bedroom every night for fear of assassination.[1] A century later, the unpopular premiership of John Stuart (the Earl of Bute) saw the Prime Minister mobbed in Cheapside and burned in effigy, subsequently becoming 'the only Prime Minister who has ever marched along Downing Street surrounded by a body-guard of prize-fighters', venturing outside in disguise to avoid attack.[2]

The Gordon Riots of June 1780, led by the Protestant George Gordon against Prime Minister Lord North, who had made concessions to Catholics, saw a huge mob march on Downing Street whilst North was entertaining friends at dinner. Around twenty Grenadier Guards were stationed on the roof, standing by ready to fire on the masses. North sent messengers to warn the crowds outside No. 10 of their presence, which proved an adequate deterrent, and the masses dispersed. North subsequently returned to his meal, before retiring to the top of No. 10, where he noticed fires across London. The 'dispersed' mob had simply gone elsewhere, and days of rioting followed.[3]

The extent to which eighteenth- and nineteenth-century Prime Ministers were exposed to risk and potential harm seems shocking today. William Pitt the Younger's premiership, for example, saw No. 10 'besieged and several windows broken' by crowds protesting over the high cost of food. The Prime Minister wrote to his mother downplaying the seriousness of the protests.[4] In fact, so lax was security that

Pitt was able to pop out of No. 10 for a duel on Putney Heath on 27 May 1798, leaving his last will and testament at Downing Street. Two shots were fired, both missed, and Pitt returned to central London for dinner.[5] In 1829, the Duke of Wellington also engaged in and survived a pistol duel, this time on Battersea Fields.

Prime Minister Spencer Perceval was not so fortunate, receiving no prior warning of his being shot at when he was assassinated at the House of Commons on 11 May 1812 by John Bellingham. Bellingham had been imprisoned in Russia for five years due to an alleged debt, and felt that he had not received adequate assistance from the British Ambassador, nor a satisfactory response to his petitions to the Prime Minister calling for compensation.[6] Similarly, in 1843 Robert Peel's Private Secretary Edward Drummond was fatally shot whilst attempting to enter No. 10, in a case of mistaken identity.[7]

During Benjamin Disraeli's nineteenth-century premierships, the Conservative activist Edward Tracy Turnerelli regularly turned up on the doorstep of No. 10, asking to meet the Prime Minister. Turnerelli had organised the production of a gold laurel wreath, funded by contributions from 52,000 'working men' around the country, and wanted to place the wreath on Disraeli's head. The Prime Minister repeatedly turned him away, however, and Turnerelli had to make do with a handshake when he happened upon Disraeli on Bond Street.[8] Despite repeated incidents of violence, it appears little improvement in security had been made over the years.

Modern era

Both Herbert Henry Asquith and David Lloyd George were thought to be the targets of failed assassination plots by suffragettes. Winston Churchill, apart from being repeatedly bombed, was allegedly targeted by the Nazis with an exploding chocolate bar. Alec Douglas-Home was the victim of a kidnap plot whilst at his country home in Scotland, but managed to talk his kidnappers – a group of left-wing students – out of their plot after providing them with beer.[9]

The informality of life at Downing Street brought a certain vulnerability to espionage, particularly in the first few postwar decades.

This was highlighted one night in May 1964 when the butler of Reginald Maudling, the Chancellor of the Exchequer, brought back to No. 11 two women that he had met at the nearby Sherlock Holmes pub, known to be frequented by Russian intelligence officials.[10] The women were subsequently investigated by Special Branch, and found to be air hostesses from Ealing, with no foul play by them or the butler suspected.[11] However, given the alarming ease with which the women had gained access to the building, and with it the opportunity to install eavesdropping equipment or indulge in countless other nefarious activities, it was decided that the interconnecting doors between No. 11 and No. 10 on every level should be firmly locked each night.

This solution was far from foolproof. Principal Private Secretary Tim Bligh confessed in a private note that 'it is not really possible or feasible to make No. 10 security tight at night from a determined attempt by an intruder who has gained access to No. 11'.[12] And whilst the front doors to both buildings were well guarded, Downing Street itself remained accessible to the public (except in exceptional circumstances) until the late 1980s, and the building's windows were frequently shattered by bottles and cans thrown by protesters as late as the 1960s.[13] Security gates preventing unchecked access to Downing Street were only installed semi-permanently at the end of the 1980s.

It wasn't always bad news, however: on one occasion during the premiership of Alec Douglas-Home, a group of Sea Scouts knocked on the door of No. 10, seeking the Prime Minister's autograph as part of an initiative test. The Prime Minister invited them in for lunch, offering a tour of the Cabinet Room to boot.[14] But not all Prime Ministers have been entirely at ease with the lack of privacy and, to some extent, security at No. 10.

Harold Wilson and No. 10

No. 10 may not have provided complete security, but at least it was a known entity. As Harold Wilson did not want to live at No. 10 during his second premiership, electing instead to remain at his private property at No. 5 Lord North Street, a security inspection was required there by the Metropolitan Police. (Grange Farm, a Buckinghamshire property owned and also used by the Wilsons, also posed an ongoing security challenge, despite being used infrequently.)[15]

A report of 7 March 1974 found that No. 5 Lord North Street's back garden was easily entered, the front of the house was susceptible to 'missile attack by pedestrians' and the roof was accessible from neighbouring buildings, with its chimney flumes acting as potential 'entries for explosive and or incendiary devices'. Ultimately, 'whilst the security can be improved [additional security measures] will not deter or prevent political extremists carrying out bomb attacks or other similar outrages'. The property was deemed 'extremely vulnerable to attack in the light of present day experiences'.[16] The Wilsons, who had lived there since 1970, were unperturbed, and remained at the house throughout Wilson's second short spell as Prime Minister – albeit with around £8,000 worth of increased security measures installed.[17] Perhaps it was during the installation of these that the Prime Minister believed that the house was first bugged by the security services – a belief that increasingly concerned him at both No. 5 and No. 10 until the end of his premiership.[18]

According to Wilson's biographer Ben Pimlott, Wilson first arrived at No. 10 in 1964 regarding the security services as 'a valuable tool'.[19] However, over time the Prime Minister came to distrust them immensely, becoming increasingly paranoid and later telling a BBC journalist that 'MI5 contained a group of right-wing officers who'd been plotting against the Labour Government, and in particular against him as Prime Minister'.[20] The Prime Minister was convinced that No. 10 was bugged by MI5, and when staying away from Downing Street he was said to have turned on the taps in hotel bathrooms before whispering to guests, gesturing up at the light fixtures to indicate that they may be monitoring the conversation.

Even the BBC was under suspicion in Wilson's No. 10, albeit by the building's civil servants rather than the Prime Minister himself. One of Principal Private Secretary Derek Mitchell's primary concerns about letting the BBC into the Cabinet Room to film an interview with Wilson was that the presence of their technicians may 'constitute a security risk because of the opportunity to "bug" the room [...] the visitors we normally receive may not have the same expertise in bugging the room, or, possibly, the same motive'.[21]

Temporary gates block the entrance to Downing Street, 1980s.

To this day, it is unclear whether Wilson was right that No. 10 contained listening devices. There is some evidence to suggest that Harold Macmillan had the Cabinet Room, Study and Waiting Room bugged on his return to No. 10 in 1963, and that the devices were not removed until 1977, with Prime Ministers potentially unaware of their existence.[22] What is more apparent is that MI5 kept a file on Wilson, unlike other Prime Ministers, ever since he became an MP in 1945, due to their suspicions that he may have had communist links.[23] Wilson's paranoia during his second premiership, whether justified or not, cannot have made life at No. 10 easy – even when the Prime Minister elected to actually live elsewhere.

In November 1975, Wilson approved the installation of bulletproof glass in the No. 10 Study, in response to a concern that 'when the study lights are on the Prime Minister can be readily seen and could be a target for a terrorist from St. James's Park'.[24] Whilst Wilson was never a specific target for Irish terrorism, a threat assessment produced by Special Branch on his retirement demonstrates just how paranoia-inducing life for even a former Prime Minister can be. Acknowledging that 'Mr. Wilson appears never to have generated animosity among the Irish in quite the same way that Mr. Edward Heath has done despite the bi-partisan policy followed by succeeding Governments', the report also cautioned that 'it was not until Mr. Heath relinquished office that two determined attacks were made on him (Mr. Heath), both being directed against his private residence'. The risk of Wilson being targeted was expected to decrease over time, and assessed as 'at least as great but certainly no greater than the general threat to other prominent British politicians who have not (i) been named in target lists or (ii) suffered attack'.[25] But the brutal reality of this evaluation of a relatively 'safe' Prime Minister demonstrates the extent to which those leaving Downing Street for the last time must be aware that life will never be the same again.

A closed shop?

Downing Street remains technically a public right of way today, but large security gates block entry to all but invited guests, with the police using common-law powers to prevent a breach of the peace. However, whilst the street has been effectively closed to the public since the end of 1989, entry had already been forbidden or restricted intermittently at several points in history, at times of heightened tensions.

In the early 1920s, large wooden barricades 'ten feet high' were erected at the end of Downing Street as a response to the conflict in Ireland, 'for fear of reprisals against the Prime Minister'.[26] The street was temporarily blocked off again during the Suez crisis, with the security risk this time coming from protests against British actions in Egypt.[27] Protesters were kept away from No. 10, but a noisy rally at Trafalgar Square, featuring speakers including Aneurin Bevan, could be heard from the Cabinet Room.[28] The Metropolitan Police discussed the acquisition of new temporary barriers to block entry to Downing Street 'when necessary' in April 1974, with sockets drilled into the road in May.[29] A temporary barrier was erected from 1981, and access to Downing Street for the general public was effectively ended following the Brighton hotel bombing of October 1984.[30] But the installation of permanent, yet demountable (removable), gates still brought great controversy.

In December 1985, an intruder on the roof at Downing Street prompted a security review by Home Secretary Douglas Hurd.[31] The invader turned out to be a twenty-five-year-old Australian lawyer named Marcus Morgan, who had climbed a nearby drainpipe before gaining access to No. 10's roof. Whilst harm to No. 10 or its occupants was neither intended nor caused, as a 'senior minister' told *The Times*, 'The man should not have been able to get anywhere near No. 10. He penetrated the citadel.'[32] A series of electronic sensors were installed along buildings and open ground around Downing Street and its immediate surroundings in response to the invasion – 'further proof that the days when sightseers could pose for photographs on the steps of No. 10 are now past'.[33] Given the increasing threat of terrorism, and following an attempt on the Prime Minister's life in Brighton, it was clear that keeping Downing Street open to the public was no longer a viable option. Plans for permanent gates were considered by Westminster City Council's planning committee in September 1989. Aesthetic considerations were as challenging as security issues, with the design drawing criticism from English Heritage, the Royal Fine Art Commission, the Westminster Society and the Georgian Group, who felt that the gates were 'too high, heavy and monumental and too obtrusive in Whitehall'.[34] Former Thatcher Cabinet Minister and chairman of the Royal Fine Art Commission Norman St John-Stevas (Lord St John of Fawsley) also objected to the gates on principle:

> The Prime Minister is not the head of state and to treat her as though she were would arouse public criticism and hostility. Railings and gates which have to be opened and shut will merely attract attention to the Prime Minister's movements and increase the security risk.[35]

The Royal Fine Art Commission went on to claim that the gates would 'make the street into a prison'. Westminster City Council also objected to the closure of the street, which it declared 'most regrettable, particularly as historically, the street has been regarded for almost 200 years as a typical London street which happens to contain the residence of the Prime Minister and, except for very limited periods, has been open to free public access'.[36]

Whilst security issues made the erection of gates an inevitability, the idea that No. 10 was 'a typical London street', with the Prime Minister's presence an interesting but almost incidental quirk, is an enduring and powerful concept. As the *Independent* insisted, 'Number Ten Downing Street is not Buckingham Palace. Nor is it the Forbidden City or the Kremlin.' The steel 'shield' that was built into the road, capable of blocking oncoming vehicles when raised, was tolerated, but it was widely felt that the apparently permanent security gates blocking entry to Downing Street would change the nature of the Prime Minister's world-famous residence in a fundamental way.[37]

The *Daily Express* dubbed the gates, which were installed over the Christmas holidays at the end of 1989, 'Mrs. Thatcher's Iron Curtain'.[38] In a 2011 documentary, broadcaster Michael Cockerell claimed that the gates meant that 'the risk of a Prime Minister developing a bunker mentality increased'.[39] The Leader of the Opposition Neil Kinnock publicly asserted that, if he were to become Prime Minister, he would make the removal of the gates one of his first priorities. Kinnock claimed they had 'helped cut off Margaret Thatcher from the real world', and symbolised 'the style of the government'. Pledging to reopen access to Downing Street to all, Kinnock said that the removal of the security measures 'will only be a symbol but an important one that we have ended government with gates'.[40] The cost of their installation was not revealed, in keeping with precedent regarding security measures, but at least one MP delighted in branding the associated controversy 'Thatchergate'.[41]

In January 1990, Tony Banks MP asked the Department of the Environment if 'public right of way through Downing Street had been extinguished' by the installation of the security gates. Responding on behalf of the government, Parliamentary Under-Secretary Christopher Chope responded, 'Access to Downing Street is controlled under police common law powers which allow them to take reasonable steps to preserve the peace and prevent threats to it.'[42] It is certainly a curious situation that Downing Street remained a public right of way, albeit one with restricted access on common-law grounds. Compared to any equivalent home and office of a world leader, Downing Street's gates seem an incredibly subtle form of security, with the building still visible from Whitehall and protests regularly held just across the road. But such is the peculiar history of No. 10, and its accidental evolution

A walk down Downing Street, 1925. Many features
remain the same today, but much has changed.

from cheap terraced house to one of the most powerful buildings
in the world, that even this small measure seemed somehow almost
unconstitutional.

Alex Allan, who served as Principal Private Secretary to John Major
and Tony Blair, recalls the arrival of the latter Prime Minister bringing

about another 'big push to take the gates down [...] The whole team, I think, were quite keen. It was symbolism, I think'.[43] However, security sensibly trumped symbolism. A debate in the House of Lords in 1998 saw the possibility of the gates' removal discussed, but they were ultimately still deemed 'the most efficient and cost-effective means of controlling access', with one peer going as far as to say that the gates 'add considerable distinction to what is otherwise a slightly dingy little street'. This was not a popular viewpoint, either on aesthetic grounds or on principle, but the gates stayed put regardless.[44] When we consider the history of No. 10 under attack, however, it is remarkable that they were not installed sooner.

Under fire

No. 10 is a remarkable survivor. The First World War saw bombs dropped by Zeppelins falling 'alarming near' the building.[45] The Second World War saw a concrete-and-steel reinforced air raid shelter constructed in the basement of No. 10, protruding under the adjacent Old Treasury building (now home to the Cabinet Office).[46] The bombing of Whitehall and Westminster, like that across much of London, was heavy and destructive. Forced to relocate (at least most of the time) to the No. 10 Annexe underneath the nearby Government Offices Great George Street, Churchill's Private Secretary John 'Jock' Colville wrote privately that he felt 'sad to leave the old building, especially as I fear it will not survive the Battle of London'.[47] In the event, No. 10 did not suffer the direct hit that it would have been highly unlikely to survive. A series of near misses left the building with impressive and expensive battle scars, but ultimately – like London itself – it survived.

In September 1940, No. 10 was the victim of friendly fire when a British anti-aircraft shell exploded on Horse Guards Parade, damaging roof tiles and windows, with a trailing barrage balloon cable causing further damage less than a week later. The enemy also did some damage in late 1940 when bombs were dropped nearby, including on Treasury Green, which runs adjacent to No. 10, separating it and the Cabinet Office building. The Treasury Green bomb caused a great deal of internal damage, as did the three bombs that fell close

by on 20 February 1944.[48] Photographs of the damage were not published during the war, due to the propaganda value they were thought
to hold for Britain's enemies.[49] But by the end of the war, as the historian R. J. Minney noted, 'The woodwork of the windows was studded
with shrapnel. There were cracks in almost every wall and in many
places portions of the ceiling had come down and lay in dusty debris
on the carpets.'[50]

No. 10 was also seriously vulnerable to fire in its dilapidated postwar
state, but also throughout most of its existence. Fire destroyed most of
No. 12 Downing Street in 1879, leaving it half the height of the rest of
the terrace. The historic building was rendered an increasingly severe
fire risk by its cheap construction and the limited and piecemeal renovation works that had been undertaken since. Whilst Clement Attlee
had banned smoking in the Cabinet Room, the rest of the house
remained vulnerable to stray cigarettes, as one former Principal Private
Secretary recalled:

I was going upstairs with some papers for the Prime Minister and I
was going up the stairs – to get the exercise – and past the door of
the study late in the evening and there was a little plume of smoke
coming from underneath the door. I didn't like the look of that. I
opened the door and went in. I found that a cigarette end had been
dropped on the floor. The floor was up and there was just workmen's
boarding there and the cigarette had not been put out properly,
had smouldered its way through the wood on the floor onto the
joist underneath and was smouldering there. So I put it out pretty
fast. But then I thought: "I'm no expert in fires. I probably ought
to make sure that somebody who is is satisfied that it is properly
extinguished." So I rang up the fire brigade. I asked them to send
round an inspector, in plain clothes, just for reassurance. Within
ten minutes – before the inspector got there – my telephone rang
and it was the *Daily Express*. "We understand that there is a fire in
Number Ten..."[51]

The Raymond Erith reconstructions of the early 1960s made No. 10
less vulnerable to fire and to the sudden, unexpected collapse of the
building's walls and floors, and the installation of security gates in

1989 shut Downing Street off, keeping would-be assailants at distance. But then, in 1991, No. 10 came under attack once more.

Mortar attack

On 7 February 1991, a meeting of Major's War Cabinet, which had gathered to discuss the Gulf War, was interrupted by an explosion. Robin Butler, then Cabinet Secretary, recalled the details:

> What I remember clearly [...] was what we were worried about was Iraq might launch a terrorist attack in London, and the last word I remember John Major uttering before the mortar bomb exploded was the word "bomb". And suddenly, there's this bomb. The room shakes, the windows shiver, shatter – not shatter, but crack. The French windows at the end of the Cabinet Room blow in and what I immediately supposed had happened was that this is a terrorist attack and people had come over the back wall and they were going to appear at the Cabinet Room windows spraying sub-machine guns at us. And so, I got under the table pretty quick, I found John Major was under the table beside me [...] After about ten minutes it was clear that there was no follow-up attack. [...] We went through the Cabinet Room to COBRA and resumed the meeting, and it wasn't for another twenty minutes, half an hour, that we were told what the nature of the attack had been.[52]

It later emerged that the IRA had launched three mortar shells at No. 10 from a parked van at the corner of Horse Guards Avenue and White-hall. Whilst two shells missed their target entirely, the third exploded in the garden of No. 10, missing the building itself by a relatively short distance and coming close to claiming the lives of the Cabinet, just seven years after the Brighton bomb.

The reaction within No. 10 to the entire incident was laced with studied British understatement. Once the initial furore had died down, with Cabinet Ministers and civil servants emerging from beneath the Cabinet table, Major initiated a relocation to the nearby Cabinet Office Briefing Room, where the meeting was resumed, with the Prime Minister saying, 'I think we'd better start again somewhere else.'[53] Major was subsequently forced to relocate to Admiralty House whilst works and repairs were undertaken at No. 10. Ultimately, despite the seriousness of this attack on No. 10, life resumed as normal. Speaking in the aftermath of the attack, Home Secretary Kenneth Baker told the House of Commons:

> We must take all reasonable security measures. That means continuing police efforts and public vigilance in support of them. But there is a limit to the sort of defensive measures that can be taken. In a democracy, people wish to be free to go about their business. To disrupt their lives any more than we need to would be a concession to terrorism.[54]

Once again, the relative ordinariness of life at No. 10 was highlighted. The Home Secretary's words could have applied to all of London at the height of the IRA's bombing campaign, and under subsequent terrorist threats since.

In some senses, much as the Queen Mother was said to have expressed that the bombing of Buckingham Palace during the Second World War allowed the royal family to 'look the East End in the eye',[55] the vulnerability of the relatively humble Downing Street houses has an important symbolic levelling quality. A balance between accessibility and safety must be struck at all times – but comparison to the sizeable security operation that travels alongside the US President, for example, makes the British Prime Minister look extremely humble.

Every living former Prime Minister, the incumbent and Her Majesty
the Queen attend an event to mark 250 years of No. 10 being the
official residence of the First Lord of the Treasury, 1985.

9

Concluding Thoughts

No. 10 Downing Street is larger than it first appears, but it remains a comparatively tiny and rather humble home for the British Prime Minister. The building's size has clearly had a constraining influence on the size of the staff that supports the premier, and serves as a reminder that the role is not a presidential one, but is much more collegiate. Harold Wilson claimed that any Prime Minister with delusions of presidentialism would find that 'his first visit to Washington should put paid to them'. In Wilson's view:

> The president [...] can hardly move for staff. [...] He is pressed on all sides for signatures, approvals, ratifications – I have seen presidents badgered to sign them in the lift, an action that must be a more or less automatic reflex. Contrast that with a *total* staff in No. 10, including private secretaries, garden room girls, the Honours and Church sections, telephone and communications operators, messengers and cleaners, of less than one hundred.[1]

In Wilson's view, the size and nature of the Prime Minister's Office therefore served as a reminder that 'British government is more cohesive, less fragmental, than a system with a single executive. The Cabinet is a force for unity'.[2]

Margaret Thatcher saw the comparatively tiny staff at No. 10 as 'an extraordinary achievement', requiring 'people of unusual qualities and commitment', particularly when compared with the larger resources available to the premier's German and US equivalents.[3] Charles Powell, who worked closely with the Prime Minister, claimed that No. 10's size brought 'great advantage':

There's no hierarchies, things don't have to wind their way up the bureaucracy or anything, if you wanted to know the Prime Minister's view you stuck your head round the door and said, you know, "Prime Minister, nuclear war or do we surrender?" You got a clear instruction and you could transmit it to the rest of Whitehall. There were no delays in No. 10, I think, in those days.[4]

External observers have suggested that the centre of the British system is 'too small to enable its leader properly to cover the waterfront of his responsibilities'.[5] It is clear that there are advantages and disadvantages to the size of the No. 10 operation, but it is also unquestionable that there has been a trend towards expansion, as the role itself has become increasingly varied and demanding over the years.

This could be interpreted as suggesting that No. 10 itself is under-sized and therefore under-resourced. However, the small size of No. 10's elite, flexible staff can also be a great strength for a Prime Minister, provided that they arrive with a clear vision of what they want to achieve, and are temperamentally suited to such an un-bureaucratic, direct and interpersonal working environment. Otherwise, the tiny building can prove a deadly pressure cooker, its small size leaving nowhere to hide. The building's Grand Staircase, lined with portraits displaying almost 300 years of fallen Prime Ministers, is a reminder that whilst No. 10 can provide the most impressive display cabinet for the best qualities of its occupants, it also has a powerful ability to expose the worst.

The building's incredible history is one of its greatest assets, but this comes at a cost. No. 10 does not lend itself to the provision of much open-plan office space, and there is no comfortable or easy space for its staff to socialise informally. New technologies have had to be awkwardly retrofitted into its creaking structure. The building has only acquired a small café in recent times, and finding space in one of its limited number of adapted 'meeting rooms' is a highly competitive process. There is no way of telling if a room is occupied – still, to this day, guides leading tours of the building must slowly crack open any closed doors, poking their heads around silently to check whether business is being conducted before entering.

This book is ultimately a work of history, and not of political science. It does not seek to argue for or against future change, only to observe the impact of No. 10 on the role of Prime Minister in the British system from 1945 to 1997. In this period, No. 10 has had a clear impact on those who have occupied it, and has proved remarkably resilient and broadly effective. Its influence on the role that it houses can be seen in its constraining effect on the number of political and non-political staff that support the Prime Minister, and in shaping access and influence for advisers. Its relatively humble nature reminds the Prime Minister that they are not a president, and provides some level of normality. Prime Ministers and their families have loved and hated aspects of life at No. 10, and premierships have been influenced by the ability of the occupant to live and work in a single, somewhat ramshackle, space.

Equally, No. 10 has in turn been shaped by its occupants. Prime Ministers have adapted the building, laid it out to suit their needs and decorated to project their personalities. Incremental, piecemeal change has led to a fascinating historical mess of a building, with only a few Prime Ministers managing to leave a lasting legacy on its material fabric. Still, due in no small part to the conservative nature of the reconstruction of Downing Street in the early 1960s, the presence of all great Prime Ministers and the powerful legacy of some of the biggest decisions in British history can still be felt at No. 10. Through the retention of the bulk of Downing Street's historic buildings, a sense of No. 10's past was preserved, and still has a powerful impact upon those who work within the building today. Wilson, who was Prime Minister for almost eight years over two separate terms, pondered the significance of the building's history in a 1975 interview with the BBC World Service, and said, 'I think that unless you have a sense of history, and of tradition, and of the people who have been there, you can't apply yourself to the problems of the present.'[6] Thatcher, No. 10's longest-serving twentieth-century resident, could keenly feel 250 years of great historical moments resonating throughout the building:

> It is a heritage which every Prime Minister guards with care and affection [...] the feeling of Britain's historic greatness which pervades every nook and cranny of this complicated and meandering old building.[7]

Whilst still 'complicated and meandering' today, despite numerous further adaptations, No. 10 Downing Street remains a house full of history, intrigue and power.

Image Credits

Notes

Introduction

1.   A. Turnbull, in: Mile End Group, 'Men of Secrets: The Cabinet Secretaries', 14/1/13, http://www.cabinetsecretaries.com, accessed 9/2/18.
2.   R. Armstrong, in: Institute for Government, '100 Years of the Cabinet Secretariat', 30/11/16, https://www. instituteforgovernment.org.uk/events/100-years-cabinet-secretaries-six-conversation, accessed 4/1/18.
3.   W. Churchill, 'House of Commons Rebuilding', *Hansard*, 28/10/43, vol 393, col 403, http://hansard.millbanksystems. com/commons/1943/oct/28/house-of-commons-rebuilding, accessed 7/6/16.
4.   House of Commons Information Office, 'Some Traditions and Customs of the House', August 2010, https://www.parliament. uk/documents/commons-information-office/g07.pdf, accessed 27/3/18.
5.   W. Churchill, 'House of Commons Rebuilding', *Hansard*, 28/10/43, vol 393, col 404, http://hansard.millbanksystems. com/commons/1943/oct/28/house-of-commons-rebuilding, accessed 7/6/16.
6.   Twitter correspondence with Richard Blyth, Head of Policy at the Royal Town Planning Institute, 16/12/16.
7.   D. Mitchell, 'Who'd want to be an MP in a sorting office in Bristol?', *The Guardian*, 17/4/16, http://www.theguardian.com/ commentisfree/2016/apr/17/david-mitchell-renovation-houses-parliament-palace-westminster-bristol-sorting-office, accessed 10/2/17.
8.   Author's interview, Robert Armstrong, 26/10/16.

1 The Building

1. American Ambassador to the UK, Guildhall speech, 1900: W. L. Stephen, *The Story of No. 10 Downing Street* (London: Arthur H. Stockwell Ltd., 1935), pp. 18–19.
2. *Ibid.*, p. 31.
3. R. J. Minney, *No. 10 Downing Street: A House in History* (Boston: Little, Brown & Co., 1963), p. 426.
4. C. Jones, *No. 10 Downing Street: The Story of a House* (London: BBC, 1985), p. 114.
5. R. Butler, in: Mile End Group, 'Men of Secrets: The Cabinet Secretaries', 16/11/12, http://www.cabinetsecretaries.com, accessed 14/12/16.
6. P. B. Guiver (Ferguson & Guiver Ltd.) to Ministry of Works, untitled letter, 8/9/53, National Archive (henceforth 'NA'), WORK 12/581; and A. Bevir to I. Wallis, untitled note, 15/9/53, NA, WORK 12/581; and I. Wallis to Ferguson & Guiver Ltd., untitled letter, 16/9/53, NA, WORK 12/581.
7. C. Jones, *op. cit.*, p. 71.
8. C. Attlee, *As It Happened* (London: William Heinemann Ltd., 1954), p. 156.
9. R. Rhodes-James, *Anthony Eden* (London: Weidenfeld & Nicholson, 1986), p. 413.
10. A. Horne, *Macmillan 1957–1986: Volume II of the Official Biography* (London: Macmillan, 1989), p. 14.
11. C. Jones, *op. cit.*, p. 113.
12. H. Macmillan, *Pointing the Way 1959–1961* (London: Macmillan, 1972), p. 24.
13. P. Hennessy, *Whitehall* (New York: Free Press, 1989), p. 383.
14. J. Colville, *The Churchillians* (London: Weidenfeld & Nicholson, 1981), p. 53.
15. P. Hennessy, *Whitehall, op. cit.*, p. 382.
16. C. Pascoe, *No. 10 Downing Street, Whitehall: Its History and Associations* (London: Duckworth & Co., 1908), pp. 139–40.
17. H. Macmillan, *op. cit.*, pp. 26–7.
18. C. Jones, *op. cit.*, foreword.
19. M. Thatcher, *The Downing Street Years* (London: HarperCollins, 1995), p. 23.

20. R. Millar, *A View From The Wings – West End, West Coast, Westminster* (London: Weidenfeld & Nicholson, 1993), p. 321.

21. P. Hennessy, *The Prime Minister: The Office and its Holders since 1945* (London: Penguin, 2000), p. 37.

22. H. Macmillan, *op. cit.*, p. 26.

23. H. Wilson, *The Governance of Britain* (London: Book Club Associates, 1976), p. 77.

24. B. Donoughue, *The Heat of the Kitchen* (London: Politico's, 2003), p. 140.

25. P. Hennessy, *The Prime Minister, op. cit.*, p. 50; and A. Seldon, *10 Downing Street: An Illustrated History* (London: HarperCollins Illustrated, 1990), p. 120.

26. A. Seldon, *10 Downing Street, op. cit.*, p. 121.

27. *Ibid.*, p. 122.

28. *Ibid.*

29. *Ibid.*, p. 132.

30. M. Williams, *Inside Number 10* (New York: Coward, McCann & Geoghegan, 1972), pp. 68–9.

31. J. Powell, *The New Machiavelli: How to Wield Power in the Modern World* (London: Bodley Head, 2010), p. 17.

32. A. Seldon, 'The Heart of Power', *Prospect*, 28/4/10, http://www.prospectmagazine.co.uk/features/anthony-seldon-inside-downing-street, accessed 4/2/16.

33. D. Kavanagh & A. Seldon, *The Powers Behind the Prime Minister: The Hidden Influence of Number Ten* (HarperCollins Kindle Edition, 2013).

34. M. Thatcher, *The Downing Street Years, op. cit.*, p. 23.

35. C. Pascoe, *op. cit.*, p. 138.

36. The phrase is widely attributed to Macmillan. The authenticity of the famous quote's exact wording has been challenged, although the sentiment has not: R. Harris, 'As Macmillan never said: that's enough quotations', *The Telegraph*, 4/6/02, https://www.telegraph.co.uk/comment/personal-view/3577416/As-Macmillan-never-said-thats-enough-quotations.html, accessed 14/6/19.

37. D. Sandbrook, 'Put him in his place', *The Guardian*, 8/4/07, https://www.theguardian.com/politics/2007/apr/08/tonyblair. labour, accessed 14/6/19.

38. W. L. Stephen, *op. cit.*, p. 42.

39. Author's interview, Robert Armstrong, 26/10/16.

40. M. Burch & I. Holliday, 'The Prime Minister's and Cabinet Offices: An Executive Office in All But Name', *Parliamentary Affairs* (1999), 52 (1), p. 36.

41. P. Hennessy, *The Prime Minister, op. cit.*, pp. 53–4.

42. A. Seldon, 'The Heart of Power', *op. cit.*

43. N. Tebbit, in: Strand Group, 'Margaret Thatcher and No. 10', 27/4/15, http://www.thatcherandnumberten.com, accessed 20/8/16.

44. M. Williams, *Inside Number 10, op. cit.*, p. 68.

45. C. Brown, *Whitehall: The Street that Shaped a Nation* (London: Simon & Schuster, 2009).

46. That £5 was worth an equally unimpressive £779.30 in 2019 prices, when calculated in real terms. 'Purchasing Power of British Pounds from 1270 to Present', MeasuringWorth, https://www.measuringworth.com/ppoweruk, accessed 1/6/19; C. Jones, *op. cit.*, pp. 26–32.

47. C. Brown, *op. cit.*

48. A. Seldon, *10 Downing Street, op. cit.*, p. 10.

49. M. H. Cox & G. T. Forrest (eds.), *Survey of London: Volume 14, St Margaret, Westminster, Part III: Whitehall II* (London: London County Council, 1931), pp. 105–12; C. Jones, *op. cit.*, p. 19; and R. J. Minney, *op. cit.*, pp. 23–4.

50. W. Churchill, *The Second World War, Volume II: Their Finest Hour* (New York: Houghton Mifflin, 1985), p. 304.

51. R. J. Minney, *op. cit.*, pp. 18–22.

52. P. Hennessy, *The Prime Minister, op. cit.*, pp. 39–40 & 43.

53. A. Seldon, *10 Downing Street, op. cit.*, pp. 16–17.

54. R. J. Minney, *op. cit.*, pp. 30–4.

55. *Ibid.*

56. A. Seldon, *10 Downing Street, op. cit.*, p. 12.

57. C. Jones, *op. cit.*, pp. 9, 43 & 46.

58. *Ibid.*, p. 45.

59. *Ibid.*
60. R. J. Minney, *op. cit.*, p. 47.
61. S. Hogg & J. Hill, *Too Close to Call – Power and Politics: John Major in No. 10* (London: Little, Brown & Co., 1995), pp. 16–17.
62. C. Pascoe, *op. cit.*, p. 128.
63. C. Jones, *op. cit.*, pp. 71 & 98.
64. S. Hogg & J. Hill, *op. cit.*, p. 16.
65. C. Jones, *op. cit.*, pp. 158–9.
66. Author Unknown, 'History of Downing Street and the Treasury', 1936, NA, T 199/420.
67. F. L. Rothwell, 'No. 10 Downing Street', 6/10/54, Royal Institute of British Architects (henceforth 'RIBA'), ErR/100/4.
68. Note by the Secretary, 'Committee on the Preservation of Downing Street: History and Present Use', 18/7/57, NA, WORK 15/579; C. Jones, *op. cit.*, pp. 66–7; and A. Seldon, *10 Downing Street, op. cit.*, p. 24.
69. C. Jones, *op. cit.*, pp. 52–5.
70. A. Seldon, *10 Downing Street, op. cit.*, p. 21.
71. C. Jones, *op. cit.*, p. 89.
72. *Ibid.*, p. 96.
73. *Ibid.*, p. 97.
74. *Ibid.*, pp. 97 & 106.
75. *Ibid.*, pp. 66–7.
76. *Ibid.*, p. 72.
77. A. Seldon, *10 Downing Street, op. cit.*, p. 182.
78. All Prime Ministers are expected to provide a portrait for hanging here at some point following their departure. A rumour that Callaghan sent a colour photograph, only for Thatcher to reject it, insisting on a black-and-white image for continuity, could not be corroborated.
79. R. J. Minney, *op. cit.*, p. 400.
80. Namely Henry Campbell-Bannerman (Prime Minister from 1905–8), and Stafford Northcote, later the Earl of Iddesleigh (Chancellor of the Exchequer from 1874–80). Coincidentally, neither figure was in his aforementioned post when he died at No. 10: A. Seldon, *10 Downing Street, op. cit.*, pp. 117 & 121; and R. J. Minney, *op. cit.*, p. 419.

81.   R. J. Minney, *op. cit.*, p. 400.

82.   D. Kavanagh & A. Seldon, *The Powers Behind the Prime Minister*, *op. cit.*; and R. J. Minney, *op. cit.*, p. 400.

2 What Goes On Inside No. 10 Downing Street

1.   P. Hennessy, *The Prime Minister*, *op. cit.*, p. 30.

2.   A. Blick & G. Jones, 'The Institution of Prime Minister', *Gov. UK*, 1/1/12, https://history.blog.gov.uk/2012/01/01/the-institution-of-prime-minister, accessed 6/10/17.

3.   *Ibid.*

4.   *Ibid.*

5.   R. E. Neustadt, 'White House and Whitehall', *National Affairs* (Winter 1966), 2, p. 56.

6.   P. Hennessy, *The Prime Minister*, *op. cit.*, pp. 53–101.

7.   A. Bevir, 'Functions of No. 10 Downing Street', NA, PREM 11/5225.

8.   A. Bevir, 'Functions of the Private Office at No. 10 Downing Street', NA, PREM 11/5225.

9.   P. Hennessy, *The Prime Minister*, *op. cit.*, pp. 45–51.

10.   *Ibid.*, pp. 59–91.

11.   *Ibid.*, pp. 91–6.

12.   F. Mount, *The British Constitution Now: Recovery or Decline?* (London: Mandarin, 1993), pp. 136–7.

13.   H. Wilson, 'A Prime Minister at Work' in A. King, *The British Prime Minister* (London: Macmillan, 1985), p. 12.

14.   *Ibid.*, p. 17.

15.   M. Burch & I. Holliday, 'The Prime Minister's and Cabinet Offices', *op. cit.*, p. 35.

16.   P. Hennessy, *Whitehall*, *op. cit.*, p. 387.

17.   D. Kavanagh & A. Seldon, *The Powers Behind the Prime Minister*, *op. cit.*

18.   A. Bevir, 'Functions of the Private Office at No. 10 Downing Street', date unknown, NA, PREM 11/5225.

19.   Office of Works, 'Official Residences at 10 & 11, Downing Street', February 1930; A. Bevir to Prime Minister, untitled note, 30/9/48; and 'The Prime Minister's expenses at No. 10,

Downing Street', attached to: D. Pitblado to Prime Minister, untitled note, 12/4/55: all in NA, PREM 11/5227.

20. 10 Downing Street, 'The Work of the Prime Minister's Office', July 1974, attached to: R. Armstrong to D. Allen, untitled note, 24/6/74, NA, PREM 16/784.

21. M. Burch & I. Holliday, 'The Prime Minister's and Cabinet Offices', *op. cit.*, p. 36.

22. H. Wilson, 'A Prime Minister at Work', *op. cit.*, pp. 14–5.

23. 10 Downing Street, 'The Work of the Prime Minister's Office', July 1974, attached to: R. Armstrong to D. Allen, untitled note, 24/6/74, NA, PREM 16/784.

24. D. Kavanagh & A. Seldon, *The Powers Behind the Prime Minister, op. cit.*

25. Although the first Principal Private Secretary to be retained across administrations, Ronald Waterhouse, who served Andrew Bonar Law, Baldwin and MacDonald, was not a permanent official himself, and therefore 'makes a murky source for a constitutional orthodoxy': A. Blick & G. Jones, *At Power's Elbow: Aides to the Prime Minister from Robert Walpole to David Cameron* (London: Biteback, 2013).

26. D. Kavanagh & A. Seldon, *The Powers Behind the Prime Minister, op. cit.*

27. C. Moore, *Margaret Thatcher – The Authorised Biography: Volume 1, Not For Turning* (London: Allen Lane, 2013), p. 434.

28. Cabinet Office, 'The Office of Prime Minister', 24/3/76, NA, PREM 16/784.

29. Author's interview, Andrew Turnbull, 6/12/16.

30. D. Kavanagh & A. Seldon, *The Powers Behind the Prime Minister, op. cit.*

31. E. Heath, *The Course of My Life* (London: Hodder and Stoughton, 1998), p. 312.

32. H. Evans, *Downing Street Diary: The Macmillan Years 1957–63* (London: Hodder & Stoughton, 1981), pp. 28–9.

33. P. Hennessy, *Whitehall, op. cit.*, p. 384.

34. D. Kavanagh & A. Seldon, *The Powers Behind the Prime Minister, op. cit.*

35. J. Colville, *The Fringes of Power – Downing Street Diaries – Volume Two: 1941–April 1955* (London: Spectre, 1987), pp. 329–31.

36. D. Kavanagh & A. Seldon, *The Powers Behind the Prime Minister*, *op. cit.*

37. A. Blick & G. Jones, *At Power's Elbow*, *op. cit.*; and D. Kavanagh & A. Seldon, *The Powers Behind the Prime Minister*, *op. cit.*

38. A. Seldon, *Churchill's Indian Summer: The Conservative Government 1951–55* (London: Hodder & Stoughton, 1981), p. 32.

39. P. Hennessy, *Whitehall*, *op. cit.*, p. 387.

40. A. Bevir, 'Functions of the Private Office at No. 10 Downing Street', date unknown, NA, PREM 11/5225.

41. A. Bevir, 'Memorandum', date unknown, NA, PREM 11/5225.

42. 10 Downing Street, 'The Work of the Prime Minister's Office', July 1974, attached to: R. Armstrong to D. Allen, untitled note, 24/6/74, NA, PREM 16/784.

43. Author's interview, Alex Allan, 8/12/16.

44. E. Heath, *op. cit.*, p. 314.

45. A. Seldon, *10 Downing Street*, *op. cit.*, p. 206.

46. *Ibid.*, p. 207.

47. *Ibid.*, p. 208.

48. Interview with M. Hunter, No. 10 Oral History Project.

49. *Ibid.*

50. R. J. Minney, *op. cit.*, p. 408.

51. R. Jenkins, *Churchill* (London: Macmillan, 2001), p. 859.

52. Jane Williams (Lady Williams of Elvel), speaking at No. 10 History event, Downing Street, 23/11/17.

53. M. Williams, *Inside Number 10*, *op. cit.*, pp. 137–8.

54. M. Williams to Prime Minister, untitled note, 6/5/75, NA, PREM 16/333; and K. Stowe to Prime Minister, 'Support for the Political Office', 13/5/75, NA, PREM 16/333.

55. M. Williams, *Inside Number 10*, *op. cit.*, pp. 137–8.

56. D. R. Thorpe, *Alec Douglas-Home* (London: Stevenson Sinclair, 2007), p. 328.

57. *Ibid.*, p. 328.

58. M. Burch & I. Holliday, 'The Prime Minister's and Cabinet Offices', *op. cit.*, p. 36.

59. D. Kavanagh & A. Seldon, *The Powers Behind the Prime Minister*, *op. cit.*

60. M. Williams, *Inside Number 10*, *op. cit.*, pp. 20–1.

61. H. Wilson, *The Governance of Britain*, *op. cit.*, p. 91.

62. M. Williams, *Inside Number 10*, *op. cit.*, p. 27.

63. M. Falkender, *Downing Street in Perspective* (London: Weidenfeld and Nicholson, 1983), p. 89.

64. A. Blick & G. Jones, *At Power's Elbow*, *op. cit.*

65. 10 Downing Street, 'The Work of the Prime Minister's Office', July 1974, attached to: R. Armstrong to D. Allen, untitled note, 24/6/74, NA, PREM 16/784.

66. H. Wilson, *The Governance of Britain*, *op. cit.*, p. 93.

67. M. Burch & I. Holliday, 'The Prime Minister's and Cabinet Offices', *op. cit.*, p. 36; and D. Kavanagh & A. Seldon, *The Powers Behind the Prime Minister*, *op. cit.*

68. D. Kavanagh & A. Seldon, *The Powers Behind the Prime Minister*, *op. cit.*

69. *Ibid.*

70. M. Cockerell, P. Hennessy & D. Walker, *Sources Close to the Prime Minister: Inside the Hidden World of the News Manipulators* (London: Macmillan, 1984), p. 68.

71. 10 Downing Street, 'The Work of the Prime Minister's Office', July 1974, attached to: R. Armstrong to D. Allen, untitled note, 24/6/74, NA, PREM 16/784.

72. A. Seldon, *10 Downing Street*, *op. cit.*, p. 127.

73. T. Burridge, *Clement Attlee – A Political Biography* (London: Jonathan Cape, 1985), p. 199.

74. *Ibid.*, p. 198; and M. Cockerell, P. Hennessy & D. Walker, *op. cit.*, p. 67.

75. M. Cockerell, P. Hennessy & D. Walker, *op. cit.*, p. 63.

76. R. Rhodes-James, *op. cit.*, p. 412.

77. M. Burch & I. Holliday, 'The Prime Minister's and Cabinet Offices', *op. cit.*, p. 36.

78. B. Donoughue, *The Heat of the Kitchen*, *op. cit.*, pp. 193–4.

79. Author's interview, Bernard Donoughue, 19/1/17.

80. H. Wilson, *The Governance of Britain*, *op. cit.*, p. 99.
81. A. Seldon, *Major: A Political Life* (London: Phoenix Books, 1998), p. 140.
82. However, George Jones and Andrew Blick have claimed, 'From 1998 a succession of official definitions of the roles of the Cabinet Office diminished its task of supporting collective decision making, by 2002 eliminating any mention of cabinet and collective': G. Jones & A. Blick, 'The PM and the Centre of UK Government from Tony Blair to David Cameron', *LSE Blogs*, 21/5/10, http://blogs.lse.ac.uk/politicsandpolicy/the-pm-and-the-centre-of-uk-government-from-tony-blair-to-david-cameron-how-much-will-change-in-the-transition-from-single-party-to-coalition-government, accessed 12/12/17.
83. R. Armstrong to N. Wicks, 'The Cabinet Office, 1916–86', 5/12/86, Thatcher Archives, PREM 19/1776.
84. J. Callaghan, *Time and Chance* (London: Collins, 1987), p. 407.
85. P. Hennessy, *Whitehall*, *op. cit.*, p. 389.
86. D. Kavanagh & A. Seldon, *The Powers Behind the Prime Minister*, *op. cit.*
87. A. Blick & G. Jones, *At Power's Elbow*, *op. cit.*
88. Cabinet Office, 'The Office of Prime Minister', 24/3/76, NA, PREM 16/784.
89. D. Kavanagh & A. Seldon, *The Powers Behind the Prime Minister*, *op. cit.*
90. C. Moore, *Margaret Thatcher – The Authorised Biography: Volume 1*, *op. cit.*, p. 432.
91. Author's interview, Andrew Turnbull, 6/12/16.
92. Interview with C. Ferns, No. 10 Oral History Project.
93. Interview with R. Penny, No. 10 Oral History Project.
94. Interview with M. Prentice, No. 10 Oral History Project.

3 The Geography of Power at No. 10 Downing Street

1. P. Hennessy, *The Prime Minister*, *op. cit.*, p. 158.
2. D. Kavanagh & A. Seldon, *The Powers Behind the Prime Minister*, *op. cit.*
3. A. Seldon, 'The Heart of Power', *op. cit.*
4. M. Thatcher, *The Downing Street Years*, *op. cit.*, p. 25.

5.   B. Donoughue, *Downing Street Diary – With Harold Wilson in No. 10* (London: Jonathan Cape, 2005), p. 16.

6.   J. Wheeler-Bennett (ed.), *Action This Day* (London: Macmillan, 1968), p. 168.

7.   H. Evans, *op. cit.*, p. 24.

8.   Author's interview, Robert Armstrong, 26/10/16.

9.   *Ibid.*

10. B. Donoughue, *Downing Street Diary, op. cit.*, p. 17.

11. C. Jones, *op. cit.*, p. 47; and R. J. Minney, *op. cit.*, p. 47.

12. Folder, 'Cabinet meeting held at Grand Hotel, Brighton, 4 October 1966: request to display commemorative plaque', October 1966–January 1967, NA, PREM 13/1723.

13. Author Unknown, 'The Prime Minister's Speech at the Dinner to Commemorate the 250th Anniversary of 10 Downing Street Becoming the House of the First Lord of the Treasury', 4/12/85, Thatcher Archives, THCR 1/7/49.

14. J. Haines, *The Politics of Power* (London: Jonathan Cape, 1977), p. 4.

15. R. Jenkins, *Churchill, op. cit.*, p. 599–610.

16. BBC Press Office, 'Victory for Churchill as he wins battle of the Britons', *BBC*, 25/11/02, http://www.bbc.co.uk/pressoffice/pressreleases/stories/2002/11_november/25/greatbritons_final.shtml, accessed 4/1/18.

17. C. Jones, *op. cit.*, p. 137.

18. *Ibid.*, pp. 118–19.

19. D. Stephens to R. Erith, untitled letter, 4/10/61, RIBA Archives (RIBA), ErR/103/3.

20. Quotation: S. Hogg & J. Hill, *op. cit.*, p. 18. Examples of Prime Ministerial donations: R. J. Minney, *op. cit.*, p. 274.

21. A. Seldon, *10 Downing Street, op. cit.*, p. 146.

22. R. J. Minney, *op. cit.*, p. 422.

23. C. Jones, *op. cit.*, p. 141.

24. House of Commons Information Office, 'Some Traditions and Customs of the House', August 2010, https://www.parliament.uk/documents/commons-information-office/g07.pdf, accessed 27/3/18.

25. E. Muir to N. Brook, 'The Cabinet Room', 28/4/55, NA, WORK 12/588.

26. E. Muir to Minister of Public Works, untitled note, 28/7/55, NA, WORK 12/588; and A. Barclay to E. F. Muir, 'Cabinet Room', 29/7/55, NA, WORK 12/588.

27. A. Bevir to D. Pitblado, untitled note, 11/5/55, NA, PREM 11/5226.

28. E. Muir to Minister of Public Works, untitled note, 28/7/55, NA, WORK 12/588; and A. Barclay to E. F. Muir, 'Cabinet Room', 29/7/55, NA, WORK 12/588.

29. Hooper to Mr. Pitblado, 'Cabinet Room', 26/10/55, NA, PREM 11/5226.

30. Prime Minister to Minister of Works, 'Prime Minister's Personal Minute', 15/4/56, NA, PREM 11/5227.

31. A. Barclay to Mr Root, 'Cabinet Room', 21/10/55, NA, WORK 12/588.

32. E. Heath, *op. cit.*, pp. 459–60.

33. M. Thatcher, *The Downing Street Years, op. cit.*, p. 23.

34. D. R. Thorpe, *Supermac: The Life of Harold Macmillan* (London: Chutto & Windus, 2009), p. 377.

35. C. Jones, *op. cit.*, p. 177.

36. A. Horne, *op. cit.*, p. 160.

37. H. Macmillan, *op. cit.*, p. 26.

38. *Ibid.*

39. A. Seldon, *10 Downing Street, op. cit.*, p. 24.

40. R. Wilson, in: Mile End Group, 'Men of Secrets: The Cabinet Secretaries', 2012, http://www.cabinetsecretaries.com, accessed 7/9/17.

41. J. Campbell, *Edward Heath: A Biography* (London: Pimlico, 1993), pp. 385–6.

42. H. Wilson, *The Governance of Britain, op. cit.*, p. 81.

43. R. J. Minney, *op. cit.*, p. 409; and C. Jones, *op. cit.*, p. 142.

44. A. Eden, *Memoirs – Full Circle* (London: Cassell, 1960), p. 549.

45. A. Horne, *op. cit.*, p. 160.

46. M. Williams, *Inside Number 10, op. cit.*, p. 82.

47. *Ibid.*; and H. Wilson, *The Governance of Britain, op. cit.*, p. 81.

48. J. Callaghan, *op. cit.*, p. 394.

49. *Ibid.*, pp. 402–3.
50. J. Callaghan, in: M. Cockerell, 'The Secret World of Whitehall – Behind the Black Door', *YouTube*, 9/9/11, https://www.youtube.com/watch?v=XfkglvhxX50, accessed 23/3/16.
51. J. Rentoul, 'Nigel Lawson back in his old office at the Treasury', *The Independent*, 3/12/15, http://www.independent.co.uk/voices/comment/daily-catch-up-nigel-lawson-back-in-his-old-office-at-the-treasury-a6758341.html, accessed 5/4/16.
52. S. Hogg & J. Hill, *op. cit.*, p. 19.
53. A. Seldon, *Major, op. cit.*, p. 191.
54. R. J. Minney, *op. cit.*, pp. 374 & 419; and A. Seldon, *10 Downing Street, op. cit.*, p. 49.
55. D. Kavanagh & A. Seldon, *The Powers Behind the Prime Minister, op. cit.*
56. A. Howard (ed.), *The Crossman Diaries – Selections from the Diaries of a Cabinet Minister, 1964–1970* (London: Hamish Hamilton and Jonathan Cape, 1979), p. 468.
57. B. Pimlott, *Harold Wilson* (London: HarperCollins Publishers, 1992), p. 341.
58. Author's interview, Bernard Donoughue, 19/1/17.
59. D. Mitchell, 'Note for the Record', 11/10/65, NA, 13/234.
60. H. Wilson, *The Governance of Britain, op. cit.*, p. 81.
61. A. E. Coules, 'Reference Letter from A. E. Coules', 23/7/59, RIBA, ErR/100/2.
62. E. Heath, *op. cit.*, p. 460.
63. Author's interview, Robert Armstrong, 26/10/16.
64. D. Kavanagh & A. Seldon, *The Powers Behind the Prime Minister, op. cit.*
65. J. Callaghan, *op. cit.*, pp. 402–3.
66. Author's interview, Bernard Donoughue, 19/1/17.
67. D. Kavanagh & A. Seldon, *The Powers Behind the Prime Minister, op. cit.*
68. M. Thatcher, *The Downing Street Years, op. cit.*, p. 21.
69. C. Jones, *op. cit.*, pp. 177–8.
70. S. Hogg & J. Hill, *op. cit.*, p. 18.

71. C. Parkinson, in: Strand Group, 'Margaret Thatcher and No. 10', 19/3/15, http://www.thatcherandnumberten.com, accessed 20/8/16.

72. W. Clark, *From Three Worlds* (London: Sidgwick and Jackson, 1986), p. 149.

73. C. Jones, *op. cit.*, p. 47.

74. A. Seldon, *10 Downing Street, op. cit.*, p. 130.

75. P. Hennessy, *Whitehall, op. cit.*, p. 384.

76. Author's interview, Robert Armstrong, 26/10/16; and D. Kavanagh & A. Seldon, *The Powers Behind the Prime Minister, op. cit.*

77. J. Callaghan, *op. cit.*, p. 405.

78. Author's interview, Alex Allan, 8/12/16.

79. *Ibid.*

80. *Ibid.*

81. Author's interview, Robert Armstrong, 26/10/16.

82. D. Kavanagh & A. Seldon, *The Powers Behind the Prime Minister, op. cit.*

83. Author's interview, Robin Butler, 18/10/16.

84. D. Kavanagh & A. Seldon, *The Powers Behind the Prime Minister, op. cit.*

85. A. Seldon, *10 Downing Street, op. cit.*, p. 192.

86. Author's interview, Andrew Turnbull, 6/12/16.

87. B. Pimlott, *op. cit.*, p. 340.

88. Author's interview, Robert Armstrong, 26/10/16.

89. B. Donoughue, *The Heat of the Kitchen, op. cit.*, p. 140.

90. *Ibid.*, pp. 140–1.

91. *Ibid.*

92. D. Kavanagh & A. Seldon, *The Powers Behind the Prime Minister, op. cit.*

93. Author's interview, Bernard Donoughue, 19/1/17.

94. A. Blick & G. Jones, *At Power's Elbow, op. cit.*

95. S. Hogg & J. Hill, *op. cit.*, p. 18.

96. A. Seldon, *10 Downing Street, op. cit.*, p. 113.

97. A. Blick & G. Jones, *At Power's Elbow, op. cit.*

98. M. Williams, *Inside Number 10, op. cit.*, p. 72.

99. *Ibid.*, p. 29.

100. B. Donoughue, *The Heat of the Kitchen, op. cit.*, p. 139.

101. B. Donoughue, *Downing Street Diary, op. cit.*, pp. 16–17.

102. A. Blick & G. Jones, *At Power's Elbow, op. cit.*

103. A. Howard (ed.), *op. cit.*, p. 138.

104. D. Hurd, *Memoirs* (London: Little, Brown, 2003), pp. 191–2.

105. D. Hurd, *op. cit.*, p. 192.

106. D. Kavanagh & A. Seldon, *The Powers Behind the Prime Minister, op. cit.*

107. *Ibid.*

108. C. Moore, *Margaret Thatcher – The Authorised Biography: Volume 1, op. cit.*, p. 434.

109. M. Williams, *Inside Number 10, op. cit.*, pp. 76–7.

110. S. Hogg & J. Hill, *op. cit.*, p. 18.

111. D. Hurd, *op. cit.*, p. 192.

112. D. Kavanagh & A. Seldon, *The Powers Behind the Prime Minister, op. cit.*

113. C. Jones, *op. cit.*, p. 138.

114. W. Clark, *op. cit.*, pp. 149–50.

115. D. Kavanagh & A. Seldon, *The Powers Behind the Prime Minister, op. cit.*

116. S. Hogg & J. Hill, *op. cit.*, p. 19.

117. R. J. Minney, *op. cit.*, p. 416.

118. T. Burridge, *op. cit.*, p. 199.

119. J. Colville, *The Churchillians, op. cit.*, p. 64.

120. D. Kavanagh & A. Seldon, *The Powers Behind the Prime Minister, op. cit.*

121. *Ibid.*

122. *Ibid.*

123. H. Evans, *op. cit.*, p. 23.

124. *Ibid.*

125. J. Haines, *op. cit.*, p. 4.

126. D. Maitland, *Diverse Times, Sundry Places* (Brighton: The Alpha Press, 1996), p. 177.

127. *Ibid.*

128. C. Moore, *Margaret Thatcher – The Authorised Biography: Volume 1, op. cit.*, p. 440.

129. S. Hogg & J. Hill, *op. cit.*, p. 22.

130. G. Jones & A. Blick, *op. cit.*

131. B. Donoughue, *Prime Minister: The Conduct of Policy Under Harold Wilson and James Callaghan* (London: Jonathan Cape, 1987), pp. 29–30.

132. A. Blick & G. Jones, 'The Institution of Prime Minister', *op. cit.*

133. F. A. Bishop to D. Stephens, 'Downing Street and Kent's Treasury', 30/6/58, NA, PREM 11/2355.

134. Prime Minister to Chancellor of the Exchequer, untitled note, 7/7/58, NA, PREM 11/2355.

135. Chancellor of the Exchequer to Prime Minister, untitled note, 16/7/58, NA, PREM 11/2355.

136. D. Stephens to F. A. Bishop, 'Downing Street and Kent's Treasury', 30/6/58, NA, PREM 11/2355.

137. Author's interview, Robert Armstrong, 26/10/16.

138. Author's interview, Robin Butler, 18/10/16.

139. A. Turnbull, in: Mile End Group, 'Men of Secrets: The Cabinet Secretaries', 14/1/13, http://www.cabinetsecretaries.com, accessed 9/2/18.

140. B. Pimlott, *op. cit.*, p. 359.

141. M. Williams, *Inside Number 10, op. cit.*, pp. 81–2.

142. *Ibid.*, p. 52.

143. D. Kavanagh & A. Seldon, *The Powers Behind the Prime Minister, op. cit.*

144. A. Howard (ed.), *op. cit.*, p. 432.

145. B. Donoughue, *The Heat of the Kitchen, op. cit.*, pp. 168–9.

146. C. Moore, *Margaret Thatcher – The Authorised Biography: Volume 2, Everything That She Wants* (London: Allen Lane, 2015), p. 28.

147. C. Parkinson, *Right at the Centre* (London: Weidenfeld & Nicholson, 1992), p. 194.

148. Author's interview, John Redwood, 19/10/16.

149. D. Willetts, 'The Role of the Prime Minister's Policy Unit', *Public Administration* (December 1987), 65 (4), p. 447.

150. S. Hogg & J. Hill, *op. cit.*, p. 21.

151. M. Williams, *Inside Number 10, op. cit.*, p. 8.

152. S. Hogg & J. Hill, *op. cit.*, pp. 45–6.

153. P. Hennessy, *Whitehall, op. cit.*, p. 655.

4 The Geography of Whitehall – and Geography Subverted

1. E. Dell, *The Chancellors: A History of the Chancellors of the Exchequer, 1945–90* (London: HarperCollins, 1996), p. 1.
2. D. Healey, *The Time of My Life* (London: Michael Joseph, 1989), p. 388.
3. H. Wilson, 'A Prime Minister at Work', *op. cit.*, p. 16.
4. D. Lipsey, *The Secret Treasury: How Britain's Economy is Really Run* (London: Viking, 2000), p. 18; and M. Thatcher, *The Downing Street Years, op. cit.*, pp. 672–3.
5. Author's interview, Robin Butler, 18/10/16.
6. 'Tony and Cherie seek elbow room at No. 10', *The Times*, 27/10/96.
7. C. Brown, *op. cit.*
8. Author's interview, Robert Armstrong, 26/10/16.
9. *Ibid.*
10. Author's interview, Andrew Turnbull, 6/12/16.
11. Author's interview, Robin Butler, 18/10/16.
12. M. Williams, *Inside Number 10, op. cit.*, p. 68
13. Author's interview, Bernard Donoughue, 19/1/17.
14. *Ibid.*
15. P. Hennessy, *The Prime Minister, op. cit.*, p. 3.
16. A. Seldon, *10 Downing Street, op. cit.*, p. 141.
17. J. Brown & B. Draper, 'Sir Winston Churchill', *Gov.UK*, https://www.gov.uk/government/history/past-prime-ministers/winston-churchill, accessed 8/7/16.
18. W. Clark, *op. cit.*, pp. 149–50.
19. D. R. Thorpe, *Supermac, op. cit.*
20. H. Evans, *op. cit.*, p. 28.
21. B. Pimlott, *op. cit.*
22. B. Donoughue, *The Heat of the Kitchen, op. cit.*, p. 153.
23. 'Rasputin with a megaphone', *Evening Standard*, 14/8/97.
24. J. Wheeler-Bennett (ed.), *op. cit.*, p. 257.
25. B. Donoughue, *The Heat of the Kitchen, op. cit.*, p. 153.
26. Author's interview, Robert Armstrong, 26/10/16.
27. B. Donoughue, *Downing Street Diary – Volume Two: With James Callaghan in No. 10* (London: Jonathan Cape, 2008), p. 3.

28. K. O. Morgan, *James Callaghan: A Life* (Oxford: Oxford University Press, 1997), p. 487.
29. D. Kavanagh & A. Seldon, *The Powers Behind the Prime Minister, op. cit.*
30. *Ibid.*
31. Author's interview, Robert Armstrong, 26/10/16.
32. Author's interview, John Redwood, 19/10/16.
33. S. Hogg & J. Hill, *op. cit.*, p. 19.
34. J. Major, *John Major: The Autobiography* (HarperCollins e-books, 2013), p. 211.
35. C. Moore, *Margaret Thatcher – The Authorised Biography: Volume 1, op. cit.*, p. 433.
36. D. R. Thorpe, *Supermac, op. cit.*
37. D. Healey, *op. cit.*, pp. 253–4.
38. S. Coates, 'It happened here: How locations affect politics', *BBC*, 11/3/10, http://news.bbc.co.uk/2/hi/uk_news/politics/8555366.stm, accessed 10/11/17.
39. J. Glover, 'It's a very good thing. Now people can see what the options were', *The Guardian*, 10/2/05, https://www.theguardian.com/politics/2005/feb/10/uk.freedomofinformation, accessed 7/1/18.
40. K. Clarke, 'In one day, our reputation went up in flames', *The Times*, 5/10/16, https://www.thetimes.co.uk/article/i-had-never-been-in-a-government-with-absolutely-no-economic-policy-before-3ssmrohpm, accessed 30/5/19.
41. Author's interview, Alex Allan, 8/12/16.
42. *Ibid.*

5 Reconstructing No. 10 Downing Street

1. Memorandum by Minister of Works, 28/3/55, NA, CAB/129/74/34.
2. *Ibid.*
3. Committee on the Preservation of Downing Street, 'Costs: Note by the Ministry of Works', 13/8/57, NA, WORK 15/579.
4. Memorandum by Minister of Works, 28/3/55.
5. C. Jones, *op. cit.*, p. 142.
6. Cabinet minutes, 21/6/55, NA, CAB/128/29/16.

7. D. Kavanagh & A. Seldon, *The Powers Behind the Prime Minister*, *op. cit.*

8. C. Jones, *op. cit.*, pp. 143 & 153.

9. Macmillan's friend and adviser John Wyndham once amended this to read, 'And if doesn't, you'll probably be shot!': A. Horne, *op. cit.*, p. 13.

10. A. Horne, *op. cit.*, p. 164.

11. Prime Minister to Minister of Works, 'Reconstruction of Downing Street', 19/6/57, NA, WORK 15/579.

12. Committee on the Preservation of Downing Street, *Report of the Committee on the Preservation of Downing Street* (London: HMSO, June 1958).

13. Committee on the Preservation of Downing Street, Minutes of First Meeting, 22/7/57, NA, WORK 15/579.

14. C. Jones, *op. cit.*, p. 178; and Committee on the Preservation of Downing Street, *Report of the Committee*, *op. cit.*, pp. 4–6.

15. Committee on the Preservation of Downing Street, *Report of the Committee*, *op. cit.*, p. 7.

16. *Ibid.*

17. *Ibid.*, p. 10.

18. D. Pitblado to F. J. Root, '10, 11 & 12 Downing Street', 31/1/56, RIBA, ErR/100/4.

19. *Ibid.*

20. *Ibid.*

21. *Ibid.*

22. *Ibid.*

23. R. Erith to C. Boyne, untitled note, 27/11/58, RIBA, ErR/101/2.

24. 'Report on the design for the reconstruction of Nos. 10, 11 & 12 Downing Street', 30/9/58, RIBA, ErR/100/1.

25. R. Erith, Handwritten note entitled 'Downing Street', 12/6/61, RIBA, ErR/100/1.

26. 'Report on the design for the reconstruction of Nos. 10, 11 & 12 Downing Street', 30/9/58, RIBA, ErR/100/1.

27. R. Erith, Handwritten note entitled 'Downing Street', 12/6/61, RIBA, ErR/100/1.

28. H. Macmillan, *op. cit.*, p. 26.

29. The total cost of the renovation was initially estimated at £400,000: Committee on the Preservation of Downing Street, *Report of the Committee, op. cit.*, pp. 8–9.
30. H. Macmillan, *op. cit.*, p. 26.
31. Committee on the Preservation of Downing Street, Minutes of Fifth Meeting, 26/11/57, NA, WORK 15/579.
32. F. A. Bishop to D. Stephens, 'Downing Street and Kent's Treasury', 30/6/58, NA, PREM 11/2355.
33. D. Stephens to F. A. Bishop, 'Downing Street and Kent's Treasury', 1/7/58, NA, PREM 11/2355.
34. *Ibid.*
35. D. Stephens to Prime Minister, 'No. 10 and the Old Treasury', 5/7/58, NA, PREM 11/2355.
36. *Ibid.*
37. Author unknown, 'Downing Street Reconstruction: Note of a meeting held at No. 10 Downing Street, S.W.1., on Thursday, November 12th, 1959, at 5.00pm', 12/11/59, RIBA, ErR/103/4.
38. D. Stephens to R. Erith, untitled letter, 27/9/61, RIBA, ErR/103/3.
39. R. Erith to D. Stephens, untitled letter, 4/10/61, RIBA, ErR/103/3.
40. D. Stephens to R. Erith, untitled letter, 6/10/61, RIBA, ErR/103/3.
41. H. Macmillan to R. Erith, untitled letter, 9/10/61, RIBA, ErR/103/3.
42. *Ibid.*
43. *Ibid.*
44. Ministry of Works, 'Post War History of Work at Nos. 10, 11 and 12 Downing Street', attached to: P. F. Hicks to PS/Secretary, 'No 10 Downing Street', 16/7/70, NA, WORK 12/580.
45. J. Hope to Prime Minister, 'Downing Street Contract', 5/4/60, RIBA, ErR/100/1.
46. D. Stephens to R. Erith, 'Downing Street Reconstruction', 28/3/60, RIBA, ErR/100/1; and Prime Minister to Minister of Works, 'Downing Street Contract', 2/4/60, RIBA, ErR/100/1; and R. Erith to D. Stephens, 'Downing Street Reconstruction' 7/4/60, RIBA, ErR/100/1.

47. Ministry of Works, 'Post War History of Work at Nos. 10, 11 and 12 Downing Street', *op. cit.*

48. *Ibid.*

49. A. Horne, *op. cit.*, p. 266.

50. C. Jones, *op. cit.*, p. 154.

51. R. J. Minney, *op. cit.*, pp. 429–30.

52. C. Jones, *op. cit.*, p. 154.

53. L. Archer, *Raymond Erith: Architect* (London: Cygnet Press, 1985), p. 55.

54. C. Jones, *op. cit.*, p. 154.

55. John Mowlem and Co. Ltd. to R. Erith, 'Nos. 10, 11 and 12 Downing Street, S.E.1', 24/4/61, RIBA, ErR/103/2.

56. *Ibid.*

57. A. S. Lee to R. Erith, untitled letter, 12/10/61, RIBA, ErR/101/4.

58. Author unknown, 'Report on Downing Street', 28/11/61, RIBA, ErR/103/2.

59. Ministry of Works, 'Post War History of Work at Nos. 10, 11 and 12 Downing Street', *op. cit.*

60. R. Erith to M. Bennitt, untitled letter, 1/5/62, RIBA, ErR/100/1.

61. R. Erith to M. Bennitt, untitled letter, 22/5/62, RIBA, ErR/100/1.

62. R. Erith to K. Newis, untitled letter, 19/4/63, NA, CM23/177; and R. Erith to F. R. Rothwell, untitled letter, 31/5/61, NA, CM23/175.

63. G. R. Lock to J. E. Jones, 'Downing Street and Treasury Reconstruction', 4/4/63, NA, CM 23/177.

64. Ministry of Works, 'Post War History of Work at Nos. 10, 11 and 12 Downing Street', *op. cit.*

65. A. Seldon, *10 Downing Street, op. cit.*, p. 34.

66. R. Erith to M. Bennitt, untitled letter, 4/12/62, RIBA, ErR/103/3.

67. *Ibid.*

68. *Ibid.*

69. *Ibid.*

70. M. Bennitt to R. Erith, untitled letter, 27/12/62, RIBA, ErR/103/3.

71. L. Archer, *op. cit.*, p. 57.

72. R. Erith to D. Hicks, untitled letter, 4/4/63, RIBA, ErR/103/2.

73. A. Horne, *op. cit.*, p. 535.

74. Ministry of Works, 'Post War History of Work at Nos. 10, 11 and 12 Downing Street', *op. cit.*

75. R. Erith to D. Hicks, untitled letter, 4/4/63, *op. cit.*

76. R. G. Jones to K. Newis, Confidential Note, 17/9/65, NA, WORK 12/580.

77. C. Pannell to Prime Minister, 'State Drawing Room', 24/11/65, NA, WORK 12/580.

78. R. Kemp to J. Stevens, 'Nos 10, 11 and 12 Downing Street', 28/6/73, NA, WORK 12/580.

79. Ministry of Works, 'Post War History of Work at Nos. 10, 11 and 12 Downing Street', *op. cit.*

80. R. Kemp to J. Stevens, 'Nos 10, 11 and 12 Downing Street', 28/6/73, *op. cit.*

81. C. Pannell to Prime Minister, 'State Drawing Room', 24/11/65, *op. cit.*

82. P. F. Hicks, 'Note of Meeting held at No 10 Downing Street on 26 January at 11am', 4/2/71, NA, WORK 12/580.

83. Committee on the Preservation of Downing Street, *Report of the Committee*, *op. cit.*, p. 7.

84. A. Horne, *op. cit.*, p. 657.

85. D. Andrews to Senior Fire Surveyor, '10/12 Downing Street', 10/7/63, NA, CM23/177.

86. A. Seldon, *10 Downing Street*, *op. cit.*, p. 29.

6 Living Above the Shop

1. C. Pascoe, *op. cit.*, p. 137.

2. R. J. Minney, *op. cit.*, p. 47.

3. A. Seldon, *10 Downing Street*, *op. cit.*, p. 105.

4. R. J. Minney, *op. cit.*, pp. 399–400.

5. A. Seldon, *10 Downing Street*, *op. cit.*, pp. 135–6.

6. C. Jones, *op. cit.*, p. 132.

7. A. Seldon, *10 Downing Street*, *op. cit.*, p. 78.

8.   C. Jones, *op. cit.*, p. 141.

9.   R. J. Minney, *op. cit.*, p. 413.

10. *Ibid.*, p. 419.

11. A. Seldon, *10 Downing Street, op. cit.*, p. 142.

12. *Ibid.*, p. 146.

13. *Ibid.*, p. 150.

14. C. Jones, *op. cit.*, p. 97.

15. *Ibid.*, p. 118.

16. *Ibid.*, p. 143.

17. R. Rhodes-James, *op. cit.*, p. 413.

18. R. J. Minney, *op. cit.*, p. 423.

19. D. R. Thorpe, *Eden: The Life and Times of Anthony Eden, First Earl of Avon, 1897–1977* (London: Chatto & Windus, 2003), p. 451.

20. H. Macmillan, *op. cit.*, p. 25.

21. D. R. Thorpe, *Supermac, op. cit.*, p. 379.

22. B. Pimlott, *op. cit.*, p. 324.

23. D. R. Thorpe, *Alec Douglas-Home, op. cit.*, p. 328.

24. B. Pimlott, *op. cit.*, p. 324.

25. Paddy the dog was said to have learned to use the lift to get down from the private flat to the garden when a trip outside was necessary: A. Seldon, *10 Downing Street, op. cit.*, pp. 154 & 214.

26. A. Seldon, *10 Downing Street, op. cit.*, p. 155.

27. B. Pimlott, *op. cit.*, p. 325.

28. Author's interview, Robin Butler, 18/10/16.

29. B. Pimlott, *op. cit.*, p. 324.

30. C. Attlee, *op. cit.*, p. 156.

31. R. J. Minney, *op. cit.*, p. 416.

32. A. Seldon, *10 Downing Street, op. cit.*, p. 139.

33. 'Callaghan did not want to enter No. 10', *The Independent*, 4/1/05, http://www.independent.co.uk/news/uk/politics/callaghan-did-not-want-to-enter-no-10–8004470.html, accessed 4/2/18.

34. Curiously, Callaghan's memoirs refer to 'No. 2 Carlton Gardens' rather than No. 1, which has been the grace-and-favour residence of the Foreign Secretary since 1945, perhaps due to the

fact that he did not actually live at the property: J. Callaghan, *op. cit.*, p. 295.

35. 'Callaghan did not want to enter No. 10', *The Independent*, *op. cit.*

36. J. Warwicker, *An Outsider Inside No. 10: Protecting the Prime Ministers, 1974–79* (London: The History Press, 2015).

37. K. O. Morgan, *op. cit.*, p. 498; and A. Seldon, *10 Downing Street*, *op. cit.*, p. 161.

38. D. Kavanagh & A. Seldon, *The Powers Behind the Prime Minister*, *op. cit.*

39. A. Seldon, *10 Downing Street*, *op. cit.*, p. 161.

40. D. Kavanagh & A. Seldon, *The Powers Behind the Prime Minister*, *op. cit.*

41. E. Heath, *op. cit.*, p. 313.

42. Author's interview, Robin Butler, 18/10/16.

43. Author's interview, Robert Armstrong, 26/10/16.

44. A. Seldon, *Major*, *op. cit.*, p. 190.

45. *Ibid.*, p. 143.

46. Author's interview, Alex Allan, 8/12/16.

47. P. Hennessy, *The Prime Minister*, *op. cit.*, p. 446.

48. Author's interview, Alex Allan, 8/12/16.

49. M. Thatcher, *The Downing Street Years*, *op. cit.*, p. 19.

50. Janice Richards, in: Strand Group, 'Margaret Thatcher and No. 10', 20/3/15, http://www.thatcherandnumberten.com, accessed 10/10/16.

51. C. Jones, *op. cit.*, p. 182.

52. Author's interview, Robin Butler, 18/10/16.

53. R. J. Minney, *op. cit.*, p. 422.

54. A. Seldon, *10 Downing Street*, *op. cit.*, p. 213.

55. E. J. Powell to L. A. Price, 'Regulations governing the occupation of Nos. 10 & 11 Downing Street and 1 Carlton Gardens', 13/8/47, NA, WORK 12/607.

56. C. Jones, *op. cit.*, p. 144.

57. M. Cockerell, *op. cit.*

58. C. Parkinson, in Strand Group, 'Margaret Thatcher and No. 10', 19/3/15, http://www.thatcherandnumberten.com, accessed 10/10/16.

59. F. Beckett, *Clem Attlee* (London: Richard Cohen, 1997), pp. 210–11.

60. A. Seldon, *10 Downing Street, op. cit.*, p. 139.

61. D. Kavanagh & A. Seldon, *The Powers Behind the Prime Minister, op. cit.*

62. J. Callaghan, *op. cit.*, p. 403.

63. W. Clark, *op. cit.*, p. 156.

64. A. Eden, *op. cit.*, p. 549.

65. R. Rhodes-James, *op. cit.*, p. 411.

66. D. Kavanagh & A. Seldon, *The Powers Behind the Prime Minister, op. cit.*

67. H. Wilson, *The Labour Government 1964–1970 – A Personal Record* (London: Weidenfeld and Nicholson, 1971), p. 1.

68. *Ibid.*, p. 2.

69. A. Seldon, *10 Downing Street, op. cit.*, p. 218–19.

70. B. Pimlott, *op. cit.*, pp. 374–5.

71. C. Moore, *Margaret Thatcher – The Authorised Biography: Volume 2, op. cit.*, p. 670–1.

72. J. Major, *op. cit.*, p. 725.

73. *Ibid.*

7 Hosting the World

1. A. Seldon, *10 Downing Street, op. cit.*, p. 196.

2. Government Hospitality Wine Cellar, 'Annual Report 2016–17', *Gov.uk*, https://assets.publishing.service.gov.uk/government/uploads/system/uploads/attachment_data/file/647038/Annual_Report_GH_Wine_Cellar_16–17.pdf, accessed 4/7/18.

3. A. Seldon, *10 Downing Street, op. cit.*, p. 198.

4. *Ibid.*, p. 28.

5. W. Douglas Home, *The Prime Ministers: Stories and Anecdotes from Number 10* (London: W. H. Allen, 1987), p. 237.

6. R. Rhodes-James, *op. cit.*, p. 413.

7. C. Jones, *op. cit.*, p. 144.

8. Miss Wallis, 'Note', 8/3/56, NA, WORK 12/607.

9. R. J. Minney, *op. cit.*, p. 428.

10. C. Jones, *op. cit.*, p. 156.

11. D. Kavanagh & A. Seldon, *The Powers Behind the Prime Minister, op. cit.*
12. J. Haines, *op. cit.*, p. 5.
13. D. Kavanagh & A. Seldon, *The Powers Behind the Prime Minister, op. cit.*
14. A. Seldon, *10 Downing Street, op. cit.*, p. 128.
15. R. J. Minney, *op. cit.*, p. 423.
16. N. Higham, 'National Archives' files reveal what happened to the UK's moon dust', *BBC News*, 30/12/15, https://www.bbc.co.uk/news/uk-35196156, accessed 3/8/18.
17. Author's interview, Robin Butler, 18/10/16.
18. R. J. Minney, *op. cit.*, pp. 414–15.
19. Author's interview, Robert Armstrong, 26/10/16.
20. M. Thatcher, *The Downing Street Years, op. cit.*, p. 24.
21. C. Powell, in: Strand Group, 'Margaret Thatcher and No. 10', 19/3/15, http://www.thatcherandnumberten.com, accessed 10/10/16.
22. E. Heath, *op. cit.*, p. 443.
23. *Ibid.*
24. R. Wilson, in: Mile End Group, 'Men of Secrets: The Cabinet Secretaries', 2/11/12, http://www.cabinetsecretaries.com, accessed 7/4/18.
25. A. Seldon, *10 Downing Street, op. cit.*, p. 172.
26. C. Jones, *op. cit.*, p. 178.
27. A. Seldon, *10 Downing Street, op. cit.*, p. 173.
28. *Ibid.*, p. 145
29. C. Jones, *op. cit.*, p. 143; and R. J. Minney, *op. cit.*, p. 422.
30. P. Hepburn to C. Eden, untitled letter, 18/4/56, NA, PREM 11/5226.
31. C. Jones, *op. cit.*, p. 156.
32. *Ibid.*, p. 157.
33. E. Heath, *op. cit.*, p. 460.
34. C. Jones, *op. cit.*, p. 156.
35. M. Falkender, *op. cit.*, p. 104.
36. *Ibid.*, pp. 104–5.
37. A. Seldon, *10 Downing Street, op. cit.*, p. 172.
38. M. Falkender, *op. cit.*, p. 105.

39. C. Jones, *op. cit.*, pp. 159–60 & 177–8.
40. M. Thatcher, *The Downing Street Years, op. cit.*, p. 23.
41. C. Moore, *Margaret Thatcher – The Authorised Biography: Volume 1, op. cit.*, p. 435.
42. C. Parkinson, in: Strand Group, 'Margaret Thatcher and No. 10', 19/3/15, http://www.thatcherandnumberten.com, accessed 20/8/16.
43. C. Jones, *op. cit.*, p. 159.
44. *Ibid.*, pp. 178–99.
45. M. Cockerell, *op. cit.*
46. C. Jones, *op. cit.*, p. 182.
47. K. Powell, 'Grandeur cannot be done cheaply', *The Telegraph*, 6/11/02, http://www.telegraph.co.uk/finance/property/new-homes/3308491/Grandeur-cannot-be-done-cheaply.html, accessed 5/8/16.
48. A. Seldon, *10 Downing Street, op. cit.*, p. 36.
49. Author's interview, Robin Butler, 18/10/16.
50. Author's interview, Alex Allan, 8/12/16.

8 No. 10 Under Attack
1. R. J. Minney, *op. cit.*, p. 24.
2. W. L. Stephen, *op. cit.*, pp. 29–30.
3. A. Seldon, *10 Downing Street, op. cit.*, pp. 63–4.
4. *Ibid.*, p. 103.
5. *Ibid.*
6. M. Dutton, 'The assassination of Spencer Perceval', 11/5/12, *National Archives*, https://blog.nationalarchives.gov.uk/blog/the-assassination-of-spencer-perceval, accessed 8/7/18.
7. A. Seldon, *10 Downing Street, op. cit.*, pp. 108–9.
8. C. Jones, *op. cit.*, p. 99.
9. G. Heffer, 'The plots to kill Prime Ministers', *Sky News*, 6/12/17, https://news.sky.com/story/the-plots-to-kill-prime-ministers-11159098, accessed 15/3/18.
10. R. Hollis to T. Bligh, untitled note, 4/5/64, NA, PREM 11/5085.
11. R. Hollis to T. Bligh, untitled note, 24/6/64, NA, PREM 11/5085.

12. T. Bligh to R. Hollis, untitled note, 23/4/64, NA, PREM 11/5085.
13. 'How to make Number Ten Safe', *The Times*, 22/12/85.
14. D. R. Thorpe, *Alec Douglas-Home*, *op. cit.*, p. 328.
15. J. Waddell to R. Armstrong, untitled letter, 17/2/75, NA, PREM 16/1105.
16. P. Jupp, Letter to Superintendent, 7/3/74, NA, PREM 16/1105.
17. R. Armstrong to W. Armstrong, untitled note, 23/4/74, NA, PREM 16/1105.
18. R. Wilkes, 'Inside story: Lord North Street', *The Telegraph*, 21/1/01, https://www.telegraph.co.uk/finance/property/4812588/Inside-story-5-Lord-North-Street.html, accessed 14/6/19.
19. B. Pimlott, *op. cit.*, p. 705.
20. *Ibid.*, p. 693.
21. D. Mitchell to L. Helsby, 'In Confidence', 5/10/65, NA, PREM 13/234.
22. J. Lewis & T. Harper, 'Revealed: How MI5 bugged Downing Street, the Cabinet and at least five Prime Ministers for 15 years', *Daily Mail*, 18/4/10, http://www.dailymail.co.uk/news/article-1266837/Revealed-How-MI5-bugged-10-Downing-Street-Cabinet-Prime-Ministers-15-YEARS.html, accessed 14/6/19.
23. 'MI5 kept file on former PM Wilson', *BBC News*, 3/10/09, http://news.bbc.co.uk/1/hi/uk/8288247.stm, accessed 14/6/19.
24. 'C.V.P.' to K. Stowe, untitled note, 21/11/75, NA, PREM 16/1105.
25. Special Branch, 'Threat assessment: Harold Wilson (On his retirement as Prime Minister)', 2/4/76, NA, PREM 16/1105.
26. C. Jones, *op. cit.*, p. 116.
27. A. Seldon, *10 Downing Street*, *op. cit.*, pp. 85–8.
28. D. R. Thorpe, *Eden*, *op. cit.*, p. 528.
29. E. Grant to M. Forrester, untitled note, 25/4/74, NA, PREM 16/1105.
30. House of Commons, Written answers, *Hansard*, 9/1/90, vol 164, col 590, https://hansard.parliament.uk/Commons/1990-01-09/debates/a9a5099e-9122-49b0-b710-6f8bd92892c4/

DowningStreet, accessed 14/6/19; and 'Anti-terrorist barrier for No. 10 Downing Street', *The Sunday Times*, 6/8/89.

31. 'Security Review at No. 10', *The Times*, 20/12/85.
32. 'How to make Number Ten Safe', *The Times*, 22/12/85.
33. *Ibid.*
34. 'The "stately" gates of Downing Street', *The Times*, 29/9/89.
35. *Ibid.*
36. 'RFAC angry over plans to seal off Number Ten', *Building Design*, 30/9/89.
37. 'Life behind bars at Number 10', *The Independent*, 4/10/89.
38. 'Building design comment – Proposed gates for Downing Street', *Building Design*, 7/10/89.
39. M. Cockerell, *op. cit.*
40. 'Kinnock would axe No, 10 gates', *The Sunday Times*, 29/4/90.
41. *Ibid.*
42. House of Commons, Written answers, *Hansard*, 9/1/90, *op. cit.*
43. Author's interview, Alex Allan, 8/12/16.
44. House of Lords, 'No. 10 Downing Street: Security Gates', *Hansard*, 21/7/98, vol 592, col 708, https://hansard.parliament.uk/lords/1998-07-21/debates/4fa95fdf-3d25-4caf-b28f-691c52728834/No10DowningStreetSecurityGates, accessed 14/6/19.
45. C. Jones, *op. cit.*, p. 114.
46. F. Bamford to A. Bevir, untitled letter, 1/4/52, NA, PREM 11/368.
47. A. Seldon, *10 Downing Street, op. cit.*, pp. 82–3.
48. *Ibid.*, pp. 27 & 33.
49. C. Jones, *op. cit.*, p. 139.
50. R. J. Minney, *op. cit.*, p. 411.
51. Author's interview, Robert Armstrong, 26/10/16.
52. R. Butler, in: Mile End Group, 'Men of Secrets: The Cabinet Secretaries', 2012, http://www.cabinetsecretaries.com, accessed 7/5/18.
53. J. Major, *op. cit.*, p. 238.
54. House of Commons, 'Terrorist Incident (Whitehall)', *Hansard*, 7/2/91, vol 185, col 413, https://hansard.parliament.uk/commons/1991-02-07/debates/c30cc575-92c2-423c-8f6c-

c1b6713478db/TerroristIncident(Whitehall), accessed 14/6/19.

55.   C. Davies, 'How the Luftwaffe bombed the Palace, in the Queen Mother's own words', *The Guardian*, 13/9/09, https://www.theguardian.com/uk/2009/sep/13/queen-mother-biography-shawcross-luftwaffe, accessed 7/6/18.

9 Concluding Thoughts

1.   H. Wilson, *The Governance of Britain*, op. cit., p. 82.
2.   *Ibid.*
3.   M. Thatcher, *The Downing Street Years*, op. cit., p. 20.
4.   C. Powell, in Strand Group, 'Margaret Thatcher and No. 10', 19/3/15, http://www.thatcherandnumberten.com, accessed 10/10/16.
5.   A. Seldon, 'The Heart of Power', op. cit.
6.   H. Wilson, *The Governance of Britain*, op. cit., p. 106.
7.   M. Thatcher, in C. Jones, op. cit., foreword.

Index